To the Memory of

JOHN BUTT

THE REVELS PLAYS

General Editor: Clifford Leech

THE CHRONICLE HISTORY OF
PERKIN WARBECK

A STRANGE TRUTH

piem varbeck nasit de Tournay suppose pour Richard
Duc d'Jorck peind fils d'Edouard IV Roy d'Angleterre l'an 1492.
sat perdu à Londres par la fin de l'an 1499

Perkin Warbeck *from a drawing in the Town Library at Arras
reproduced in James Gairdner's History of the Life and Reign of
Richard the Third*

The Chronicle History of
Perkin Warbeck
A Strange Truth

JOHN FORD

EDITED BY
PETER URE

THE REVELS PLAYS

METHUEN & CO LTD
LONDON

This edition first published 1968

Introduction, Apparatus Criticus, etc.
© 1968 Peter Ure
Printed in Great Britain by
The Broadwater Press Ltd, Welwyn Garden City, Herts

General Editor's Preface

The Revels Plays began to appear in 1958, and in the General Editor's Preface included in the first few volumes the plan of the series was briefly sketched. All those concerned in the undertaking recognized that no rigid pattern could be proposed in advance: to some extent the collective experience of the editors would affect the series as it developed, and the textual situation was by no means uniform among the plays that we hoped to include. The need for flexibility is still recognized, and each editor indicates in his introduction the procedures that have seemed best in relation to his particular play.

Nevertheless, we were fairly convinced that in some matters our policy would remain constant, and no major change in any of these respects has been made. The introduction to each volume includes a discussion of the provenance of the text, the play's stage-history and reputation, its significance as a contribution to dramatic literature, and its place within the work of its author. The text is based on a fresh examination of the early editions. Modern spelling is used, archaic forms being preserved only when rhyme or metre demands them or when a modernized form would not give the required sense or would obscure a play upon words. The procedure adopted in punctuation varies to some extent according to the degree of authority which an editor can attribute to the punctuation of the copy-text, but in every instance it is intended that the punctuation used in a Revels volume should not obscure a dramatic or rhetorical suggestiveness which may be discerned in the copy. Editorial stage-directions are enclosed in square brackets. The collation aims at making clear the grounds for an editor's choice wherever the original or a frequently accepted modern reading has been departed from. Annotations attempt to explain difficult passages and to provide such comments and illustrations of usage as the editor considers desirable.

When the series was planned, it was intended that each volume should include a glossary. At an early stage, however, it was realized that this would mean either an arbitrary distribution of material between the glossary and the annotations or a duplication of material. It has therefore become our practice to dispense with a glossary but to include an index to the annotations, which avoids duplication and facilitates reference.

Act-divisions are employed if they appear in the copy-text or if the structure of the play clearly points to a five-act division. In other instances, only scene-numbers are inserted. All act- and scene-indications which do not derive from the copy-text are given unobtrusively in square brackets. In no instance is an editorial indication of locality introduced into a scene-heading. When an editor finds it necessary to comment on the location of a scene, this is done in the annotations.

The series continues to use the innovation in line-numbering that was introduced in the first volume. Stage-directions which occur on lines separate from the text are given the number of the immediately preceding line followed by a decimal point and 1, 2, 3, etc. Thus 163.5 indicates the fifth line of a stage-direction following line 163 of the scene. At the beginning of a scene the lines of a stage-direction are numbered 0.1, 0.2, etc.

The Revels Plays have begun with the re-editing of a number of the best-known tragedies and comedies of the later Elizabethan and Jacobean years, and there are many such plays to which the techniques of modern editing need to be applied. It is hoped, however, that the series will be able to include certain lesser-known plays which remain in general neglect despite the lively interest that an acquaintance with them can arouse.

The present volume is the first in which a new procedure is followed in the handling of '-ed' verbal terminations. Previously we have used '-ed' in past tenses and past participles when the termination was probably syllabic, and '-'d' elsewhere. Here we use '-ed' for non-syllabic terminations and '-èd' for syllabic. This seems in line with our attempt to give the reader an edition with modernized spelling while at the same time indicating the metrical pattern. It follows that in such a form as 'studied' we now imply a probably dissyllabic pronunciation, and have dropped the form 'study'd'. Moreover, in verbs and adjectives ending in '-e', the second person singular and the superlative are given as '-est', whether or not the termination appears to be syllabic.

It has always been in the forefront of attention that the plays included should be such as deserve and indeed demand performance. The editors have therefore given a record (necessarily incomplete) of modern productions; in the annotations there is, moreover, occasional conjecture on the way in which a scene or a piece of stage-business was done on the original stage. Perhaps, too, the absence of indications of locality and of editorial scene-headings will suggest the advantage of achieving in a modern theatre some approach to the characteristic fluidity of scene and the neutrality of acting-space that Shakespeare's fellows knew.

CLIFFORD LEECH

Toronto, 1967

Contents

GENERAL EDITOR'S PREFACE   *page* vii

PREFACE   xiii

ABBREVIATIONS   xv

INTRODUCTION   xvii

  1. The Text   xvii

  2. Date and Authorship   xxviii

  3. The Sources   xxxv

  4. The Play and its Critics   xlv

  5. Majesty and Passion   liv

  6. Biographical Index of Historical Characters   lxxxiii

THE CHRONICLE HISTORY OF PERKIN WARBECK:
A STRANGE TRUTH   I

APPENDICES

  I. Extracts from Thomas Gainsford's *True and
    Wonderfull History of Perkin Warbeck*   143

  II. William Warner's *Albions England*   179

  III. Various Enquiries   181

GLOSSARIAL INDEX TO THE COMMENTARY   185

Illustrations

Perkin Warbeck   *frontispiece*

L1ʳ of the Quarto of 1634   xx

Title-page of the Quarto of 1634   2

Preface

Ford's *Perkin Warbeck* is arguably the last really good play on a topic drawn from British history ever to have been written by an Englishman. It revived the tradition of the Shakespearian history-play, but ought not to be judged entirely by that standard, for it combines a broad and vigorous design with a serious commitment to values and interests which are Ford's own. It is over three hundred years since it was first performed, and it ought to be revived on our stage. Like Shakespeare's *Richard II* (which obviously influenced Ford), it has two major rôles in dramatically efficient contrast with one another; it also has—what Shakespeare's play lacks—a splendid part for an actress.

My thanks are due to the University of Newcastle upon Tyne for granting me a period of leave, during which much of the work on this edition was done. I would like to thank my colleagues at the University, who assumed my teaching duties during an exceptionally overcrowded time, and especially Mr J. C. Maxwell, who took over the administrative part of my job—only a small portion of a huge and unrepayable debt to him accumulated over the many years during which we were colleagues. I am very grateful indeed to Professor Clifford Leech, and not only for his own published writings on Ford and Stuart drama; he has tirelessly scrutinized and improved every page of this volume and has guided and encouraged me throughout, with characteristic generosity and patience.

PETER URE

Newcastle upon Tyne, January 1968

Abbreviations

Abbott	E. A. Abbott, *A Shakespearian Grammar*, London, 1905 reprint.
Anderson [*A* in collation]	*Perkin Warbeck*, edited by Donald K. Anderson Jr, London, 1966.
Bacon	*Bacon's History of the Reign of King Henry VII*, edited by J. Rawson Lumby, Cambridge, 1892.
Baskervill [*B* in collation]	Edition of the play in *Elizabethan and Stuart Plays*, ed. Charles R. Baskervill, Virgil B. Heltzel, and Arthur H. Nethercot, New York, 1934.
Bentley	*The Jacobean and Caroline Stage*, by G. E. Bentley, 7 vols., Oxford, 1941–68.
Brereton (*Sources*)	'The Sources of Ford's Perkin Warbeck', by J. Le Gay Brereton, *Anglia*, xxxiv (1911), 194–234.
Dyce [*D* in collation]	Edition of the play in *The Works of John Ford*, edited by Alexander Dyce, London, 1869.
Gainsford	*The True and Wonderfvll History of Perkin Warbeck Proclaiming himselfe Richard the fovrth* [by Thomas Gainsford], London, 1618.
Gairdner	'The Story of Perkin Warbeck' in *The History of the Life and Reign of Richard the Third*, by James Gairdner, new and revised (third) edition, Cambridge, 1898.

Gifford
  [*G* in collation]

Edition of the play in *The Dramatic Works of John Ford*, edited by William Gifford, London, 1827.

Hall

Hall's Chronicle containing the History of England, London, 1809.

Holinshed, Hol.

The Historie of England, by Raphael Holinshed, London, 1586–7 [references are normally to the page, the column, and the first line of the passage cited].

Mackie

The Earlier Tudors, by J. D. Mackie, Oxford, 1952.

O.E.D.

Oxford English Dictionary.

Pickburn

Ford's Perkin Warbeck, edited by J. P. Pickburn and J. Le Gay Brereton, Sydney, 1896.

Rowse

Tudor Cornwall, by A. L. Rowse, London, 1941.

Sargeaunt

John Ford, by M. Joan Sargeaunt, Oxford, 1935.

Speed

The Historie of Great Britaine, third edition, by John Speed, London, 1632.

Shakespeare's England

Shakespeare's England: An Account of the Life and Manners of his Age, 2 vols., Oxford, 1916.

Stow

The Annales or Generall Chronicle of England, by John Stow, London, 1615.

Struble

A Critical Edition of Ford's Perkin Warbeck, by Mildred Clara Struble, Seattle, 1926.

Tilley

A Dictionary of the Proverbs in England in the Sixteenth and Seventeenth Centuries, by M. P. Tilley, Ann Arbor, 1950.

Weber
  [*W* in collation]

Edition of the play in *The Dramatic Works of John Ford*, edited by Henry Weber, Edinburgh, 1811.

NOTE. References to Shakespeare's plays are normally to *The Complete Works*, ed. Peter Alexander (London and Glasgow, 1951).

Introduction

The play was entered in the Stationers' Register on 24 February 1634:

> Hugh Beeston. Entred for his Copy vnder the hands of S^r. Henry Herbert & m^r Aspley warden (observing the Caution in the License) a Tragedy called Perkin Warbecke by Io: fford.

The unusual phrase in this entry, 'observing the Caution in the License', means at least that when Sir Henry Herbert, the Master of the Revels, passed the play for performance he issued some sort of warning to the players either to alter or to suppress certain passages; or perhaps it may have been a general warning not to depart from the text as duly licensed. Herbert might have been nervous about possible departures because of the ticklish nature of the subject, an attempt on a throne—and an English throne at that—which had already caused or was to cause trouble to him in connexion with another play.[1] That the 'Caution in the License' is mentioned in the Register suggests that the manuscript presented at Stationers' Hall was the Phoenix company's prompt-book bearing Herbert's certification and the additional warning. Greg considered it unlikely that prompt-books presented in this way were themselves made over to the printer;[2] but, as suggested below, there is some reason to believe that the copy for Q had been annotated by a prompter.

It was printed with the following title-page:

THE / CHRONICLE / HISTORIE / OF / PERKIN VVAR-BECK. // A Strange Truth. // Acted (some-times) by the Queenes / MAIESTIES Servants at the / *Phœnix* in *Drurie* lane. // *Fide Honor.* / [double rule] / LONDON, / Printed by *T.P.* for *Hugh*

---

[1] See Appendix III.   [2] *Editorial Problem in Shakespeare*, p. 107.

Beeston, and are to / be sold at his Shop, neere the *Castle* in / *Cornehill.* 1634.

T.P. was Thomas Purfoote Jr, a master printer since 1591 and Senior Warden of his Company in 1634. He undertook the printing of a number of play-quartos beginning with Marston's *Dutch Courtesan* in 1605 and including the fifth quarto of *Richard II* in 1615 and the 1622 quartos of *Richard III* and *1 Henry IV.*

The collation is A–K4, L1. Copies of the Quarto are fairly numerous: nineteen are recorded in Greg's *Bibliography*; Bishop's *Checklist* records fifteen copies in the United States alone. The present edition is based upon a photocopy of the British Museum copy catalogued as C. 12. g. 3/5, which has been collated with B.M. 644. b. 38, with the three copies at the Bodleian, and with those at Manchester (John Rylands), London (London University Library), and Worcester College, Oxford.

The Quarto is divided into Acts, but not into scenes, each Act being headed *Actus primus [Secundus,* etc.]*: Scæna prima.*[1] The scene-divisions were established in Weber's edition of 1811, but there is never any possibility of confusion about where they occur. The Quarto, with its dedicatory epistle and commendatory poems, is carefully printed, and it seems reasonable to suppose that Ford had something to do with the preparation of the play when it was being sent to the printer. Some stage-directions may be authorial,[2] and there is plentiful use of *Exeunt omnes* to mark the ending of scenes. Of more than ordinary interest are the many places where capital or italic letters are used for words or phrases of special import. These seem clearly to reflect a practice of Ford's which may be studied in his other quartos. Stressed or passionate speech is often indicated in this way, as, for example, with the terms of abuse thick-sown in I. i: *this Woman-Monster,* the *vpstart Duke,* This *gewgaw, French dissimulation,* this *smoake of straw,* this *eager Whelpe.* In I. ii. 14 we might doubt 'This whoresome tale of honor, (*honor Daliell*)' as merely an example of a contiguous word being attracted

---

[1] The ending of an Act is marked only once: *Finis Actus primi.*

[2] For example, those at II. i. 39.1–7, II. iii. 71.1–3, III. i. 0.1–2, III. ii. 85.1–3, III. iv. 3.1, III. iv. 54 ('*Exit Durham cum suis*'), IV. iii. 0.1, IV. iv. 23.1, v. i. 0.1, v. ii. 138.1–2.

into the italics commonly used for proper names (as frequently happens in seventeenth-century texts), of which *noble Gourdon* a few lines later may be an example. But there can be no doubt about this specimen:

> Thou standst betweene a *Father* and a *Suiter*,
> Both striving for an interest in thy heart:
> *Hee* Courts thee for affection, *I* for dutie;
> *Hee* as a servant pleads. . .[1]   (I. ii. 95–8)

Hee/wee spellings, incidentally, are not necessarily emphatic in themselves without italicization or capitalization. In the same speech Huntly further advises Katherine: 'I am confident / Thou wilt proportion all thy thoughts to side / Thy *equalls*, if not equall thy *superiors*'. Katherine herself in the same scene presents us with several examples of combined capitals and italics as in

> I want skill
> To choose without direction of EXAMPLE:
> From *which* I daily learne, by how much more
> You take off from the roughnesse of a *Father*,
> By so much more I am engag'd to tender
> The dutie of *a Daughter*. . .   (I. ii. 129–34)

or in

> So every vertuous praise, in after ages,
> Shall be your heyre, and I in your braue mention,
> Be Chronicled *the* MOTHER of that *issue*,
> *That glorious issue*.   (I. ii. 154–7)

In this last example it is not so much passion (although that of course is present) that is being underlined as meaning, the meaning of the complex metaphor.[2] Other striking examples of the combination of capitals and italics might include the passage from Warbeck's address to James in II. i:

> For your bountie,
> Royall magnificence to him that seekes it,
> WEE vow hereafter, to demeane our selfe,
> As if wee were your owne, and naturall brother:
> Omitting no occasion in *our person*. . .   (II. i. 97–101)

[1] Compare: 'When Counsailes faile, and theres in *man* no trust, / Even then, an arme from *heaven*, fights for the just' (I. iii. 137–8) or 'Great King *they* spard my life, *the butchers* spard it' (II. i. 65).

[2] See note on I. ii. 153–7.

Innocent *Warwick's* head, (for we are Prologue
But to his tragedie) conclude the wonder
Of *Henries* feares ; and then the glorious race
Of *foureteene Kings* PLANTAGINETTS, determines
In this *laſt iſſue male*, Heaven be obeyd.
Impoveriſh time of its amazement (friends)
And we will proue, as truſtie in our payments,
As prodigall to *nature* in our debtes.
Death ? piſh, 'tis but a ſound; a name of ayre ;
A minutes ſtorme ; or not ſo much, to tumble
From bed to bed, be maſſacred aliue
By ſome *Phyſitians*, for a moneth, or two,
In hope of freedome from a Feavers torments,
Might ſtagger manhood ; here, the paine is paſt
Ere ſenſibly 'tis felt. Be men of ſpirit!
Spurne coward paſſion ! ſo illuſtrious mention,
Shall blaze *our names*, and ſtile vs KINGS O'RE DEATH.
  Daw: Away - Impoſtor beyond preſident :   *Ex: all Officers*
No Chronicle records his fellow.   *and Priſoners.*

  Hunt: I haue
Not thoughts left, 'tis ſufficient in ſuch caſes
Iuſt Lawes ought to proceede.

            Enter King Henry, Durham, and Hialas.

  K: H: Wee are reſolv'd :
Your buſineſſe (noble Lords) ſhall finde ſucceſſe,
Such as your King importunes. *Hunt*: You are gracious.

  K: H: Perkin, wee are inform'd, is arm'd to dye :
In that weele honour him. Our Lords ſhall followe
To ſee the execution ; and from hence
Wee gather this fit vſe : that publicke States,
" As our particular bodyes, taſte moſt good
" In health, when purged of corrupted bloud.

                                    Exeunt omnes.

F I N I S.

L1r of the Quarto of 1634, illustrating Ford's use of capitals and
italics

or Henry's comment, making one of the play's heaviest accents, at
v. ii. 132–3:

> The custome sure of being stil'd *a King*,
> Hath fastend in his thought that HE IS SVCH

or Warbeck's final appeal:

> Spurne coward passion! so illustrious mention,
> Shall blaze *our names*, and stile vs KINGS O'RE DEATH.
>   (v. iii. 206–7)

When James of Scotland finally addresses the Pretender as '*Cosen of
Yorke* ... Welcome to *Iames of Scotland*', the italics certainly represent in this context something more than the mere convention (also
rigidly followed throughout the printing) of italicizing proper
names. Nor can we avoid, in a reading of the Quarto, the added
force of phrases such as *death-daring Scotts*; *truth it selfe*; A *Queene*,
perhaps a *Queene*;[1] ENGLISH RICHARD; *our Prince* (spoken by John
a Water); 'Arrowes hayled in showers vpon us / *A full yard long at
least*'; some *unnatural subject* (spoken by Warbeck); EDVVARDS
bloud in me; the honor of an *English name and nature*; *A handsome
youth indeede* (Henry at his first sight of Warbeck), and of many
other examples ranging from royal irony to passionate exclaims.
Especially in the dedication and the commendatory poems we can
observe the practice fully manifested as when Ralph Eure writes of

> The GLORIOVS PERKIN, and thy Poet's Art
> Equall with *His*, in playing the KINGS PART.

It is strange that all Ford's friends should take delight in the device,
but the obvious explanation is that when the copy was being sent to
the printer Ford fair-copied the preliminary pages at least, including his own dedication and his friends' offerings, improving the
latter as he went. Very little seems to have been worked out concerning this practice as a whole, but it is plain that Purfoote's workman considered it his business to reproduce very carefully this
feature of his copy. The use of these italics and capitals constitutes
an element in the play which is a genuine and irreducible part of its
author's conception. Unfortunately, modern convention makes it

[1] See note on II. iii. 47.

impossible to represent it properly, if at all, in a modernized edition. All that it has been possible to do in this edition has been to record the capitalized words in the apparatus and, normally, to give the appropriate words initial capitals in the text.

A number of the stage-directions in Q may represent or incorporate prompter's additions. Such are: I. i. 0.3, 'A Guard.' (the authorial phrase would appear to be 'a guard of Souldiers' [v. ii. 0.1], and A Guard. looks from its position as though it might have been added later in copy to the rest of the stage-direction); I. iii. 0.1, 'Lights.' (similarly detached from its stage-direction); II. i. 0.1, 'aboue:' in 'Enter aboue:', the colon indicating that an original 'Enter Countesse . . .' had been disturbed; II. i. 16, 'Flourish', a misplaced stage-direction in Q, probably originally in the margin of the printer's copy; II. i. 39, 'Hoboyes''; II. i. 39.6–7, 'Salutations ended: cease Musique.' The author is perhaps less likely than the prompter to have thought it necessary to give direction for the music to stop so that Warbeck may begin to speak. II. ii. 0.1, 'Flourish.': again unitalicized, it is medially placed in Q above the rest of the stage-direction; this suggests that it may have been a marginal addition to the copy (cf. I. i. 141.1); II. ii. 52.1–2, the punctuation of Q's 'Enter Stanly; Executioner: Vrswick and Dawbney' suggests that the third word was an interpolation; II. ii. 83.1, the stage-direction, squeezed into the margin of Q, may not originally have been authorial (cf. v. iii. 209.1); II. iii. 70, the Quarto has 'Enter' at this point (in the margin): this indicates the actual moment of appearance of the head of the procession which is catalogued in the subsequent stage-direction as it is printed on page 54 of this edition (in Q this stage-direction is found between lines 72 and 73); III. i. 42, another misplaced 'A Flourish', this time actually in the margin in roman (and a line too late, probably because the compositor could not squeeze it into its proper place); III. ii. 81, in the Quarto 'Flourish' is in roman in the middle of the line above 'Enter King Iames . . .' and is five lines late. It may have been misplaced because it was written vertically or diagonally in the margin as a prompter's indication that the music was to start sounding at Huntly's 'Oh harke . . .' and was to continue until the king and all his court had taken up their positions; III. ii. 111.3, 'Musicke', from its position and roman type seems clearly to represent an addition to the clearly authorial stage-direction; v. iii. 0.2, '*A payre of Stocks*' may, for similar reasons, be regarded as deriving from a prompter's note.

The evidence so far set out, together with the evident cleanness of its copy, suggests that the basis for Q was a fair copy, perhaps one prepared by the author himself, which had been annotated for use as a prompt-book. The compositor (I have found no evidence that there was more than one) was a careful workman, or carefully supervised; he could not manage *Phaëthon*, but he got the Latin right.

Miss Sargeaunt was the first to give a reliable account of the corrections that were made while the sheets were passing through the press.[1] These all occur on the outer forme of sheet F and on the last leaf (sheet L) in the copies collated. Anderson in his edition[2] states that some copies have H2^v in an uncorrected state signalized by the omission of both the speech-prefixes *Omnes* on this page; these prefixes are printed rather far over in the left-hand margin quite out of alignment with the rest of the type and in several of the copies examined have been almost (but not quite) cropped away altogether by the binder; it seems likely that in the copies referred to by Anderson cropping may have caused them to disappear altogether, thus giving him the impression that they had been omitted in the printing. In any case, these speech-prefixes must have been added in the printing-house, by compositor or press-corrector, after the page had been set up. They may have been added later in the copy, too, or perhaps omitted from it altogether. The other substantive alterations are confined to F and are recorded in the apparatus, one of the Bodleian copies (Mal. 238 (5)) being the only one to show these variants amongst the copies examined. The variants on L1 recto and verso, found in several copies, are not substantive: there is a long and short 's' alteration in *last* (v. iii. 195), an adjustment of spacing in relation to the stage-direction '*Ex: all Officers and Prisoners*' at v. iii. 209.1, and there are three rows of ornaments above the Epilogue in some copies and only two in others.

[1] Sargeaunt, p. 200.   [2] Anderson, pp. xx, 75, 76.

In the modernizing of a seventeenth-century text problems arise which are very hard to solve without the generation of some anomalies. All such problems and anomalies are aspects of the conflict between the desire not to lose certain effects which may be characteristic of the author and his play on the one hand and the need on the other to present a text which will not too disturbingly violate modern conventions of spelling, pronunciation, and lexical form. Very often this process entails substituting one archaism for another, which for historical or accidental reasons is currently regarded as more acceptable, though it is often no more 'modern'. Thus, in this edition *th'art* and *th'ast* are replaced by *thou 'rt* and *thou 'st*. Q's distinctions between syllabic and non-syllabic -ed terminations in preterites and past participles, which are fairly conscientiously made, are here represented, perhaps not quite adequately, by the -ed/èd system. Ford is well known, at least in the history of authorship-tests, for certain of his pronominal forms, especially his use of *'ee* for *ye*. Here it has not been possible to achieve absolute consistency: I have retained a large number of the 27 occurrences of *'ee* (in Q sometimes printed *ee* or *ee'*), but have felt it necessary to abandon it on certain occasions, as when dealing with 'Kneele to the King 'ee Rascalls' (v. ii. 102) or when 'modernizing' *w'ee* (to *wi' ye*); the occasional *y'are* has been replaced by *you're*; but the 28 occurrences of *a'* (for *he*) have been retained. The Quarto generally (but not invariably) has this form in preference to *a* or *'a*. The apostrophe, since it is placed *after* the *a*, seems not to be being used as an indication that a letter has been omitted but as a sign to distinguish this weak form of the third personal pronoun from the indefinite article. The normal Quarto form has been retained in this edition in order to avoid confusion with the indefinite article. It is hard to tell how far *a'* is deliberately intended as a characterizing device, since it is used by personages as different from each other as the grave Henry and the bluff Huntly. The spelling of proper names has naturally been modernized. This has meant in several cases the abandonment of forms preserved so long in previous modernized editions that they have become misleadingly traditional: thus Q's (and Dyce's) *Huntley* becomes *Huntly*; Q's *Dawbney* (to which Anderson, though a modernizing editor, reverts[1]) cannot properly be *Dawbeney* (as in Weber, Gifford, and Dyce, and editions which derive from them) but must be either *Daubeney* or *D'Aubigny* (I have chosen the former). There is no good reason for reverting, as both Armstrong and Anderson do, to Q's *Sketon* (for the historical character whose name was Skelton); the playwright was merely compounding an error, which was originally no more than a misprint, by the Gainsford source. But obviously there must be a limit—I have not thought it right to give the character whom Ford calls Hialas his proper name of Ayala.

The punctuation of the Quarto is heavier than is now customary and is seemingly careful in general. As is common in texts of the period, the question-mark is often used as an exclamation-mark and brackets are employed where we would use, at the most, dashes. Colon and semi-colon are frequently used to indicate dramatic pauses or changes of direction and to accent rhetorical movement in places where a modern text cannot do more than sprinkle commas, as, for example:

> Death ? pish, 'tis but a sound; a name of ayre;
> A minutes storme; or not so much; to tumble . . .
>
> (v. iii. 199–200)

or

> I had never sought
> The truth of mine inheritance with rapes
> Of women, or of infants murthered; Virgins
> Defloured; olde men butchered; dwellings fir'd;
> My Land depopulated; and my people
> Afflicted with a Kingdomes devastation.
>
> (III. iv. 59–64)

This is the place to make the usual declaration that I have tried to avoid more than the unavoidable degree of falsification which the substitution of modern for Jacobean punctuation entails. In all cases where changes may be thought to affect sense, the apparatus and commentary show what has been done.

After the Quarto of 1634 *Perkin Warbeck* was not printed again until 1714. In that year, no doubt as an instructive analogue for the

---

[1] In pursuit of his perfectly defensible policy of retaining Q spelling for all character-names.

Jacobite times, it was issued 'for *J. Roberts*, at the *Oxford Arms* / in Warwick-Lane'. The text is a reprint of the 1634 Quarto with a few obvious mistakes corrected; it is preceded by a short prose account of Warbeck's life.

There were no other editions in the eighteenth century, but there is a manuscript version of the play in the Bodleian (Rawl. poet 122) which may be mentioned here. It has been shown that this manuscript was probably intended for use as a prompt-copy for the performance of the play at the theatre at Goodman's Fields on 19 December 1745.[1] This version is an 'improved' one, altered by cuts, rewriting, 'and in other ways adapted for a Hanoverian audience', says Miss Crum. She brings evidence to show that the source of the manuscript was probably the 1714 reprint rather than the 1634 Quarto.

After two centuries of virtual neglect, the play came back into circulation in the editions of Henry Weber in 1811 and of William Gifford in 1827. Both these have been collated for the apparatus of this edition, as has the other major nineteenth-century edition, that of Alexander Dyce in 1869. The editions which have not been collated may be briefly described. The edition in the anonymous Ford's *Dramatic Works* of 1831 is the same as the one (also published by John Murray) in 'Murray's Family Library' in 1847. The notes are mostly Gifford's; some are slightly rearranged or shortened and one or two are omitted; the text is slightly bowdlerized but otherwise follows Gifford. The edition of the play in *The Dramatic Works of Massinger and Ford* edited by Hartley Coleridge in the Routledge 'Old Dramatists' series (1839 and many later reprints) has a long introduction by Hartley Coleridge (to the volume as a whole) and follows Gifford's text of *Perkin*. Havelock Ellis's edition

---

[1] See 'The Date and Handwriting of a Manuscript Copy of Ford's "Perkin Warbeck"' by D. K. Anderson (*Notes and Queries*, CCVIII [1963], 340–1) and the 'Additional Note' in the March 1965 issue of the same periodical by Margaret Crum. It may be added that the stage-history of *Perkin* is minimal: the 1745 performance is the only one mentioned in Clifford Leech's Appendix on 'Ford on the Stage' (see *John Ford and the Drama of his Time* [London, 1957], p. 136). The revival of Ford's play, again exploiting the Jacobite theme, succeeded in getting to the stage before two other new plays (no longer extant) on Warbeck which were written to exploit the parallel between Warbeck and the Young Pretender.

in the Mermaid series *John Ford*, first published in 1888, follows
Dyce's text (with some unintended departures) and there is an introduction by Ellis to the volume as a whole, with a brief prefatory
note to the play itself. In 1890 H. Macaulay Fitzgibbon included
the play in his *Famous Elizabethan Plays Expurgated and Adapted
for Modern Readers*, a title which tells its own story; the text is
based on Gifford and Dyce, but even in *Perkin* Fitzgibbon managed
to expurgate twenty-two lines. In 1895 Dyce's edition of Ford was
re-issued by Lawrence and Bullen in three volumes (like its original); the text of our play in this edition is a reprint of the 1869 printing; the 'additions' advertised on the title-page of the second Dyce
consist of a prefatory 'Note' by A. H. B[ullen] in the first volume
and a reprint of Henry Goodcole's pamphlet about Elizabeth
Sawyer the witch. In 1896 there came another bowdlerized edition
in *English Historical Plays . . . Arranged for Acting as Well as Reading* by T. Donovan, who undertook the work in the praiseworthy
hope that 'these superb historical plays will be at length rescued
from the semi-oblivion of our libraries to be assigned . . . an honoured place on our national stage'.[1] The text is taken from Dyce
but scenes are transposed and run together. Also in 1896 J. P.
Pickburn and J. Le Gay Brereton issued at Sydney an edition of
the play which, in respect of annotation at least, was by far the best
so far published. It is a school edition in format, and was perhaps
intended for school use. It seems to have been strangely overlooked
by most writers on Ford, and is admittedly very hard to come by.
The commentary of this edition owes a large debt to it. Their text,
the editors say, is 'in the main that of Gifford and Dyce . . . but the
editors have ventured to differ from it in some minor points and in
a few cases have restored the reading of the quarto'.

The first edition during this century was that by Mildred Clara
Struble (1926), a University of Washington (Seattle) Ph.D. thesis.
The edition is valuable for its study of the play's historical sources,
especially Gainsford. The text is a not very accurate reprint of the
Quarto; the long commentary, which is mainly concerned with the
fifteenth-century historical background, is often stupefyingly ir-
relevant and astray. The edition of the play in Henry De Vocht's

---

[1] Preface, I. vii; *Perkin* is in the second of the work's two volumes.

John Ford's Dramatic Works (Louvain, 1927) is an accurate attempt to reproduce a copy of the Quarto formerly in the possession of Wilhelm Bang and is without accompanying editorial matter. During the time that this Revels edition has been in preparation there have been two useful editions of the play, both published in series which have acquired good reputations. The first is William A. Armstrong's in *Elizabethan History Plays* (World's Classics series, 1965) and the second that of Donald K. Anderson Jr, in the University of Nebraska Regents Renaissance Drama series (a paperback, issued in the United States in 1965). Armstrong's edition is based on the Quarto. Dyce's punctuation is sometimes altered accordingly, but in general the modernization is very close to Dyce, as is the handling of such matters as locations and stage-directions, and even the text is sometimes led astray by him.[1] Consequently this edition presents an altogether more nineteenth-century appearance than does Anderson's, which is based on a fresh collation of six copies of Q and which has been itself collated for the Revels edition. The Anderson apparatus, however, is so minimal and eccentric as to make one wonder why it was thought worth having at all; it is also somewhat inaccurate—unfortunately in its attempt to record the substantive variants amongst the press-corrections, a task which it was the first edition to undertake.

2. DATE AND AUTHORSHIP

Ford's earliest datable plays are all collaborations with Dekker belonging to the years 1621 to 1624. Only three of the six, *The Witch of Edmonton* (1621), *The Welsh Embassador* (?1623), and *The Sun's Darling* (1624) are extant. The dates of composition and performance of his other plays are a notoriously intractable problem.

Perkin Warbeck was entered on the Stationers' Register on 24 February 1634, and the title-page of the Quarto bears the date 1634. An approximate lower limit for composition is provided by

[1] Thus it perpetuates the Gifford/Dyce compounded error *and/an* (for Q's *that*) at IV. ii. 57. Anderson, by contrast, is reluctant to emend Q, even when it seems essential to do so (as at, for example, I. iii. 100, 136, II. ii. 33, III. iv. 37); he retains a number of obsolete spellings. For Armstrong's edition, see *Notes and Queries*, CCXI (1966), 312.

the year, 1625, in which Queen Henrietta's Men, to whom the play is accredited on the title-page, are presumed to have started work at the Phoenix (Cockpit) private theatre in Drury Lane under the management of Christopher Beeston.[1] Except for this *c.* 1625–34 span for composition and first performance, all else is conjecture.

A date fairly late in the sequence of Ford's unassisted plays has been traditional, until quite recently. Thus Clifford Leech thinks of it as his 'last tragedy', and H. J. Oliver of it as coming after the 'main group' of Ford's plays.[2] These are reasonable inferences from its being placed, in the order of Quarto publication, third in the series formed by *Love's Sacrifice*, *The Broken Heart*, and our play. These were all published by Hugh Beeston and were entered under his name in the Stationers' Register on dates in January 1633, March 1633, and February 1634, respectively.

In a yet longer series, *Perkin* is one of a group of five plays by Ford which were all acted by Queen Henrietta's Men or its successor, the King and Queen's Company, at the Phoenix. The others in this group are *The Fancies Chaste and Noble*, *The Lady's Trial*, *Love's Sacrifice*, and *'Tis Pity*. Bentley has suggested[3] that all the members of this group may be later than the three plays—*The Lover's Melancholy* (licensed 1628), the lost *Beauty in a Trance* (acted at court in 1628) and *The Broken Heart* (? also 1628)—which were written for the King's Men at the Blackfriars. The pattern of Ford's career may be that after he had stopped collaborating with Dekker about 1624, he had a period of writing for the King's Men before going over to their rivals, Queen Henrietta's.

Bentley also suggested,[4] however, that the allocation of *Perkin* to this group of Phoenix plays did not mean a date of composition and performance as late in the series as the Stationers' Register entries just mentioned suggest. The statement on the title-page: 'Acted (some-times) by the Queenes Maiesties Servants at the *Phœnix* in *Drurie* lane' has no parallel, in its use of 'some-times', with other Ford title-pages. It appears to be equivalent to *formerly*, not 'occa-

---

[1] Bentley, I. 218, VI. 62–3.

[2] Clifford Leech, *John Ford and the Drama of his Time* (London, 1957), p. 96; H. J. Oliver, *The Problem of John Ford* (Melbourne, 1955), p. 100.

[3] Bentley, III. 441–2.   [4] *Ibid.*, III. 456.

sionally' or 'infrequently' (which is an improbable meaning on a title-page). It may therefore refer to a period a good deal earlier than the 1634 printing. Taking Bentley's two suggestions together, we are still left guessing at a date in the late 'twenties (after 1628) or the very earliest 'thirties.

There is, of course, nothing impossible in the supposition that the play was written quite soon after the publication of its second major source, Bacon's *Henry VII*, in 1622, and that its staging was for some reason delayed. The death of Thomas Gainsford, author of the first major source, in 1624, is followed or accompanied by a little flurry of references to him in plays of 1624–6, which suggests that the theatrical world had its eye on his activities.[1] This might have been an atmosphere in which the playwright would turn to read or re-read Gainsford's book on Warbeck, printed six years earlier. This would place the composition of the play in or very near the 1621–4 period of collaboration between Dekker and Ford.

Alfred Harbage has proposed[2] an earlier date for the sufficient reason that he believes that the play *was* written in collaboration between Dekker and Ford. He is the first writer to have suggested that *Perkin* is not the unassisted work of Ford.

Harbage sets out facts which in his view suggest, or at least do not contravene, a theory that 'Dekker wrote part of *Perkin Warbeck* and shaped the whole' (p. 131). These may be tabulated as follows: (i) Collaborative work is often different from work turned out by the collaborators when they are writing independently. This might help to explain what is, for Harbage, the great 'mystery' about *Perkin*: why it is so different—as everybody agrees it is[3]—from the rest of Ford's work. (ii) Like the best-known of the Dekker/Ford collaborations, *The Witch of Edmonton*, our play is a revival of an obsolete dramatic kind.[4] (iii) *The Witch of Edmonton* uses its prose-pamphlet source immediately after the publication of the pamph-

---

[1] See Appendix I, editorial note, p. 143.

[2] 'The Mystery of *Perkin Warbeck*' in *Studies in the English Renaissance Drama in Memory of Karl Julius Holzknecht* (New York, 1959), pp. 125–41.

[3] See p. xlix below.

[4] Harbage might have added that the same is true of the other Dekker/Ford collaborations extant (*The Sun's Darling* and *The Welsh Embassador*); the titles of the lost plays also sound old-fashioned.

let; this suggests that Gainsford and Bacon, too, would have been taken up in the same rapid way. (iv) In such a collaboration, Dekker, as the senior man, would be the 'informing spirit'. (v) The name Warbeck occurs as the name of a character in *The Witch of Edmonton*: this suggests that the collaborators had picked it up already from Gainsford. (vi) Number 43 in the list of early plays in manuscript written by the seventeenth-century book-collector Abraham Hill (published by J. Q. Adams in 1939, shortly after its discovery)[1] is an otherwise unrecorded title, *Believe It Is So and It Is So*. This would be a good alternative title for *Perkin*.[2] Hill's attribution is to 'Th. Decker', presumably copied from the manuscript which he was looking at. (vii) 'some-times' on the *Perkin* title-page suggests the earlier date.

As Harbage insists, these points do not prove collaboration; they are merely not incompatible with the idea. Having marshalled this circumstantial evidence, it is disappointing that he cannot identify more places and elements in the play where he thinks Dekker's hand reveals itself than he does; for it seems to be from his sensing the presence of Dekker that the theory originally sprang and not from any pointer supplied by the circumstantial matter. According to Harbage, there are the following signs of Dekker in *Perkin*: (viii) Huntly is a Dekker-like character, in his relationship with his daughter (compare the Friscobaldo–Bellafront scenes in *2 Honest Whore*) and in being a humorous old man like Old Carter in *The Witch of Edmonton*. (ix) Katherine reminds Harbage of Bellafront (in *2 Honest Whore*):

> In the case of Katherine the stress is not upon gentle resignation to impotence and misfortune, but upon the assertion of the principle of fidelity. Thus she is nearer to Dekker's Bellafront than to Ford's Calantha.[3]

It is a difficult argument. Harbage wants to maintain that both authors are working 'under restraints' because they are collaborating with each other. Thus, their work in *Perkin*, if it is a collaborative play, will be characteristic enough to remind us of their un-

---

[1] 'Hill's List of Early Plays in Manuscript', *Library*, 4th ser., xx (1939–40), 71–99.

[2] See note on v. ii. 132–3.   [3] Art. cit., p. 140.

assisted work and so enable their hands to be recognized, but at the same time will not be *so* characteristic as it would have been if either were writing independently. Thus *faintness* of resemblance to an author's known work is no disproof of his presence, and tests become even more subjective than they usually are in matters affecting collaboration.

Since Harbage wrote, Sidney R. Homan Jr[1] has supported him with a few more points: (x) There are parallels in situation between the Warbeck/Somerton/Old Carter/Susan/Frank Thorney group in *The Witch of Edmonton* (especially I. ii) and the Dalyell/James IV/Huntly/Katherine/Warbeck group in *Perkin*. (xi) Huntly may also be compared with Simon Eyre in *The Shoemakers' Holiday* and Janicola in *Patient Grissill*, two of Dekker's 'sentimental old men'. (xii) Dekker's contribution to the play roughly corresponds to the invented, non-historical material (centring on the Dalyell/Huntly characterization and Katherine's relation to Warbeck).

My own views are: (i) The comparative isolation of *Perkin* from the rest of Ford may be more straightforwardly explained by the unique choice of the English history-play form and subject than by collaboration. (ii) There is not much in the alleged resemblances between character and situation in *The Witch of Edmonton* and our play, with the exception noted below (no. iv). Those detected by Homan are strained. Harbage's seem to be inferences from the older play about how the collaboration in *Perkin* might have worked, once it is assumed. (iii) The supposed likeness between Katherine and Bellafront seems very remote. Bellafront's fidelity is in the face of a *husband*'s provocation and a courtier's attempted seduction. Allowing for the presence of a marriage-topic in either play, the situations of the two women could hardly be more different. (iv) I agree that Huntly has a good deal in common with Dekker's 'humorous' or 'sentimental' old men, often with daughters to look after, although such persons occur in at least three of Ford's unassisted plays.[2] I see no reason why Ford should not have taken a leaf out of his erstwhile collaborator's book: if Dekker was his senior partner for three years and they produced up to six plays together,

---

[1] *English Language Notes*, III (1965), 104–5.
[2] See Sargeaunt, p. 129.

this fact alone is probably enough to explain impressions of Dekker in the work of the younger man. (v) *Believe It Is So and It Is So* seems a plausible alternative title for *Perkin*, though our play is already equipped with a second title, *A Strange Truth*. It would be interesting to learn what theory could account for the substitution if it took place (it presumably happened before the play was presented for licensing or registration, *Believe* etc., therefore, being the original title). If Hill was copying down on his list from the manuscript before him (as Harbage supposes) not only the title but the 'Th. Decker' attribution as well, why has Ford's name disappeared altogether, if *Believe* is the same play as *Perkin*? Something similar may have happened in the case of another play *The Welsh Embassador*, no. 13 on Hill's list and also attributed to 'Tho Dekker'; but Ford had only a tiny share in that, whereas his name, if any name at all, would surely be on the manuscript of *Perkin*. It should be remembered, when Hill's list is thought about, that of the fifty-one titles which he lists a very high proportion are otherwise quite unknown; even if we allow all J. Q. Adams's most tentative guesses at the identification of Hill's titles with extant plays, the number of such identifications does not rise above eleven: so the chances are high that a play on Hill's list is not extant. (vi) It seems likely that the appearance of the name Warbeck in *The Witch of Edmonton* means that Gainsford's book was known to Dekker or Ford or both when they were writing that play in 1620–1;[1] (vii) and that 'some-times' means 'formerly'. The last two details point to an earlier date than the traditional one, but not to a great deal else.

By far the greatest difficulty in the way of Harbage's theory remains the authority deriving from the title-page and preliminary matter in the 1634 Quarto. Harbage rightly says that 'we ourselves must not grow too legalistic about the evidence of old title-pages and dedicatory epistles';[2] but it seems curious to regard Abraham Hill's equally 'old' list as though it possessed equal or superior authority.

Like three of Ford's other Quartos the title-page has his anagram *Fide Honor* and is the second such Quarto so inscribed; the dedication to the earl of Newcastle is signed 'Iohn Ford' and its phrases,

[1] See also below, p. 181, Appendix III.   [2] Art. cit., pp. 128–9.

C

such as 'Ovt of the darknesse of a former Age . . . I haue endevoured, to personate a great Attempt', imply sole authorship; three of the five commendatory poems are addressed to Ford by name. Of all this Harbage writes:

> If charged with appropriating the work of others, Ford might have said that he had done nothing of the kind—as witness the reticent title-page and the allusion to 'a late both learned, and an honourable pen', which we assume to be Francis Bacon's but was intended as Thomas Dekker's. Dekker died in 1632, and the play was published in 1633. Ford, who was legally trained, would have been technically in the clear. These insinuations of sharp practice are not seriously intended . . .[1]

But why are they not seriously intended? For, however unlikely the interpretations entailed (anagrams, for example, are not by their nature 'reticent', since they invite solution), either the 1634 Quarto involved a deliberate and fairly elaborate attempt to deceive patron and public or it did not. Harbage, claiming that 'rights in dramatic authorship were lightly held', says that Dekker 'would have been the first to encourage Ford to publish the play as he did'. This light-hearted assumption is supported by an unhappily selected example: Harbage writes of Dekker having 'let Middleton sign the preface to *The Roaring Girl*'; but the title-page of this Quarto does bear the names of both authors, and the preface is not a dedicatory epistle to a single patron but an address to 'the Comicke Play-readers, Venery, and Laughter', which Middleton signed obviously for the sufficient reason that he and not Dekker wrote it.

If Harbage is right, there must also have been a bit of fraud in connexion with the Stationers' Register entry for our play,[2] where it is again stated to be 'by Io: fford'. If it was the licensed prompt-book that was submitted as authority for the publication,[3] this implies that the manuscript submitted to the Master of the Revels for his licence bore Ford's name alone as given in the Stationers' Register entry itself. Bentley has pointed out the extremely high degree of accuracy in author-attributions of plays known to have been entered 'under the hand of' Sir Henry Herbert:

> I suggest that manuscripts of plays licensed for publication at the

---

[1] Art. cit., p. 128.   [2] Quoted on p. xvii.   [3] See above, p. xvii

Revels Office in Herbert's time were not handed on with patently false attributions, and that for some reason publishers were chary of adding fanciful guesses at authorship in the registration of manuscripts which Sir Henry or his deputies had handled.[1]

Title-page, dedication, commendatory poems, and Stationers' Register entry all tell the same story. It is not as though the fact of collaboration was normally disregarded when such things were being drawn up. Hundreds of title-pages, Stationers' Register entries, and entries in the Revels office-books exist to demonstrate that it was a regular and frequent practice to indicate collaboration by recording the names of the two (or more) authors involved.

A theory of collaboration can, I think, be rejected with some confidence. But the question of a date earlier than the traditional placing of about 1633 remains open. Some further, but inconclusive, matters which may in the end be shown to have a bearing upon the date are discussed in Appendix III.

3. THE SOURCES

The principal sources are the account of Warbeck in Bacon's *History of the Reign of King Henry VII* (1622) and Thomas Gainsford's *The True and Wonderfull History of Perkin Warbeck* (1618). The former is presumably alluded to in the dedicatory epistle; the latter Ford is discreetly silent about.

These were the only historians of whose writings it is certain Ford made direct use. Until Miss Struble revived Gainsford's name in 1926 (a suggestion originally made by Gerard Langbaine in 1688), it was believed that Hall's chronicle was the second major source. This is no longer tenable. Of the forty or so instances which Brereton in his 1911 article on the sources[2] believed to be examples of an exclusive debt to Hall nearly all either can or must be explained as debts to Gainsford, whose own chief authority, from whom he remorselessly copies, was Hall. Very few examples re-

---

[1] Bentley, III. 258.

[2] 'The Sources of Ford's Perkin Warbeck', *Anglia*, XXXIV (1911), 194–234. The publication of Miss Struble's article (in *Anglia*, XLIX (1926), 80–91) coincided with that of her edition and is therefore taken in conjunction with it.

main of what appear to be direct debts to Hall.[1] I see no real reason for believing that Holinshed's chronicle, whose account of Warbeck is a condensation of Hall's, was used by the playwright. I have found nothing that convinces me that he directly consulted Polydore Vergil, Stow,[2] or Speed, or Grafton—all names which have at one time or another been mentioned in connexion with the play. He did not use the relevant tragedy in *The Mirror for Magistrates*, so far as I can tell, although it is possible that he read the relevant chapters in Warner's *Albions England*.[3]

Both the major sources give very full and handsome accounts of Warbeck's career. Bacon's is far more penetrating and incomparably better written than Gainsford's; he has no illusions about Warbeck or about Henry. He weighs men and therefore weighs men's words. Gainsford is naïve, derivative, and conventionally minded. He faithfully works away at propagating jejune notions about the necessity of obedience to princes, sees everything in black and white, and cannot redeem this with any artistry worth speaking of. Bacon can kill with a blow of the lion's paw, but Gainsford nags away rancorously at the unhappy Warbeck. He writes high head-voice speeches for his characters and feebly attempts to dramatize their concerns by interlarding their discourses with quotations from Lucan and Euripides. This passage, which is Gainsford's imagining of how Henry received the news of the Cornish rising, is slightly more ridiculous than usual but characteristic enough:

> When the King was aduertized of these troubles and exorbitant attempts, which gathered like a clowd, threatning a tempest round about him, and saw into what perplexity he was now detruded, hauing warre on euery side, he compared himselfe to a man rising in a darke night, and going into an vndrest roome, hitting his head against that post, running against that table, meeting with his shinnes such a stool or forme, and staggering vp and downe against one blocke or another: and so stood (for the time) amazed, not knowing what to say, what to do, or with whom to find fault, till with a kind of sigh he vented out this saying of *Euripides*. . .[4]

[1] See notes on I. i. 64, I. iii. 46, II. i. 69, v. i. 67–8.
[2] But see note on IV. v. 41.
[3] See note on I. iii. 131 and Appendix II.
[4] Sig M2ᵛ; the rest of the passage may be read in Appendix I, p. 157.

Ford was not much affected by Gainsford's clumsy attempts to improve and dramatize situations in this way; he had an acumen which keeps his own text clear of Gainsford's worst 'literary' asininities. But the importance of Gainsford as a source is very great indeed. Ford comes to rely upon him more and more as he works through the play and often finds in him historical details and colours which Bacon's broader and more radical treatment dispenses with. One gets the impression that, close though he often steers to Bacon, it was to Gainsford that he turned more readily. But often, also, the two sources are very markedly used in tandem; they are interwoven and conflated from line to line in a way that suggests that, so far as play-making at least went, Ford regarded them as having more or less equal authority.

Ford adheres to the historical narrative and to the order of events as described in the two sources, which are in substantial agreement in those respects. But he does of course make some departures, telescoping time and re-arranging events. In the accompanying table the sequence of the scenes (I. i to V. iii) can be correlated with the sequence of the historical episodes (numbered A to AA) so that Ford's manipulations can be seen at a glance. It will be observed that the most striking departure from historical accuracy involves considerable backdating of the first Cornish rising (M) and its terminating battle (N). Here Ford is really exploiting a pattern which is already laid down in the sources. Both Gainsford and Bacon found it convenient to deal with the Cornish episode so as to have it cleared out of the way before they came to describe events in Scotland which really occurred simultaneously with the rising. Although of course the historians are clear that these events *were* simultaneous, and Ford leaves it to be quite powerfully inferred that they were not, the narrative *pattern* is much the same in either case. Episode Q is an interesting anticipation of a different kind, and seems designed, as Anderson has suggested,[1] to increase the impression that Henry had anticipated trouble in Scotland long before it actually came; but I doubt the view that the separation of events in Scotland from those in Cornwall (in point of time) is more than a case of both the playwright and the historians hitting upon a

[1] See pp. xliii, lxviii below.

Act & Scene	Date	Place	Synopsis of Principal Events numbered A to AA	
I. i	Dec.–Jan. 1494–95	Westminster	A	Sir R. Clifford returns to England (c. Christmas 1494).
			B	Henry removes his court to the Tower (4 Jan. 1495).
I. ii	Nov. 1495	Edinburgh	F	News of Warbeck's imminent arrival in Scotland.
I. iii	Jan. 1495 July 1495 June 1497	Tower of London	C	Clifford's betrayal of Stanley to Henry (Jan. 1495).
			E	Warbeck's attempt to invade at Deal (July 1495).
			M	The first Cornish rising (June 1497).
II. i	Nov. 1495	Stirling or Edinburgh	G	Reception of Warbeck by James IV.
II. ii	Feb. 1495 Nov. 1495 summer 1497	Tower of London	D	Execution of Sir W. Stanley (16 Feb. 1495).
			G	Reception of Warbeck by James IV (Nov. 1495).
			M	The first Cornish rising (June 1497).
			Q	Preparations for defence against Scotland (summer 1497).
II. iii	Jan. 1496	Edinburgh	H	Warbeck's marriage to Katherine.
III. i.	17 June 1497	Westminster	N	Day of the battle against the Cornish rebels at Blackheath; end of first Cornish rising.
III. ii	Jan. 1496 autumn 1496 July 1497	Edinburgh	H	Warbeck's marriage to Katherine (Jan. 1496).
			K	Preparations for the Scottish raid into Northumberland (autumn 1496).
			O	Preparations for the siege of Norham (July 1497).

Act & Scene	Date	Place	Synopsis of Principal Events numbered A to AA	
III. iii	summer 1496	Westminster	J	Pedro Hialas sets out for Scotland.
III. iv	autumn 1496 July 1497	Norham	L/P	The Scottish raid into Northumberland (autumn 1496) and the siege of Norham (July 1497), treated as one event.
IV. i	July 1497	Ayton, Berwickshire	R	The English raid into Berwickshire.
IV. ii	July 1497	Jedburgh	S	Treaty between England and Scotland entailing Warbeck's departure from Scotland.
IV. iii	July 1497	Jedburgh	S	—ditto—
IV. iv	summer 1497	Westminster	T	Henry prepares for Warbeck [see notes on ll. 69, 83].
IV. v	7 (10) Sept. 1497	Whitesand Bay, Cornwall.	U	Warbeck lands in Cornwall.
V. i	Sept. 1497	St Michael's Mount	V W	Warbeck flees to sanctuary at Beaulieu (21 Sept. 1497). Katherine is taken (Sept. 1497).
V. ii	Sept.–Oct. 1497	Woodstock/ Taunton	V Y X	Warbeck flees to sanctuary at Beaulieu (21 Sept. 1497). Warbeck is brought before Henry (Oct. 1497). Katherine is brought before Henry (Oct. 1497).
V. iii	June 1498 Nov. 1499	Cheapside/ (?) The Tower, or Tyburn	Z AA	Warbeck in the stocks (15 & 18 June 1498). Warbeck hanged at Tyburn (23 Nov. 1499).

similar narrative pattern as being the most effective and the easiest
to handle. If two big events occur simultaneously it *is* possible to
interweave the accounts of them, 'imitating' the simultaneity in
narrative form; but it is far easier to dispose of them one by one,
and, in a play of the type that Ford was writing, it is virtually impossible to do otherwise. It is certain that events L and P, the two
Scottish incursions into Northumberland of 1496 and 1497, were
combined into one incursion to avoid repetition and for the sake of
dramatic impact. After this point in the play (III. iv) it will be observed that the order of the episodes corresponds pretty exactly to
the order of history as Ford knew it from his sources.

Narrative and characterization always interact, of course; invention by the playwright of material not found in his sources
within either realm is likely to affect them both. But in *Perkin
Warbeck* it seems fairly safe to say that the truly significant inven-
tions centre on characterization. There are one or two characters,
of whom Dalyell is the most important, who are purely fictional,
that is, who are not mentioned in the sources at all; virtually in the
same category is Huntly, whom the sources name as Katherine's
father but disclose nothing else about. I discuss elsewhere the contribution made by these two personages to the play. It is a very vital
one, but can only be properly viewed as proportionate to the rest.
Apart from whatever debt may be owing to Dekker for Huntly,[1]
it is quite independent of source-material. The most important
member of this group is Katherine herself. She is a magnificently
unsentimentalized idea, virtually flawless in the coherence of its
imagining. From her first moments of shrewd appraising as she
emerges from her circle into individuation in II. i to the severe and
exciting logic of her final decisions in V. iii, she brings home to us
what a great novelist Ford might have made had he lived in the age
of Henry James. This brilliant *persona* has no real counterpart in
the sources. In seeking an origin for her, we are reduced to those
rather unsatisfactory suppositions about 'germs' and 'hints' that
are used to beg so many questions in Shakespearian source-study.
It can be placed on record that in Bacon there is a sentence, in
Gainsford a few pages, and in *Albions England* the crudest of adum-

---

[1] See pp. xxxi, xxxii–xxxiii above.

brations—of all three of which we can say that at the least they would not have proved inimical to Ford's invention of Katherine and that at the most they would have given him some slight warrant, or even (in the case of Bacon's sentence) something resembling the inspiration, for what he did.[1]

The master-stroke of invention in the play relates to Warbeck's characterization, in particular to the attribute which he possesses of appearing at no point to waver in his inward conviction and outward assertion of his royalty, that he is in reality Dick the Fourth, Edward IV's younger son. All the sources contradict this flatly, in the first place by recording his confession that he was in reality the son of John Osbek, in the second place by the mordant undercutting of his pretensions proceeding from the narrator. This second element is of course represented in *Perkin* (since it is a play and not a historical narrative) by what characters other than Warbeck say and do about him; it therefore has less authority than the several narrators wield; or, at least, its authority is of a different kind, only to be exerted by means of our imaginative participation in the work of art, in which it is only one element amongst several others. I have described elsewhere, in the critical account of the play, how I think this works out. It cannot be too strongly emphasized (since in the study of Shakespeare it has so often been neglected) that when a historical narrative is being 'translated' into a five-act drama, all the perspectives shift around and all the elements alter their relation to each other. The implications are without end, and the opportunities magnificent. It is no longer of any interest, for example, to try to establish whether Ford believed in the same way that Bacon and Gainsford did that Warbeck was a fraud; the point has a relevance to the narrator of a history which virtually disappears when it is a playwright that is being defined. Ford simply, in inventing the Warbeck we have, seized the magnificence of his opportunity; that he was able to do so is perhaps as much due to his basic gift for seeing things as a playwright should as to anything traceable in his sources. Another sentence in Bacon[2] is sometimes quoted as

[1] See notes on III. ii. 139–86, v. iii. 81–184, and Appendix II.

[2] 'himself, with long and continual counterfeiting, and with oft telling a lie, was turned by habit almost into the thing he seemed to be; and from a liar to a believer'; see note on v. ii. 132–3.

though it were the 'key' or 'germ' of the Warbeck of the play, the idea that generated Ford's *persona* (which is presumably imagined as a kind of 'clothing' of the idea—source-study is rotten with these questionable metaphors). But this sentence is nothing more than an *explanation* of Warbeck's behaviour, satisfactory to Bacon, and represented by Ford in the play as satisfactory to king Henry, who duly incorporates it into the structure. But it is not a *description* of the behaviour of the character in the play, and it is therefore hard to see why it should be presumed to have inspired Ford to seize his opportunity. As a description of Warbeck's behaviour, indeed, it falls a good deal short. For the absolutely essential thing about Ford's portrayal of Warbeck, the real stroke of genius, which makes the whole thing worthwhile and validates the labours of commentators, is this: Warbeck never does anything in the play to suggest either that he is playing a part and knows it, or—and this is the vital point—that he is, in Baconian fashion, playing a part and no longer knows it. Others within the play may offer their explanations—which, as we have seen, include Bacon's—and may comment to their hearts' content on his stage-like greatness and impostorous presumption. These comments are, from one point of view, what may be called protective or adjusting devices; they ensure the 'balanced comment' which is supposed to be favoured by television companies; they must have warranted the soundness, moral and historical, of the artefact from the point of view of such men as Sir Henry Herbert. What they provide is coincident with the disabling contempt found for Warbeck in Bacon and the nagging orthodoxies of Gainsford, and, *mutatis mutandis*, mirrors them both. But beyond these, there is, in the heart of the artefact, something which is not wholly susceptible to their modes of qualification or explanation, something therefore free and anarchic: the Warbeck whose convictions about his own nature appear both sane and noble and appeal as such directly out of the play to its spectators. *That* is the stroke of genius, and it is that that appears independent of anything identifiable in the sources. It is done of course not for the sake of trying to persuade us that Warbeck is what he thinks he is but because it is what Ford perceived would 'make' his play as a dramatic experience: one in which the spectators must measure the impact and appeal of Warbeck against the assured testimony of Henry and a whole range of witnesses, including the source-historians themselves. It should be stressed that this is for the spectators primarily a dramatic and literary experience, not one in which they are asked to judge like a jury or a court of law. But we are here moving beyond the range of source-study, where nothing less than the analysis of the whole play which is offered in another section of this introduction will serve.

Plainer debts and departures from the sources in the realm of characterization may be briefly outlined. Henry, perhaps, is basically, in his sombre strength and his absolute mastery over his servants, Bacon's figure; but a little of Gainsford's fictionalized Euripides-quoting moodiness and flamboyance has rubbed off on him. He is to some extent assimilated to the idealized stereotype of the seventeenth-century monarch by being gifted with additional foresight and mercifulness; but Anderson's view that he is so far an improved figure upon that found in the sources as to constitute an 'ideal king' seems to me more doubtful.[1] The portrayal of James of Scotland stays about equally close to the sources, except that James is represented in the matter of his dealings with Huntly over his daughter's marriage as a headstrong autocrat, designedly neglecting the advice of his counsellors and thus affording an instructive contrast to Henry. Whether his conduct at the end of his part in the play—his dismissal of Warbeck—is intended to represent a growth in political realism of a morally improving sort will depend upon one's interpretation of the nature of the play as a whole, but, with the one exception noted, all the material for views of him as an exemplary realist, a callow and despicable opportunist, a young and clumsy tyro in the art of government, or 'perfect Stuart', or any number of combinations of all these, will be found alike in the sources as in the play.

Most of the subordinate characters surrounding Henry, such as Urswick, Surrey, Oxford, and Daubeney, are purely functional and very slightly characterized both in the chronicles and in the play. The names of Warbeck's followers, Frion, Skelton, Heron, Astley, and a-Water, occur in the historians. There is very little,

---

[1] See pp. liii–liv, lxviii; nn. on II. ii. 154, III. i. 80–5, IV. iv. 83, V. ii. 43–5.

however, unless it be their trades, to warrant the clownish carica-
tures offered us by Ford, although both Bacon and Gainsford make
it clear that they were a poor lot.[1] The notion of making Frion
devious and treacherous and full of contempt for his associates
may be a fair inference from the playwright's knowledge that he
had been Henry's French Secretary and had deserted him. On the
stage at the Phoenix he may well have been represented as a stage-
Frenchman. By contrast, Hialas and Bishop Fox are described in
the sources as wise, and temperately wise they are too in the play.
Ford wrote into his play a number of stereotypes, triggered off by
a few names and arrangements in the sources. This was a perfectly
proper thing to do if, with so large a cast, scale was to be kept and
the larger characters seen in their exact and various dimensions.

One puzzle remains: the episode in II. ii when Stanley marks
the face of his betrayer Clifford with a cross before going to the
block. It is hard to believe that Ford simply invented this. It has the
air of a traditional story deriving from some fact of history or custom. I have not traced it in the historians, and its original, if there
was one, might well be quite unconnected with Warbeck or even
with the reign of Henry VII. But that Ford had somewhere come
across a story involving a condemned man, his betrayer, and the
sign of the cross seems very likely.

A last issue that might count as source-study is that of Shakespeare's direct influence on the play, especially through *Richard II*
and *Henry IV*. This has been discussed in another section as in-
separable from a description of the play's major design and purposes.

A good deal of attention has been paid in the commentary to
Ford's moment-by-moment dependence upon his sources, and to
the many small informational debts and artistic decisions which
were entailed by the business of 'translating' narrative histories into
Jacobean or Caroline drama. In the commentary there are approxi-
mately a hundred entries whose principal substance is the relation

---

[1] This must now be modified in the light of Michael Neill's discovery
that Ford derived the personal characteristics of his John a-Water from
Gainsford's account, in the Lambert Simnel portion of his narrative, of the
earl of Lincoln (sig. D3^v): see M. Neill, 'Ford and Gainsford: an Unnoticed
Borrowing', forthcoming in *Notes and Queries*, N.S., xv (1968).

of text to the historical sources. This in itself is a sufficient indication of Ford's very great dependence on them. He obviously worked with Bacon and Gainsford open on the table in front of him; he allowed their words to shape his rhetoric (often, especially with Gainsford, a process of verbal osmosis can be detected) and practically all the facts of history in the play, however insignificant, are authenticated from their pages. It is all the more splendid that Ford understood wherein his ultimate responsibility as a playwright rested; and that by a few handsome strokes of inventive insight he was able to make all the drab dependence and crowding details glitter and cohere.

4. THE PLAY AND ITS CRITICS

Perkin Warbeck has not really set off vast disagreements amongst its select company of commentators, although some pleasing little see-saws of opinion can be discerned. Lamb's enormous enthusiasm for *The Broken Heart*, as represented in his *Specimens*, originated a general feeling of approval for Ford. Hazlitt (*Lectures on the Dramatic Literature of the Age of Elizabeth* in 1820) dissented—his deadliest thrust was to compare Ford's plays with Joanna Baillie's: but he had nothing to say about our play. Nor had Jeffrey, although his essay in the *Edinburgh Review* includes an admirable description of Ford's 'singular, though very beautiful' style:

> almost always coloured with a modest tinge of ingenuity, and fashioned, rather too visibly, upon a particular model of elegance and purity.[1]

In the *Quarterly Review* at the same time—the simultaneity is accounted for by the publication in 1811 of Weber's edition, which was being cut up with relish—Gifford thinks poorly of *Perkin*, because it

> follows with injudicious fidelity the narrative delivered by Lord Bacon. . . He seems in fact to have aimed at nothing beyond that kind of compliment which he might conceive he was paying the noble historian, by bringing his work on the stage; no attempt is made at embellishment, no delineation of character (with one ex-

---

[1] *Edinburgh Review*, August 1811, no. XXXVI, p. 287.

ception, the Earl of Huntley) is even attempted . . . a chronicle and
nothing more; a chronicle, too, in its most exceptionable shape;
for while we hesitate to allow it the merit of truth, it comes recom-
mended by none of the graces of fiction, and for the mere purposes
of entertainment, the narrative [Bacon] deserves the preference.[1]

This, probably the first critique of any extent that the play had
earned, is careless, as well as being a bad augury. There is no reason
to suppose that Gifford had at that time looked beyond the first
relevant page in Bacon in drawing his hasty conclusion about the
play's improper fidelity to that source. His judgement reflects little
credit on his charge that Weber hadn't bothered to look at Bacon
at all.

The bad augury may be countered, though, with the opinions of
a writer in the *Monthly Review* the following spring, who was probably the scholar and translator J. H. Merivale.[2] He wrote a page or so
of exceedingly warm praise for *Perkin*, particularly for its delinea-
tion of Henry, Warbeck, and Dalyell:

> One of the most remarkable circumstances attending the play is,
> that, on reading it, we can scarcely help imagining that the author
> was secretly persuaded of the justice of Warbeck's pretensions.
> His character from first to last is that which would have become
> the real duke of York—not a moment of weakness or despondency
> occurs, in which, *even to himself*, he acknowledges the guilt of im-
> posture. On the other hand, Henry is (at least in his conduct to-
> wards this unfortunate young man) nothing but the cold, wary,
> and relentless tyrant, for whom the most devoted loyalists can feel
> no attachment, and from whom every ardent and independent
> spirit must turn with disgust and hatred.[3]

It is amusing to compare this view of Henry with those of modern
moralistic commentators, more Tudor than the Tudors, who see
Henry as their favourite monster, the 'ideal king'.

Merivale at least makes it possible to understand the spirit in
which Ford was read in the Shelley circle. Shelley refers to Ford in
the preface to *The Revolt of Islam* in a context which suggests that
he was thinking chiefly of *Perkin*.[4] Mary Shelley's three-decker

---

[1] *Quarterly Review*, December 1811, p. 473.
[2] See Sargeaunt, p. 220.   [3] *Monthly Review*, April 1812, p. 379.
[4] *Poems*, ed. C. D. Locock (1911), I. 39.

The Fortunes of Perkin Warbeck: a Romance (1830) cannot really be reckoned a critique of our play, but must be noticed. Three of its chapters carry epigraphs from *Perkin* and prove that she knew Ford. This barely readable fiction is based on the idea that Warbeck really was the son of Edward IV; its villain is Sir Robert Clifford (connexions with *The White Doe of Rylstone* might be interesting to trace), whom we encounter first as a page-boy and who later becomes Warbeck's betrayer. From somewhere there strays into the tale Moonina, a Moorish maiden; but Mrs Shelley's chief debt to the play is the character of Katherine Gordon, handled with a truly dreadful sentimentality.

After this accomplishment of Mrs Shelley's there is something of a pause, filled mainly with the work of Gifford and of Dyce on their editions; editors in those days were not expected to write critical studies of individual plays.[1] During this period also Ford laid the foundation of his continuing reputation in France with the work of Taine (*Histoire de la Littérature anglaise*) and Mézières (*Contemporains et Successeurs de Shakespeare*). I cannot find that any significant views were expressed about *Perkin*. A noticeable nineteenth-century criticism came from Swinburne, who gave three or four pages of his 1875 essay on Ford to *Perkin*. Once more, we have a strong personal reaction to royalty, of the Scottish breed this time:

> The two kings are faithful and forcible studies; the smooth resolute equanimity and self-reliant craft of the first Tudor sets off the shallow chivalry and passionate unstable energy of the man of Flodden. The insolent violence of constraint put upon Huntley in the disposal of his daughter's hand is of a piece with the almost brutal tone of contempt assumed towards Warbeck, when he begins to weary of supporting the weaker cause for the mere sake of magnanimous display and irritable self-assertion. His ultimate dismissal of the star-crossed pretender is 'perfect Stuart' in its bland abnegation of faith and the lofty courtliness of manner with which engagements are flung over and pledges waved aside; whether intentionally or not, Ford has touched off to the life the family habit of repudiation, the hereditary faculty of finding the most honourable way to do the most dishonourable things.[2]

---

[1] But see Dyce, II. 217.
[2] *Essays and Studies* (London, 1875), pp. 293–4.

The play has 'perfect unity of action, a perfect straightforwardness of design'; although 'rigid and bare' by comparison with *The Broken Heart*, it manifests 'completeness of stage effect and careful composition':

> The simple and lofty purity of conception, the exact and delicate accuracy of execution, are alike unimpaired by any slip or flaw of judgement or of feeling. The heroic sincerity of Warbeck, his high courtesy and constancy, his frank gratitude and chivalrous confidence, give worthy proof of Ford's ability to design a figure of stainless and exalted presence. . . .

Swinburne's diapason concludes with what is now an ingloriously cracked note:

> It is the one high sample of historic drama produced between the age of Shakespeare and our own; the one intervening link—a link of solid and durable metal—which connects the first and the latest labours in that line of English poetry; the one triumphant attempt to sustain and transmit the tradition of that great tragic school founded by Marlowe, perfected by Shakespeare, revived by the author of 'Philip van Artevelde'.[1]

Swinburne's observations have a sugary vehemence which is no longer an acceptable critical tone, at any rate in the discussion of minor Elizabethan dramatists;[2] but in their emphases they remain broadly representative of modern opinion about the play. Respect warming towards admiration has been, and is, the keynote. Because high feelings about Tudors and Stuarts have been replaced by a cautious understanding of Elizabethan concerns *de regimine principum*, critical opinion in our own time has not oscillated even to the extent it once did in the times of Merivale or Swinburne. The point may be illustrated even by the most famous and startling of all modern opinions about *Perkin*: T.S. Eliot wrote of the play:

> it is unquestionably Ford's highest achievement, and is one of the very best historical plays outside of the works of Shakespeare in the whole of Elizabethan and Jacobean drama. . . Ford for once

---

[1] *Essays and Studies*, p. 295. The first edition of Sir Henry Taylor's dramatic romance *Philip van Artevelde* appeared in 1834.

[2] For a brilliant analysis of Swinburne's style as a critic, see Edmund Wilson, 'Swinburne's Letters and Novels' in *The Bit between my Teeth* (London, 1965), pp. 248–50.

succeeded in a most difficult attempt; and the play of *Perkin War-beck* is almost flawless.[1]

As the quotations from Swinburne have shown, much of this is orthodox, however high or low may be our estimate of the non-Shakespearian history-plays.[2] No one will be inclined to deny that *Perkin* must be included in any group constituted by Marlowe's *Edward II*, the anonymous *Woodstock* and the anonymous (and maybe Shakespearian) *Edward III*, Munday's and Drayton's *Old-castle*, or the English history-plays of Heywood. In so far as Eliot's comment has to do with the status of *Perkin* in relation to the non-Shakespearian English history-play, nobody has ever shown much sign of wanting to contravene it. But it is also a comment on the relation of *Perkin* to Ford's other plays. Looked at straightforward-ly, that is a good deal more startling. But its edge can be fairly quickly turned in a way that preserves the consensus. This, for ex-ample, is skilfully done by H. J. Oliver. Against Eliot, he can quote Havelock Ellis:

> In *Perkin Warbeck* he laid aside his characteristic defects, and also his characteristic merits, to achieve a distinct dramatic success. It is the least interesting of his plays for those who care for the pe-culiar qualities which mark Ford's genius, but it certainly ranks among our best historical dramas. Ford's interest in psychological problems may be detected in his impartial, even sympathetic, treatment of Warbeck; but for the most part this play is an excep-tion to every generalization that may be arrived at concerning his work.[3]

Or, as Una Ellis-Fermor said:

> Like *Edward II* in the series of Marlowe's plays, it is likely to please best those who least appreciate the author's individual flavour.[4]

Oliver's is a perfectly sound strategy, for it directs attention to the

[1] *Selected Essays* (London, 1934 edn), pp. 200–1.
[2] I am of course going on the assumption that Eliot meant—though he did not say—the history-play from *British* history. Even if other kinds of history-play had to be included, *Perkin* would almost certainly, so far as general critical feeling goes, qualify for a high place in the larger group.
[3] *John Ford* (Mermaid Series), London, n.d., pp. xii–xiii. See H. J. Oliver, *The Problem of John Ford* (Melbourne, 1955), p. 99.
[4] *The Jacobean Drama* (London, 1947 edn), p. 233.

D

area of likely agreement: that *Perkin* is *different* from Ford's other plays, not that it is the *best* of them. It averts attention from the latter claim, and quite fairly. For Eliot's 'highest' as a verdict on the merits of *Perkin* as compared with those of other plays is not discussable as such. This is because Eliot himself makes no real attempt to justify it. His long paragraph on the play contains only one sentence that enforces the *comparative* part of the judgement, and that is somewhat negatively phrased:

> To make this base-born pretender to the throne of England into a dignified and heroic figure was no light task, and is not one which we should, after reading the other plays, have thought Ford competent to perform; but here for once there is no lapse in taste and judgement.

It is, then, 'taste and judgement' which appear to distinguish the play from Ford's other works (a position which is close to Swinburne's praise for it as a 'sample of regular and classic form, a sedate study after a given model'). But I do not believe that it can safely be inferred, given the context of the rest of Eliot's essay, where the feeling for Ford comes through especially in the selection of the quotations and the praise for the versification, that Eliot wished it to be assumed that 'taste and judgement' were the final criteria which would ordinarily serve to distinguish the 'highest' from the rest. Greatly though he may have valued 'taste and judgement', and important though they are, it is difficult to believe that it was for their sake in chief that Eliot singled out Ford for commentary. Was it not rather for the sake of a cadence, a drift of colour, a tone of voice?

> Remember,
> When we last gathered roses in the garden,
> I found my wits; but truly you lost yours.[1]

Those marvellous lines of the mad Penthea are the quintessence of Eliot's Ford.

At the least, the rest of Eliot's paragraph about *Perkin* does not support the comparative (and startling) part of his verdict. It constitutes a more or less conventional selection of the special ex-

[1] *The Broken Heart* (ed. B. Morris, London, 1965), IV. ii. 120–1.

cellences that his predecessors had seen in the play without wanting to claim that therefore it was the best: Warbeck's constancy, Katherine's loyalty, Dalyell's decency. Here is the stress on characterology which has always dominated the criticism of Ford in general and of this play in particular. Eliot's criticism, then, does not markedly disturb the consensus, if only because critical opinion has not been able to rise to a challenge which is virtually unsupported by its context, and one which, in the light of that context, begins to look more like the expression of a private a-critical fondness for the play. Eliot's nineteenth-century predecessors were worried about Ford's subject-matter in his other plays, his 'decadence' and sensationalism. They found relief from these matters in the severe nobility, the sedate and orderly qualities of *Perkin*. Although only Eliot went so far as to say—without, as I have impertinently suggested, actually *meaning*—that these qualities make *Perkin* the best, the consensus consists in the common recognition that *Perkin* is not like the others, that it is, as Havelock Ellis put it, the least marked by the peculiar qualities of Ford's genius.

As an admirer of those peculiar qualities, especially as they are displayed in '*Tis Pity She's A Whore* and *The Broken Heart*, I regret that this is so, but I can see no way of evading the facts. These tend, rather disappointingly, to rob of one large dimension any critical performance that may be attempted on the play's behalf. On the other hand, they also mean that the critic of *Perkin* escapes from under, as it were, the general argument about Ford's work, which finds its polarities in, say, the essay by Stuart Sherman and the book by G. F. Sensabaugh on the one side and in the books by Robert Davril and Clifford Leech on the other. National styles in the approach to English literature are a forbidden subject, otherwise one might be tempted to enlarge on the separation here, which is by no means without significance, between a European and an American school.

The 'general argument' just referred to is about in what sense Ford was a 'decadent'; about whether he was a 'modernist' or whether he shared much more deeply in his own historical context —a point neatly taken in the title of Leech's book *John Ford and the Drama of his Time*. It is also an argument about whether, in Sensabaugh's phrase, he endeavoured to 'turn the moral order upside down' by, amongst other things, questioning the 'laws of conscience and of civil use', or whether, as Leech puts it, he was a good deal less antinomian than all that implies and was not very much victimized either by Caroline *préciosité* or by a 'scientific determinism' derived from Burton's *Anatomy*. As a long-standing proponent of the latter view,[1] which is now gaining ground even in the United States, I am sorry that the whole argument can largely be conducted without any real need for such evidence as *Perkin* may supply. While it considerably simplifies the discussion of *Perkin*, this state of affairs considerably sharpens our sense of the reason for it: the comparative isolation of our play from the rest of the Fordian canon. And this in itself is only another aspect of a larger condition: the comparative isolation of *Perkin* from the rest of Caroline drama.

At this point can be discerned taking shape what *lack* of critical consensus there is likely to be about this play. For, if it is isolated from the rest of Caroline drama, is it perhaps more nearly related to the drama of an earlier period? And will this relationship, if it can be established, detach *Perkin* even more than has hitherto been perceived from other plays by Ford which share his concern for 'psychological subtleties', for the depiction of emotional states, for pathos, pity, and for that love's sacrifice which, as Richard Crashaw unblushingly observed, is 'but the broken heart'? On this kind of ground we must tread warily. The polarities are not so clear, although the contingent implications are at least as far-reaching and sensitive as those which attend upon the argument about the modernist and traditional elements in Ford's work. For they touch in the end on the problem of how the Elizabethan history-play ought to be read. I put it with blunt emphasis on extremes which may yet meet: is the history-play to be regarded as a piously didactic tract for the times or as a work of dramatic art? Is *Perkin*, or other plays like it, an impersonal performance, during which the playwright loses his identity in his putative 'intellectual milieu'?

---

[1] See 'Cult and Initiates in Ford's *Love's Sacrifice*', *Modern Language Quarterly*, IX (1950), 298–306, and 'Marriage and the Domestic Drama in Heywood and Ford', *English Studies*, XXXII (1951), 200–16.

Or is it a personal achievement in which the dramatist who traced out the lineaments of Henry VII is still recognizable as the same man who conceived the aboundingly different ones of Penthea or Giovanni ?

The modern commentator who wishes to supply a reasonably full account of the play's individuality must try to give proper weight both to the 'Truth and State' which Ford talks about in his prologue and to the 'strength of passion' which he celebrates in his epilogue. As he perfectly well knew from his devoted study of Shakespeare, it was entirely possible, if you had the genius, to create a history-play in which the dialogue between the two elements makes a great harmony. Modern criticism has shown some tendency towards deafness in this matter. Miss Sargeaunt, for example, wrote:

> Ford is not really concerned at all with the fortunes of England, with its traditions, its politics, and its countryside; of these he treats solely because of their effect on the somewhat fantastic character, as he has conceived it, that chance has called on to play a leading part for a short while in the historical scene.[1]

This view must have seemed more true at a time when students of the history-play had scarcely heard of the Homilies and were altogether less conscious than they are nowadays of the didactic functions of the genre. That awareness may, however, lead us to over-stress that very element of 'State' whose presence in the play Miss Sargeaunt minimized. Thus Irving Ribner's account, in a book which has many of the virtues of a standard work on *The English History Play in the Age of Shakespeare*, is virtually *Perkin* without the Pretender. Squeezed between his exemplary monarchs, little is left of the 'somewhat fantastic character' that for Miss Sargeaunt and a long line of her predecessors constituted the chief appeal of our play. Of the same school of procedure is Donald K. Anderson Jr, who begins his knowledgeable piece on the play with this paragraph:

> John Ford is not generally considered a political dramatist, but he would seem to be one in *Perkin Warbeck*. Illustrating the pragmatic viewpoint of such theorists as Machiavelli and Bacon, Ford

[1] Sargeaunt, p. 69.

portrays his ideal king in the person of the wise and eminently
practical Henry VII, and so considerable is the playwright's attention to competent and incompetent governing that *Perkin Warbeck*
might well be called a lesson in kingship.[1]

A study in a 'fantastic character' or a 'lesson in kingship'—it is a
debate about this kind of issue that some recent commentary enforces.

5. MAJESTY AND PASSION

For the audience at the Phoenix the opening scene must have had
an unaccustomed taste. The largeness of scale and high pitch, the
sense that a great crisis in the English polity is being unsentiment-
ally plucked out of the haze—all this is something which had grown
unfamiliar during the years of decline. Ford is aware that he is re-
newing a great tradition. The echoes of *1 Henry IV* point to this.
So does the brusquely classical spectacle of the English king 'supported to his throne' by his councillors. There are many high personages on the stage; the sympathies course strongly between them
and the highest of all. No other of Ford's opening scenes engages
his theatre in action of this size and variety (his plays usually begin
with a quiet conversation between two persons). The throne itself
physically dominates this stage. Henry, upon it, is like a sea-mark
against which beat the varying tides of the national fortunes, as
they are reported to us by all these vigorous and high-languaged
men.

The language itself is resonantly filled with figures of effort and
violence, of gross disturbance and harsh irony. We hear in Henry's
first speech (I. i. 5–6) of his lavishing 'sweat and blood / In scorn
and laughter to the ghosts of York'—a terrific, indeed Conradian,
image of a man sweating his life out for the amusement of phan-
toms; vengeance pours down like rain; there is a 'rent face / And
bleeding wounds', the 'blood-shrunk commonwealth' (I. i. 9–10,
25), 'this poor, panting island' (I. i. 40), and other great thrusts
of violent gesture. The princes in the Tower have been 'Forced
to a violent grave', the black usurper 'struck . . . to a carcass' (I. i.
30–5); the 'headless trunk' of her father and the bodies of her

---

[1] 'Kingship in Ford's *Perkin Warbeck*', *ELH*, XXVII (1960), p. 177.

smothered nephews are shored up against a 'woman-monster' (I. i. 45–52) who is figured as a bottomless mine venting ore; a cub, an 'eager whelp', is to be hunted to death 'even in the beldam's closet' (like David Rizzio), tall striplings are to be crushed to pieces by a steel hammer (I. i. 122, 63). Proportioned to this past and threatened violence is the brutal fantasy of Margaret of York's supposed birth-pangs. All the evil, we are given to understand, flows from a Duessa-like creature from whose unnaturally burdened womb come stripling-pretenders, 'even the youngest . . . fifteen years of age' (I. i. 54–62). It is a verbal cartoon. Men's thoughts are distended by the weird turbulence of the time, and 'troubles and sedition' agitate every mind. One of the functions of the scene is to expound these. The frantic enumeration of the ninety years during which there perished 'Threescore great dukes and earls, a thousand lords / And valiant knights, two hundred fifty thousand of English subjects' (I. i. 16–19) is only a prelude to a sketch of Richard's bloody reign, of Margaret, fruitful with confusion, and of the 'spectacles of ruin' ensuing upon Lambert Simnel's enterprise and the battle at Stoke. Finally, we are informed of Warbeck's career to date—one which has brought French and Irish allies to his side, and set Europe by the ears. All this sufficiently warns us that a fever of a long and exhausting sort has reached a point of crisis. At the same time we are offered the spectacle of a monarch who is stoutly weatherproofed against the political storm, if not actually, at present, riding it in full confidence. Whenever they are given a chance, his servants eagerly affirm their allegiance with loyal noises and gestures, and they are bitterly contemptuous of the conspirators. In a quieter moment at the end of the scene Henry takes control. All this is one of those unimpeachable openings of the old-style history-play—processional entry, storm-battered conference, the great king and his ministers. Ford has even seized the opportunity to convey that one of those ministers is a traitor (I. i. 81–2, 101–2). This scene is vigorously multi-dimensional, old-fashioned perhaps, but unquestionably in the great tradition.

With scene ii Ford returns to what is, for him, a more ordinary opening. We would expect an experienced dramatist, especially one who had learned from Shakespeare, to contrive such juxtapositions. The first scene is one of disturbing and at times unnatural pressures; the second, of high civility, where the pressures have been organized according to a code which reconciles etiquette and natural merit. The scene is specially interesting to anyone who has remarked the theme of enforced marriage in Ford's other plays. The point of reference for the first scene will be the great tradition which it reanimates; for this one, it will be the Fordian ethos as we find it in his personal tradition. Dalyell seeks Katherine's hand in marriage; Huntly will neither approve nor forbid what might be, because of Katherine's royal blood, a disastrous mistake from his point of view. He leaves his daughter to make her own decision. When she takes charge of the scene her language is plainly designed to mime the high ideal of civility and awaken our admiration for her charm and good sense and for the moral elegance of the world to which she belongs. She 'manages', as Henry James would say, beautifully. Her airs and graces, like those of a Scott heroine, have a positively bravura effect:

> My worthiest lord and father, the indulgence
> Of your sweet composition thus commands
> The lowest of obedience; you have granted
> A liberty so large that I want skill
> To choose without direction of Example:
> From which I daily learn, by how much more
> You take off from the roughness of a father,
> By so much more I am engaged to tender
> The duty of a daughter.   (I. ii. 126–34)

Huntly is delighted with her 'performance', which, in cold blood, will seem to us absurdly stiff and formal. But it should not be viewed in cold blood, but as the presentation of a young, untried girl triumphantly rising to an occasion. Acted with the right measure of charm and vivacity, the scene as a whole should serve, as it is plainly intended to do, to centre this trio of persons firmly in our imaginative sympathies for the rest of the play. They have very creditably accomplished, without anger or fuss or ill-breeding, their little domestic negotiation. They employ few striking lines or clamant images. It is not that kind of scene; it depends instead upon the rhythms of civility, which are not necessarily always those of fine involution or stiff compliment, as witness Huntly's:

Settle
Thy will and reason by a strength of judgement;
For, in a word, I give thee freedom; take it.
If equal fates have not ordained to pitch
Thy hopes above my height, let not thy passion
Lead thee to shrink mine honour in oblivion.
Thou art thine own; I have done.   (I. ii. 118–24)

This has the strength and containment which it advocates. These personages will not subject each other to vulgar enforcements arising out of either Huntly's ambition or Dalyell's desire. The only importunity comes, ominously, from outside in the form of the message from king James summoning Huntly, which he disregards until it is repeated at the end.

There could hardly be a greater contrast between Henry's England, with all its disturbed and stained colour, and Huntly's Scotland, coolly organizing its human pressures. But I do not think that Ford is striving to build up a contrast that can be fully stated in national terms. The differences are of a more subtle sort. They are often to be deployed as the play works itself out.

The return to England and Henry in scene iii is a return to darkness, lit by ragged lights. It is the Tower, and a betrayal, an act of shame, sombre, and jagged with Henry's passion of disappointment and shock. Ford is trying to give us a further insight into the disturbed kingdom—more inward still, for we trench on the darker secrets of state. Henry is not on his throne now, but prudently housed in his London fortress and political prison; everything is *in camera*. The impression, both visual and verbal, is of darkness pierced by lights and shocks. They enter with lights (I. iii. 0.1); it is very late at night in the private closet (I. iii. 5–6); Warbeck is figured as a meteor and comet, his flames momentarily sparkling in the night, flashing, flourishing in the sky like a popish firework (I. iii. 35–42). When Clifford finally names Stanley—a black deed against which the rays of his conscience feebly struggle—the king cries out:

Urswick, the light!
View well my face, sirs; is there blood left in it?
(I. iii. 87–8)

The bloodless face looks white under the glare of the lamp against the surrounding shadows (an effect contrivable at the Phoenix). Henry's shocked cries about his love for Stanley match this tearing open of the pall of concealment. The whole scene, indeed, figures forth the thrust of light into dark places and the blinding shocks which this can administer to both the subjects and the agents. There are other meanings. Warbeck's perversion of such men as Stanley is dangerous to Henry's balance ('You lose your constant temper', Bishop Fox says to him), but there is no relaxation of the contempt felt for Warbeck himself or of the assurance that he will be easily dealt with. We hear about his 'confused rabble of lost bankrupts' (I. iii. 57); their 'dull capacities' become linked with the rascal Cornish, whose insurgence we hear of in the last minute of the scene. Henry's worries are not in that quarter; it is Stanley, Stanley who torments him, the ruler's nightmare, treachery in the inner cabinet. This is the emphasis of the concluding couplet as he looks forward to a sleepless night, brooding on Stanley: 'When counsels fail, and there's in man no trust . . .' (I. iii. 137). The episode serves to bring nearer to us the much remoter, throned figure of the first scene. Ideal king though he be, and always one step ahead in policy (as this scene clearly demonstrates), he is subject to grief and perturbation to the point of wishing to give up (I. iii. 110–12); like Henry IV he is pinched by majesty and sleeps, or does not sleep, with golden care upon his pillow. The echoes, it is sad to say, only serve to remind us of powers that lie utterly beyond Ford's reach. Although the lines have been admired, Ford fails to charge Henry's exclaims of passion (I. iii. 104–19) with high poetic force and interest. He sticks too slavishly and too lazily to the second-rate phrases invented by Hall and Gainsford.

By delaying until the second Act the appearance of Warbeck himself Ford has exploited certain opportunities inherent in his design. No doubt, in any production, including the one at the Phoenix, the company's leading actor plays the pretender. So we have, for as long as possible, something, together with whatever extra skill or interest the chief man may command, to keep us looking forward. Anticipation of that kind is after all one of the chief pleasures of going to the theatre. Ford has also employed the time in giving us a great deal of loaded information about the

pretender. There is his company of lost bankrupts and the shame-
fully abortive attempt at Deal; there is the Henrician version of
him as a 'gewgaw', a 'smoke of straw', the fruit of Margaret of
York's unnatural hatreds, her idol, the false blaze that fooled the
Irish. All this (and there is a lot of it) is germane to the matter;
but it does not bind the playwright. We are not shown it but only
told it, and by his enemies, too, however indignant and trust-
worthy. Ford does not want us to disbelieve it, but it is doubtful
if he wishes us to tot it up as evidence which inoculates us for
ever against Warbeck's 'jugglery' of appeal. The design is more
subtle and more truly dramatic. All the contre-Warbeck material,
if we have been attending to it, surely prepares us for a contemptible squib and joker, a shabby tool already blunted by failure and
panic, a 'painted' creature and caterpillar of the commonwealth.
If he is nasty, it is only with the nastiness of the 'Pestilent adder'
who lackeys him (I. iii. 67); the danger comes from the great men
—the Austrian emperor, the French king—who are using him.
This is the Warbeck whom Henry and all his ministers think so
little of. When we do finally see him, we are not, I think, expected
to discount his every air and grace by measuring it against the
Henrician image of him, of which we have heard so much. The
playwright has surely calculated, with greater theatrical aplomb,
upon an effect of *surprise*. There is to be a vivid surge of interest
because of the difference between what we have been told and
what we now see and hear. The prudent dramatist may prepare us
for his effects precisely by not preparing us; what we are told about
a character before he appears is not given us always or exclusively
in order to inform us about him. It would be as naïve to neglect this
point as to suppose that a theatrical surprise simply annuls all fore-
knowledge.

The pleased astonishment and interest, which is the dominant
feeling aroused by II. i, the scene of Warbeck's first appearance, are
qualified by suspicions inherited from the Henrician version and
accented here by the Countess of Crawford's irony and Huntly's
pained resignation to James's headstrong will. In this scene, the
play, like most sensitive dramas, is much at the mercy of its pro-
ducer. He can easily take the glow and burnish from Warbeck's

first appearance, if he wishes to; he can guy its ceremony and inter-
polate clownish gambols for Warbeck's followers. But even if this
is done, Ford's conception of Warbeck's playing a difficult part
with full conviction and self-dependence must come through. The
throne is again used, this time for James. James's 'Present him to
our arms' (II. i. 38) is the climax to a Stuart exordium on the theme
of kings as exiles and witnesses; it suggests that when Warbeck,
elaborately ushered through rows of gentlemen, presents himself
before the throne, James descends so that king and pretender may
embrace in the centre of the stage. It is a rehearsed state-ceremony
to the clamour of hautboys (II. i. 38–9), and of course has something theatrical and 'staged' about it. To the whole situation belongs
an in-built and indispensable theatricality. This lends its ambiguous charm to any play about a pretender. For how are we, in the
theatre, to distinguish between the man who plays the king and
the man who plays the man who plays the king? When the chain of
communication between actual man and player-king is lengthened
in this way, our leading actor has an almost irresistible temptation
to display his skill by numbering its links, and in the age of Piran-
dello or Ionesco we are only too likely to accept, or demand, much
clever manipulation of the two masks. Here again the play is much
at the mercy of its director. The absence of soliloquy, to which
several critics have called attention, and a great deal of other evidence, shortly to be discussed, go to show that Ford would have
asked for a reading that permits Warbeck to play the king (or at
least the son of Edward IV) with precisely the same degree of cere-
monious conviction as his fellow-actors may be presumed to be
lavishing on the rôles of Henry VII and James IV. He must, in
short, behave, in Bacon's words,[1] like a 'believer' and not like a
'liar'.

From our first direct encounter with him onwards, it ought to
be emphasized that Ford chose not to represent Warbeck as an expressive rogue, or even as a poor, verdant fool, sporting, like the
grasshopper, in the gilt beams of Scottish favour. The dramatist
probably felt constitutionally less disposed to agitation about his
rights and wrongs than, say, Mrs Shelley did. C. V. Wedgewood

[1] See note on v. ii. 132–3.

has remarked, very truly, of Ford that 'the apparent injustice of fate moves his heart but does not engage his intellect'.[1]

Warbeck's long speech (II. i. 40–79) establishes his identity not of course as the son of Edward IV but as a dramatic character. It comprises the Warbeck version of the Henrician facts, but it is doubtful if we are meant to weigh it against them one way or the other like a jury considering the evidence. Yet the comparison with a jury may hold, if only because the impression made by what the defendant appears to *be* may count at least as much as what he actually claims about the case in trial. The speech is primarily a plea for attention to his wrongs and ill-fortune. It is couched in the language of civility that is specially esteemed in this Scottish court. The speech is deeply indebted to the corresponding place in Bacon; but Bacon's units are longer and heavier, his sounds fuller, while Ford, by comparison, flows and tinkles, continually shaped by the neat lift and drop of the feminine ending. Ford omitted, for example, this striking bit in the middle of Bacon's version of the speech:

> But Almighty God, that stopped the mouth of the lion, and saved little Joash from the tyranny of Athaliah, when she massacred the King's children; and did save Isaac, when the hand was stretched forth to sacrifice him; preserved the second brother. For I myself, that stand here in your presence, am that very Richard duke of York, brother of that unfortunate Prince King Edward the fifth, now the most rightful surviving heir male to that victorious and most noble Edward, of that name the fourth, late King of England.[2]

That has more resonance than Ford desires, and, with its faint suggestion of the worm-eaten faces in the old tapestry, hardly sounds like the speech of a young, elegant prince; indeed, it is closer to tapestry and heraldry than to the more abstract and lighter patternings in Ford. There is in Bacon's attempt to re-create the occasion a groaning and sighing note, a touch of the homilist, which Ford has converted into a cooler and sprightlier tone. The violence of the events which Warbeck describes is subdued beneath closely-woven rhythms and that sense of rising to the courtly

---

[1] 'John Ford' in *Penguin New Writing*, XXXVIII (1949), p. 96.
[2] Bacon, p. 137.

occasion which we have already met in Katherine herself; consider the tripping (or bouncing) movements of such antithetical constructs as these:

> The softness of my childhood smiled upon
> The roughness of their task, and robbed them farther
> Of hearts to dare or hands to execute   (II. i. 62–4)

or the way in which the story of ancient wrongs is kept at a distance by not being permitted to break through the tight-meshed fabric of rhythm and syntax in these lines:

> How from our nursery we have been hurried
> Unto the sanctuary, from the sanctuary
> Forced to the prison, from the prison haled
> By cruel hands to the tormentor's fury,
> Is registered already in the volume
> Of all men's tongues.   (II. i. 49–54)

The climax comes not harshly with the 'fury' but subduedly with the 'registering' conceit of the last line and a half. From moment to moment Warbeck knows what he is going to say; the speech visibly demarcates the channels along which it is going to flow:

> But as I grew in years I grew in sense
> Of fear and of disdain: fear of the tyrant . . .
>
> (II. i. 70–1)

There is a fairly high proportion of circumlocution and of abstraction:[1] 'our misfortunes', not 'me'; the 'roughness of their task', not 'their rough task'; disdain prompts, hire pays wages, a tragedy (not a murdered prince) quenches the thirst for blood. There is a cumulative tendency to suspend a gauze in front of the brutal past, which is very different from the methods of actualization adopted in the first scene of *Perkin*.

This thin, rapid elegance of locution, then, is what the Scottish court understands by 'The language of a king' (II. i. 104) or at least of 'a gentleman' (II. i. 115). Katherine is reduced by it to tears of sensibility, while retaining an open mind: 'I should pity him / If a' should prove another than he seems' (II. i. 119–20). The different

[1] On Ford's fondness for abstractions see especially R. Davril, *Le Drame de John Ford* (Paris, 1954), pp. 430 ff., and many notes in this edition.

ways in which king James and the ladies of his court react indicate
sufficiently that Ford is not trying merely to bemuse us, to make
us suppose that Warbeck is what he claims to be.[1] All of them are
touched by an irreproachable manner. For James, the rash un-
tutored politician, albeit assured by his letters from Charles VIII
and Maximilian (II. i. 29–31), this is sufficient to determine the
policy of his state; for the ladies, who are not anyway concerned
with deciding policy, it is enough to establish Warbeck as a sharer
in their high civility. Either way, Warbeck has earned such places
as either group can offer him, by methods poetical and spectacular.
It has been the playwright's chief concern to mediate these to us as
vividly as possible. Now that we have been shown what Warbeck
is, we become, like Katherine and James, involved with him rather
than with the evidence about him.

The next two scenes of the second Act carry forward the narrative and also reflect upon one another in the ideological area of the
play, chiefly in relation to the conduct of the two kings. The first—
the execution of Stanley—concludes unfinished business; the
second—the marriage of Warbeck and Katherine—starts a fresh
sequence. Each incident results directly from either ruler's nature
and flows from his personal decision (in the sources, James con-
sents to the marriage, but does not initiate it himself, as he does in
the play). We are therefore silently invited to compare them. At the
same time, and theatrically speaking, it is difficult to gauge how far
this comparatively intellectual exercise takes precedence over the
contrasted excitements of an execution and a royal wedding. Ford
was as opportunistic as the next playwright; he was hardly likely to
sacrifice the short-term advantage of the excitements to the struc-
tural and ideological values of the exercise. None the less, there is a

---

[1] I am not able to agree with Oliver (*The Problem of John Ford*, pp. 103–4)
that the audience entertains until the end of the fifth Act the 'theoretic
possibility that Warbeck has a genuine claim on the throne'. Indeed, much
of the evidence that Oliver himself presents seems to rule out this possibility. Having the authority of Henry, we hardly need to wait for Lambert
Simnel's, as Oliver suggests we should. Katherine's and even James's
reservations (II. i. 119–20, 105) at moments of high triumph for Warbeck
are certain signs; James's belief in him, such as it is, is too plainly wishful
and conditional from the start. But it depends on how much weight is
borne by the word *theoretic*, I suppose.

manifest invitation, enforced by structure, to consider James and Henry as, in their different ways, exemplary at this point. The mistake would be to forget that both are caught up also in a good deal of purely natural and human turbulence. Henry would like to be merciful to his treacherous chamberlain, 'one whom I esteemed a friend' (II. ii. 41), yet he accepts the advice of his ministers, realizing that he must cherish their loyal anxieties in preference to his own inclinations. Against Huntly's desperate pleas, those in his eyes merely of a 'peevish father' (II. iii. 43), James insists on the politic marriage. Correspondent sketches of the practical consequences ensue, on either hand. In England, there is a new chamberlain, and urgent counter-measures against the revolted Westerners, every sign that the decks are cleared and Henry instated in close command of the future. In Scotland, the scene suffers a take-over by Warbeck's bankrupt advisers and by the sharp-witted Frion who despises them as 'abject scum of mankind'. This is our first real meeting with Astley, Skelton, and the rest. It is a depressing experience. Ford would have done well to have looked more carefully still at the pages of his master Shakespeare. The assumption that the terms of honest trades are in themselves degrading and ridiculous is a bad piece of unthinking snobbery. It is of course right in the design of the whole that Warbeck's followers should be an insufferable and thoughtless lot, but Ford tries to achieve this effect by lazy and thoughtless methods.[1] The result is that what repels us from Astley and his companions is not anything in themselves (they are hardly well enough realized for any positive effects at all) but something in the mind and assumptions of their creator. We can dimly see, however, the place that these ineffectual and unamusing sketches are intended to occupy in the larger design. They are unedifying; and they are a bad prognosis for Warbeck's future and Scotland's. In the one scene, the civility that Warbeck in his own person has hitherto represented becomes ambiguous and muddled; while, in the other scene, the troubles of Henry's realm begin to look more and more like the sufferings that must be endured for the sake of a final success. 'War must breed peace' (II. ii. 162) says the

---

[1] Some readers (e.g., Dyce) have had a much higher opinion of Warbeck's men: see Dyce, II. 217.

political realist Henry at the end of his scene of salutary blood-letting; 'our tide / Runs smoothly' (II. iii. 185–6) says the befooled Frion at the end of a scene of enforced marriage.

It would be as wrong to exaggerate these symmetries as to over-look them. Both, narratively speaking, evolve clearly towards the Anglo-Scottish squabble, which is the main occupation of the next Acts. Both give us some useful comparative knowledge about the political chiefs on either side. We can denominate this a 'lesson in kingship' if we are accustomed to generalize such matters in such a form. A modern audience may prefer to reflect upon some emer-gent paradoxes. Stanley's execution is politically wise and just, Warbeck's marriage politically unwise and unjust. By means of the execution, Henry, physician to his commonwealth, purges cor-rupted blood and converts treason into a means of clearing the decks in his kingdom; by the marriage, James converts Warbeck's civility into a means of muddying the waters in his. It is obvious which realm has been fashioned into the better instrument for fighting the other. We may award our prize to the wiser king. But is that all ? This is also a world where personal and political are interdependent and may yield an oxymoron as readily as a lesson. Katherine's po-litically stupid marriage is transformed by the married pair into the most memorable personal and individuating element in the whole play; what was, in its way, an act against civility translates itself into a great celebration of it. Stanley's death is not by any means represented as a coldly satisfactory paradigm in political logic. His last scene, with that odd incident of the cross as a traitor's badge, flings open the windows; we think of Buckingham, we think, as Ford thought in *A Line of Life*, of the earl of Essex and of Charles, duke of Biron. On Stanley's behalf Ford risks some surprising plangencies, the fruit, no doubt, of his turning the pages of his copies of *Richard III* and *Henry VIII*:

> Tell him he must not think the style of Derby,
> Nor being husband to king Henry's mother,
> The league with peers, the smiles of fortune, can
> Secure his peace above the state of man. (II. ii. 104–7)

Henry's political wisdom, having generated Stanley's painful and noble *casus*, may blow back in his face Merivale's words about a

E

wary and relentless tyrant.[1] There are dimensions and symmetries which transcend mere narrative; there are correspondences and thematic variations which cannot quite be grasped except in the words and actions of the play itself; these are by no means confined to its functions as a *speculum*, but have to do with its 'strength of passion' as well as its 'Truth and State'.

From the beginning of the third Act we move away from the presence-chamber on to the margins of action in the field. Until the play's last scene but one most of the characters are away from home and the campaigns are on. Some of the diplomatic and all the military activity comes to us at second hand. No attempt is made to stage events such as the battle at Blackheath, the siege of Exeter, or the surrender of Warbeck at Beaulieu, although they are fully documented in the sources. In choosing Norham rather than Exeter, Jedburgh instead of Taunton, Ford was no doubt showing a proper sense of historical proportion, for it was in Scotland and on the Border that Warbeck's fate was really decided. But the playwright's motive may also have resembled that of the author of *Richard II*, who likewise limits his generals and soldiery to parleying and news-bearing: the wish that the play should have something of the order and shape of biography. King and no king are at the centre of our play, like king and usurper at the centre of Shakespeare's.

The two plays are in some respects quite like each other in construction. In *Perkin*, one line traces out Henry's ascent towards virtual mastery of fate and shows us the wise governor at his work. Another line develops Warbeck's destiny, as luck falls away from him. There are no signs that he was ever a good strategist, but his other special qualities, the 'fantastic' part of him, come gradually into their own; he becomes more individual, and more expressive in his relations with others, with Katherine, and then, later, with Dalyell and with Huntly even. As in the case of Richard II, this happens when, on his graph, the line that represents his capacity for sustaining a passion soars high above that representing his possession of actual authority and power in the polity. The movements that can be identified as those of 'governor' and 'pretender' (or 'believer'), if plotted on another graph, would form a pattern so

[1] See above, p. xlvi.

narrowly resembling the one which relates supplanter to supplant-ed in *Richard II* that one cannot doubt Ford's close attention to Shakespeare's tragedy.

The implied comparison between Richard and Warbeck must not be pressed too far. Ford can write nothing for Warbeck ap-proaching the great tropological arias that Shakespeare composed for the falling Richard, and perhaps, since styles had changed, pre-ferred his own 'particular model of elegance and purity' anyway. *That* difference is indeed crucial and far-reaching. But Richard and Warbeck are people, or rôles, of the same kind. Their natural place is, as it were, the world's stage, and both, as Pater said of Richard, fall gracefully enough upon it. It is as though some of the qualities that we especially associate with actors—an expressive-ness, a sweet kind of egotism—are built into the temperaments of both men, so that it can be more comfortably said of them than of the rest of us that in their lives they 'act a part'. As we have seen,[1] there are special complications when the part is that of a pretender and not that of a genuine king, but I am far from implying that in either case the 'actor' metaphor is more than a metaphor for identi-fying certain individuating elements in the man's character. These elements account for the congeniality of the parts, the readiness with which an actor, if he were ever to be given the chance, might seize upon them and successfully interpret them. But neither Richard nor Warbeck is conceived by his creator as a man who bleeds merely in sport; they truly give their heart's blood to their 'rôles', which they play out as expressively as they can, not because they are really only actors of them but because they feel they have been chosen by them.

The theatrical metaphors that we might wish to apply in seeking a disclosure of Warbeck's nature, which would include a gift and taste for ceremony, a love of the centre of the stage, an emotional capacity for rising to the occasion in words rather than in action, would seem misplaced if they were applied to Henry VII or to Bolingbroke, that common man of rough energy, as Yeats described him. It seems plain that the idea of lodging two such antithetical types together in a play of dynastic crisis must be part of Shake-

[1] See above, p. lx.

speare's legacy to Ford. This fact is probably in itself sufficient to account for what has been called 'the mystery of *Perkin Warbeck*'.[1]

The next two scenes to be discussed (III. i and ii) resemble the pair that precede them in that they, too, seem deliberately juxtaposed for the sake of contrast. This seems to be the last occasion in the play on which Ford uses this device. It is an emblem of the clash of personalities and of values that, in this play, mediates 'war' to us. In III. i (which would be perhaps somewhat dull in the theatre) Ford doubtless wants us to see Henry as the wise governor. His clemency (III. i. 80 ff.), greatly heightened from Bacon's altogether more conditional evaluation, shows this. So do the firmness, foresight, and consistency exhibited in his earlier speech (III. i. 16 ff.).[2] Feelings will differ about whether the facts of history— which obliged Ford to keep Henry himself off the battlefield and leave the fighting to his generals—advantage our opinion of the king here or not. While it is good that the exemplary governor should not personally hack and hew the revolted lieges, it is perhaps bad, in the theatre, that we get the battle at Blackheath from a not very eloquent *nuntius*, who is shackled to Gainsford. Nevertheless, the scene has a clear purpose. We get our news, and its accompanying gloss of exemplary characterization; we get, in the larger structure, the end of the sequence that began when Stanley's death cleared the decks: the sword-hand is now free for Scotland. Ford cheats a little on the dates, representing Blackheath as precedent to certain events in Scotland. His motive may have been, as Anderson suggests,[3] to exalt Henry by detaching Cornish grievance from Scottish opportunism. But narrative impact by means of the tidy conflation of two similar events (the two Scottish incursions into

[1] See above, p. xxx, n. 2.

[2] In his enthusiasm for the ideal king, Ribner (*English History Play*, London, 1965 edn, p. 302) misreads when he claims that the lines 'we must learn / To practise war again in time of peace, / Or lay our crown before our subjects' feet' (III. i. 11–13) are a particularly clear acknowledgement of 'a king's responsibility to his subjects'. They are an ironic joke: 'We must learn to make war in peace-time or humble ourselves to our own subjects, must we not?' Henry is not proposing a democratic test of his prerogatives but the exact opposite—mocking the idea that he's answerable to anyone; he is God and they are rebels (3–4).

[3] 'Kingship in Ford's *Perkin Warbeck*', *ELH*, XXVII (1960), p. 179.

Northumberland) must also have been a motive. The salient fact about the scene is its orderliness. This is accompanied by an absence of rhetorical interest, but is politically and characterologically significant. In its orderliness and its bareness of figure it affords a sharp contrast with I. i. The contrast is a measure of the control which Henry *now* has over events. Bacon tells us that he was glad when matters came out into the open—at his best when riding rather than waiting for the storm.

The second scene of this third Act is opportunist without being merely that. It is a clear source of what one writer has called the 'double impression' made upon us by Warbeck's cause.[1] The high civility of Scotland, as mediated to us chiefly through the existence as a group of Huntly, Dalyell, and Katherine, has been smashed. First, they are no longer a group, having been drawn apart by the powerful attraction of the new planet Warbeck, who has brought Katherine to his side. Secondly, what is left outside that orbit are the two men, father and lover, who now have nothing to share but their deprivation. That sharing is what we see in the first hundred or so lines of the scene, as they try to assuage their bitterness by registering themselves as partners in affliction. Even here, the instinct for civility finds its expression. It is traceable in what, in cold blood, may seem to us some too exquisitely managed verbal etiquette[2] and in their whole idea of seeking for a new combination of amity over the grave of their loss. The language of the scene conveys the essential courtliness of Huntly and Dalyell—one still bluff and gamesome, the other youthfully silky and deferential; but it also gives expression to the roughness of the intrusion that has spoiled it all. We hear of the rude junketings ('Hotch-potch of Scotch and Irish twingle-twangles' and other incivilities of that sort), of the gout, the stone in the bladder (III. ii. 34–5), of a blow on the face (III. ii. 43), the fever shrinking every limb (III. ii. 36), the 'rape done on mine honour' (III. ii. 56). The playwright's opportunism comes in in the staging of the masque of the Scotch antics and the wild Irish in their trowses. This is doubtless meant to be

---

[1] 'Artifice or High Design?' [review of Clifford Leech's *John Ford and the Drama of his Time*], *Times Literary Supplement*, 19 July 1957, p. 434.
[2] See notes on III. ii. 49–52, 78.

relished for its own sake, but it also has a constructional rôle as civility's anti-masque. Fun though it may be, it is also what Scotland has come to.

A bold stroke after this noisy interlude is the staging immediately after it of what may permissibly be called the main masque: the quiet episode of Warbeck's and Katherine's 'parting ceremony' (III. ii. 141). This is the only occasion in the whole play that we ever see them quite alone together. Here, in a scene where everything has been running against him, Warbeck must reassert his own participation in that civility which his coming has paradoxically tarnished. It rests on him to reanimate the gentler aspect of the 'double impression'. Again Ford seems to be contriving an effect of surprise. Warbeck does rise to the occasion, and so does Katherine. There is the sweet heaviness of his own spoken requiem. It is characteristic of the closeness and extension of its rhythms that they are unfairly abrupted unless almost the whole of this speech is quoted:

> If thou hear'st
> A truth of my sad ending by the hand
> Of some unnatural subject, thou withal
> Shalt hear how I died worthy of my right
> By falling like a King; and in the close
> Which my last breath shall sound, thy name, thou fairest,
> Shall sing a requiem to my soul, unwilling
> Only of greater glory 'cause divided
> From such a heaven on earth as life with thee.
>
> (III. ii. 150–8)

The amount of working out that this takes, the architectonic of it —the way the two big syntactical units (separated by the semicolon) are softly shored up against one another—makes one comprehend why Milton was a reader of Ford. What has been called the Fordian 'soft fervour' of it is another matter, of tone and not of construction. In the second half, the two properties are united by the way in which the lulling movement of the two longer lines (155 and 158), answering one another, is gently restrained by their share in the elaborate syntactical scheme. This is what Katherine means by his 'noble language' (III. ii. 163). His earlier and, in movement, more sprightly lines (III. ii. 143–6), more resonant, perhaps, but still mobile and sensitive—tracing 'the paths which lead / Through various hazards to a careful throne'—have a touch of Marvell or Lovelace, or of those Caroline portraits where shining steel casque or gorget is lit against velvet and linen. In this scene, too, Katherine herself enunciates for the first time what is to make her rôle specially memorable: Warbeck is 'king of me' (III. ii. 168); but as to what else he is king of she reserves her rights. The resulting ambiguity of flavour, the mixture, very apparent in this episode, of fervour and doubt, constitute one of the chief distinctions of the play.

The next six scenes (III. iii–IV. iv) are a sequence dramatizing events in Scotland and Northumberland during 1496 and 1497, and may fairly be taken as a unit. They render clearly a complicated movement—the detachment of James IV from Warbeck's cause by stubbornness in the field and initiative in the chancellery. Much of this clarity, of both detail and development, Ford owes to his sources. When the sequence begins, Warbeck's fortunes are ostensibly waxing: he is, after all, now leading an army into England, backed by the Scots. But few in the audience will be deceived by this, knowing what they now know of Henry and also having watched the scene (III. iii), with which the sequence starts, and which demonstrates Henry's potent influence on the immediate future through Hialas. Another highly conditional element in the whole series of episodes is the temperament of king James. This is the only element amid this run of the historical events in which there is much room for play. As Anderson has pointed out,[1] Ford

[1] Art. cit., pp. 180–1. Ford cannot have wished to portray James as an exemplary illustration (or 'lesson') in kingship to the same degree as Henry is so portrayed in III. i (see above, pp. lxviii–lxix). The two kinds of exemplariness are incompatible; I doubt if Ford would have expected an audience capable of recognizing Henry's wisdom to react with any special warmth of admiration to James's 'political realism': one remembers Swinburne's feelings about 'perfect Stuart' and the 'hereditary faculty' of doing dishonourable things in an honourable way. This is unjust to young James, whose conduct Bacon at least (p. 161) described as 'noble'; and yet, however much James may grace his dismissal of Warbeck, the combination of weakness towards an enemy and of foul-weather unfriendliness towards a protégé is so very far from exemplary as to be almost damning in the eyes of ordinary men; Ford *may* have shared Bacon's view, but does little to persuade us of it.

had in II. iii departed from his sources in representing James as a headstrong autocrat bent on disregarding in the matter of Warbeck's alliance and marriage the advice of his grave elders. James's abandonment of this posture, leading eventually to the treaty with England, is the most absorbing bit of character-development in this series of scenes. His instability (or possibility of growth) is the lever on which Henry's emissaries would like to get their hands and which Warbeck would like to protect from them. The fourth scene of Act III is a convincing study in this process. James, hitherto captivated by the 'language of a king', begins to measure his enterprise by starker criteria, such as the failure of the Northumberlanders to come rushing to his standard. Of the episode when Warbeck pleads that they should not, in revenge, be raped and massacred, Gairdner dryly remarked that 'the request was humane, but does not seem to have been accounted princely'.[1] It is hard to tell whether Ford and his audience, which could not have contained many Northumberlanders, would have been moved by it to admiration for Warbeck or to derision; as Gairdner remarks, the old chroniclers make merry about it (the mockery of Gainsford can, I think, be discounted, since to him everything that Warbeck did was contemptible). At any rate, the sharpness of the reply that it earns from James is taken as a clue for developing the Scottish king's character; to him, as he exults over an adroit political bargain, is given the only true soliloquy (IV. iii. 56–61). Yet James, too, can rise to an occasion: his noblest speech comes just before (IV. iii. 30–48). At this point, also, both the real Warbeck and his fictive shadow agree in a gesture of true civility, in their temperate response to James's 'realism'.

Throughout all these military and diplomatic affairs, Warbeck has plainly been out of his depth. There is one moment (IV. ii. 5–7) when he swoops perilously near to panic and self-betrayal. It seems, for one sickening minute, that the dramatist is going to make an artistically intolerable miscalculation and show us after all a pretender *conscious* that he is an impostor. Yet the very closeness that he comes to such a point, without actually touching it, seems to underwrite Ford's conception of the character as one whose 'belief'

[1] Gairdner, p. 306.

in himself can safely swing him out over the worst abysses. This prepares us for the sustained imaginative triumph of the hero in the final scenes of the play. In order that that last phase should properly shine out, it is probably right that during the sequence that we have just been examining Warbeck should yield some of his prominence to James, and that his performance, though it does not contradict any impression that we have hitherto acquired of him, does not add a great deal either.

At length, in IV. v, Warbeck lands on the coast of Cornwall, inter-volved with the comely and plaintive shadow of king Richard, to begin the last phase of his tragedy.

The presentation of Warbeck in this part of the play is essentially a matter of sleight of hand with perspectives. One is reminded of those Renaissance toys made out of pleated paper to which Shake-speare and Chapman refer:

> So cunningly to optick reason wrought,
>   That a farre of, it shewd a womans face,
> Heauie, and weeping; but more neerely viewed,
> Nor weeping, heauy, nor a woman shewed.[1]

Any one who has followed his fortunes so far is bound to ask 'How will Warbeck bear it out even at the edge of doom? What sustains him? What really *is* he?' The question is, as E. M. Waith saw,[2] something to do with the 'nature of reality', or at least with his reality, although there seems no reason why that question should be separated, as Waith argues it should, from another one about the 'nature of heroism', as heroism has been developing during the time since Chapman, in *Bussy d'Ambois*, produced a model for his pupil Dryden. Sooner or later, Ford will bring us up against both these questions and in his own fashion answer them. For the time being, we may watch him arranging and re-arranging the screens about his protagonist. These arrangements, as they shift about and give coarse or subtle accentuation to the figure, help to enliven the his-torical narrative as it winds its way to the end fixed for it in history.

In the course of this last phase two historical analogues are used, which are, in their opposed ways, extreme versions of the Warbeck

---

[1] *Ovid's Banquet of Sense*, stanza 3, ll. 6–9 (*Poems*, ed. Bartlett, 1941, p. 54).
[2] *The Herculean Hero* (London, 1962), p. 144.

enterprise. One comes from Lambert Simnel when he compares Warbeck to himself (v. iii. 35–52), and the other from Warbeck when he compares himself to Harry Richmond (v. ii. 58–74). It may seem insufficiently subtle that at this stage in the play Ford should judge it necessary to work with such broad strokes: for even the least attentive auditor must surely have glimpsed by now that the question who Warbeck *is* can hardly be answered either by 'He is a kind of failed Richmond' or 'He is just another Lambert Simnel, whose proper destination is the scullery'. (When Daubeney suggested that he might serve as a 'swabber', that was after all in I. i.)

Yet the offering of analogues so extremely various may at least be interpreted as a way of indicating that our perspectives of him, the means we have for identifying him, are going to shift and oscillate in rapid dependence both on what he claims about himself and on what the other *personae* feel about him. They alter their points of view and do not always agree on what they see; their disagreements are not at all about his dynastic pretensions, but about what can possibly be his motives for 'keeping it up' and about whether that is anyway the right way of putting it. As the auditors attend to these disagreements, they are also called upon to respond, as their 'clearer judgements' enjoin them, to Warbeck's own manifestations of his 'strength of passion'.

But first these judicious spectators are subjected to what must surely be regarded as a discordant and not very salutary shock. It occurs as a result of the juxtaposition in IV. v and v. i of Warbeck's finest apostrophe to his partisans ('A thousand blessings guard our lawful arms . . .', IV. v. 47) and the news transmitted in the later scene that he has, from Taunton, 'Fled without battle given' (v. i. 58). Ford himself is not in perfect control here, for he feels obliged to invent a reason for Warbeck's conduct, but it only just saves his face, if indeed it does do so.[1] It is a point where the historical personage's imputed cowardice, or at least total incompetence, in the campaigning seriously inconveniences the playwright. A figure of the stature that Warbeck has to assume in the play cannot really afford such extreme ineptitude; it makes him look too like the 'maumet' made of straw and painted cloth of whom Hall

[1] See note on v. i. 67–8.

and Gainsford write. In so far as it tends to empty his threat of credibility it tends to reduce to a storm in a tea-cup the whole ado that has been organized about him in the play, including the chief organizer, the exemplary Henry himself. Scotland was bad enough, but this is dreadful. One cannot help feeling that Ford ought to have contrived a more impressive and more strategically disposed justification of his hero's behaviour. As it is, he either has not bothered or has been unable to prevent the perspective here almost blotting out his protagonist altogether. But in the next scene the confrontation of Warbeck and Henry considerably mends matters.

The entrance of the captured Warbeck is accompanied by some rousing words from Daubeney:

> Life to the king, and safety fix his throne!
> I here present you, royal sir, a shadow
> Of majesty, but in effect a substance
> Of pity; a young man, in nothing grown
> To ripeness but th' ambition of your mercy:
> Perkin, the Christian world's strange wonder.
>
> (v. ii. 31–6)

Henry's answer mordantly disables most of this: 'We observe no wonder . . .'; he scrutinizes the prepossessing exterior: 'An ornament of nature, fine and polished, / A handsome youth' (v. ii. 38–9). Then he becomes the stern pastor: 'Turn now thine eyes, / Young man, upon thyself and thy past actions!' (v. ii. 48–9). When this fails, there come the irritated comment 'The player's on the stage still' (v. ii. 68) and the speech beginning 'A pretty gallant!' (v. ii. 75–9). Both of these are explanations, such as might first appeal to the rational mind, of Warbeck's responses and are on the lines of 'he's just keeping it up'. At length, Henry has to admit into his mind the notion that Warbeck is self-deluded, what might be styled the Baconian theory of his behaviour: 'Time may restore their wits, whom vain ambition / Hath many years distracted' (v. ii. 126–7), and, most plainly of all:

> Was ever so much impudence in forgery?
> The custom, sure, of being styled a king
> Hath fastened in his thought that he is such.
> But we shall teach the lad another language;
> 'Tis good we have him fast. (v. ii. 131–5)

Henry has covered the whole ground and arrived with impressively Tudor aptitude at the 'medical' explanation, as Daubeney sees when he prescribes an old-fashioned remedy: 'The hangman's physic / Will purge this saucy humour' (v. ii. 135–6; *humour* in the sense of 'diseased excess').

Doubts may soon begin to arise as to whether this explanation *tout court* is going to prove adequate to sustain us for the rest of the piece. In v. iii Ford has radically altered history. In the sources Warbeck confesses his identity as the son of John Osbek. He was ultimately hanged not because he persisted in maintaining that he was the son of Edward IV but because he became implicated in the destruction of the earl of Warwick.[1] In the play, however, he is offered the alternative of being executed or confessing that he is an impostor. That there is a clear choice for him is made plain by Urswick: 'Yet, yet, confess / Thy parentage; for yet the king has mercy' (v. iii. 20–1), and by Lambert Simnel: 'Let my example lead thee; be no longer / A counterfeit; confess, and hope for pardon!' (v. iii. 51–2), as well as by Daubeney and Surrey:

> *Dau.* What has a' yet confessed?
> *Urs.*   Nothing to purpose;
>   But still a' will be king.
> *Sur.*   Prepare your journey
>   To a new kingdom, then.   (v. iii. 155–7)

Warbeck, of course, persists in affirming his pretensions and ignores the conditional offers of pardon. Not surprisingly, the standers-by find it hard to distinguish between wickedness (or extreme impudence) and madness in explaining this behaviour. Self-destructive obstinacy carried to the height to which Warbeck is carrying it can itself be seen as a kind of madness.[2] But in general their diagnosis certainly does not exclude that offered by Henry— and by Lawrence Babb[3]—that Warbeck's wits are distracted. The most clinical of the descriptions of Warbeck's condition comes from

---

[1] See note on v. iii. 13–19.

[2] If we read at v. iii. 157 *madman* (Gifford's emendation of Q's *Madam*) and take the remark as applying to Warbeck, it does, especially because self-contradictory, represent this feeling; but see note on the passage.

[3] 'Abnormal Psychology in Ford's *Perkin Warbeck*', *Modern Language Notes*, LI (1936), 234–7.

Urswick, who appears to have been recently studying Reginald Scot's treatise on witchcraft:

> Thus witches,
> Possessed, even to their deaths deluded, say
> They have been wolves and dogs and sailed in egg-shells
> Over the sea and rid on fiery dragons,
> Passed in the air more than a thousand miles
> All in a night; the enemy of mankind
> Is powerful but false, and falsehood confident.
>
> (v. iii. 104–10)

This amounts to saying that Warbeck is in the grip of something irresistible—either the Devil or melancholia or the former working through the latter—and cannot help himself. His choice of death rather than confession in the last scene, therefore, is merely further evidence for the depths of his delusion. It is a delusion which, although a morbid condition, exempts him from nothing. Witches were wicked as well as crazy.

It is not easy to believe that the audience in general was expected to look quite with Urswick's perspective upon the matter. What in the dramatic experience counts at least as much as the clinical verdict is Warbeck's 'strength of passion', his performance in the rôle he has created. Immediately after his first entrance in bonds he gives us his own perspective. His rejoinder to Henry is a moment of astounding force and beauty:

> *Hen.* . . . What revels in combustion through our kingdom
> A frenzy of aspiring youth hath danced,
> Till, wanting breath, thy feet of pride have slipped
> To break thy neck.
> *War.*   But not my heart; my heart
> Will mount till every drop of blood be frozen
> By death's perpetual winter.   (v. ii. 50–5)

Amongst the things that account for this (the most thrilling moment in the play) are the masterful anaphora by which Warbeck takes the speech away from Henry and raises it to a higher pitch, and the potent but discreetly concealed link in the imagery between the mounting of the heart and the mounting upwards of a wounded bird; both speeches, too, if taken together, read as a verbal paradigm of death by hanging and the soaring upwards of the released soul. The poetic interest here is matched later on in the scene by Warbeck's unerring ear for the princely code of conduct, as idealized in many a Jacobean courtly spectacle, when he begs for clemency for his 'poor creatures' but not for himself (v. ii. 90–9).

The choice between confession and death in the next scene is—and this is all the playwright's invention—presented to Warbeck as a choice between death and a life such as Lambert Simnel's. In their interchange, Lambert's level-headedness is set off against Warbeck's heroic madness and pride of blood; and there is no doubt which is more designed to arouse our sense of 'wonder'—the word that Huntly is to use to Warbeck in his last complimentation (v. iii. 173). Caught up in such juxtapositions, it becomes splendid to be like Warbeck, base to be like Simnel, whose sanity is put down below the pretender's Bedlamite vision. Yet this is not a spectacle intended to have didactic effect or to act as an exemplary illustration. We are not to imitate Warbeck but to be astonished by him and to be carried away by the air of absolute conviction with which he lives up to his rôle. We are trenching, indeed, upon the 'nature of heroism', at least as that was understood in some seventeenth-century literature. We can glimpse the degree to which Warbeck may be assimilated with the figures of heroic drama, who generate a special amazement because they are, as Dryden declared, 'as far above the ordinary proportion of the stage, as that is beyond the common words and actions of human life'.[1]

There follows a last ceremony of civility, the sealing of the 'testament of honourable vows' with Katherine (v. iii. 147), a renewal of marriage which reminds us of Calantha's last mysterious pledge in *The Broken Heart*; then come the exchanges with Huntly and Dalyell, the cheerful inspiriting of his followers, the final unfaltering rationalization of death.

This whole diapason of the conjugal, courtly, princely, and stoic suggests that Warbeck has turned the ending of his life into an amazing work of human art—a creation virtually independent of the melancholy delusion within which it has grown, like the pearl in the oyster. It is this artefact that we are called upon to admire,

---

[1] 'Of Heroic Plays, an Essay', *Essays of J. Dryden*, ed. W. P. Ker (Oxford, 1900), I. 151.

composed to a series of heroic gestures by an imputed magnitude of mind that holds its sceptre steady before the scaffold itself. The softness and civil sober-suitedness of the verse, when compared to some other examples of heroic apotheosis (such as Chapman's or Fletcher's), the absence of complacent loquacity in the self-display, should not deceive us about the affinities; for that quietness of tone is Ford's special property. The terms that one might, in cold blood, be tempted to use for the behaviour—stagy, attitudinizing, and so on—transform themselves, for this kind of dramatic contrivance, into terms not of derogation but of compliment. For everything depends upon the exalted performance of a rôle. When man and actor draw as close together as this, when to be a man and hero is to be one who performs excellently the chosen rôle, who creates it, and stands by it in his imagination, and prefers to die rather than abandon it—then what matters is the quality of composition and performance, their stageworthiness, the degree of accomplishment achieved. If these satisfy and convince, it really does not matter if the little boy points out that the emperor has no clothes, that the hero strutting it out before us is 'really' the son of John Osbek. We have known that all along, in much the same sense that we have known that Henry VII is not 'really' Henry VII but a member of the Phoenix company. Unless it is intruded too brutally (or with some ulterior theatrical purpose), such knowledge cannot spoil our pleasure in the spectacle. That such knowledge is present is true; Simnel's scepticism and Urswick's diagnosis criticize without disabling the aesthetic display, and contribute, like all the shifting perspectives in this part of the work, to that flavour of ambiguity which is the persistent aftertaste of the play as a whole. But for the moment this element is overridden by Warbeck's presentation of himself as a man who still retains the capacity not only for meaningful but for exalted choice.

It is of some importance that Warbeck should have attained, or retained, this stature; for he has a heroine to match with. If what Warbeck gives us in this part of the play is mainly heroic and aesthetic, Katherine's contribution is moral and critical. Commentators have always thought her admirable, no doubt because, in Davril's words, '[elle] symbolise surtout l'inlassable fidélité de

l'épouse liée à son mari en dépit de tout'.[1] Davril justly adds that
she is a perfect wife in point of possessing 'un sens sublime du
devoir, à défaut d'une très grand passion'. Katherine would ordinarily have married Dalyell. Her first comments on Warbeck are
shrewd as well as interested; she is not borne by an irresistible tide
of passion into his arms but by an unduly arranged marriage, and
her passionate allegiance to him in the last Act springs from something other than a passionate devotion to him as a lover. What that
something other is, much in the play has been at pains to show and
to define for us. It is what has been denominated, in this account, as
civility, the value that she, her father, Dalyell, and, in his ambiva-
lent way, Warbeck have in common. It is odd that out of an evil of
which Ford in *The Broken Heart* showed himself peculiarly aware
—the enforced or unduly arranged marriage—the 'épouse parfaite'
should come; but civility conquers all. As we have seen, it is the
keynote of Katherine's circle—it is magnificently demonstrated in
I. ii, right at the beginning of the play. It even expresses itself in
her relation with her servants. Ford was doing more than manifest
his allegiance to the Shakespearian capacity, never to be too much
admired, for making the least of persons interesting when he
created Jane and the anonymous groom of v. i. 34–41. Huntly,
Crawford, and Dalyell remain true to the spirit of I. ii in the last
moments of the play, when they accord to the dying husband the
respect they cannot give to the dying duke of York. The whole
conception of Dalyell's character is founded upon civility and
helps to define it—sprightly, honourable (the adjectives are
Huntly's), but, in his personal disaster, subdued to serve without
hope.

Above all, the value inheres in Katherine, and acquires with her
a new vigour, which is not that of self-effacement. For Katherine's
loyalty to her husband comes to imply a criticism of the larger
society with which it brings her into contact. When she is brought
before Henry (v. ii), she cannot cope with the great king who
blandly ignores her attempts to mention Warbeck; each of his
ferociously overwhelming compliments makes her feel worse. She
comes into her own in the final scene. To give this its full value, it

[1] *Le Drame de John Ford*, p. 259.

ought to be staged so as to present a Warbeck who shows some signs of having spent some months in a fifteenth-century political prison—his clothes ought to be foul and his body, at the least, worn (in history, he was tortured; there are plenty of examples to supply modern analogies to the director, should he run short of older ones). This is the victim whom Katherine embraces in the open street as he goes on his way to the kind of 'shameful' death from which the nobility were exempted. It is not surprising that John de Vere, the thirteenth earl, is profoundly shocked. He refers to Katherine's 'strange subjection in a gaze so public', dazedly wonders what her father will think, and angrily urges her not to disgrace herself (v. iii. 80 ff.). Katherine's reply is distinguished and unanswerable:

> You abuse us:
> For when the holy churchman joined our hands,
> Our vows were real then; the ceremony
> Was not in apparition, but in act.
> Be what these people term thee, I am certain
> Thou art my husband, no divorce in heaven
> Has been sued out between us. (v. iii. 112–18)

These are the accents of civility at its toughest and most self-contained. They are sounded in the presence of another 'holy churchman', Urswick, whose reactions are not recorded; he has just diagnosed Warbeck as a witch; what he thinks of Katherine we shall never know. The director must, however, tell the actor to do something; perhaps he casts up his eyes to heaven.

Warbeck himself appears thoroughly to understand what Katherine is doing:

> Why wouldst thou prove so much unkind to greatness
> To glorify thy vows by such a servitude? (v. iii. 98–9)

That difficult word *greatness* here means something like 'rank, high social position': 'why do you derogate from your rank by glorifying your marriage-vows by such a "low", slave-like obedience to them (or to me)?' The glory and the servitude are inextricably confused together. Is this a society in which obedience to our vows is reckoned slavish and disgraceful when it shakes degree? Is greatness the only ladder to all high designs? We can see Katherine, at any rate,

F

gradually deciding during the episode to go as far as she can in showing where civility has brought her to stand. This is the point of her final pledge to 'die a faithful widow to thy bed' (v. iii. 152). She does not do this because she is conceived as a sentimental heroine, luxuriating in the emotion of the moment, still less because she is besotted with Warbeck. She wishes to demonstrate to the standers-by that her pledge to the marriage is absolute, the very bond that Henry in the earlier scene had deflected attention from, and that his representatives in this scene are willing (unlike Huntly) to disavow.

Thus, as civility is joined to heroism in the play's last phase, there emerges something resembling a counter-truth to its politico-historical world. It is not surprising, in view of material in Ford's other plays, that he here so exalted the faithful wife and staged once again the renewal of a marriage on the edge of the tomb. The episode specially relates, as does Warbeck's own participation in its solemn splendours, to all that part of the play which the epilogue styles 'strength of passion'; for Katherine's passion of allegiance is as much passion as if it were what it emphatically is not, the passion of love-melancholy. It is hard to tell how far her conduct is intended to reflect upon greatness itself, upon its throne. Although they are in some respects elements quite differently compounded and with different pasts and futures, what distinguishes *Perkin* is the way in which it mediates—and even 'marries'—the two elements that have been provisionally titled 'heroism' and 'civility'. Or, to put it in a less questionable way, it is Warbeck and Katherine that we remember and the several things that are exceptional about them both. It is to neither of them, however, that the last lines of the play are assigned, but to the legitimate physician-king who re-enters upon the scene flanked by a bishop and a diplomat.

For, at other times, and in a different chamber of thought, we shall remember that *Perkin* is the last good English history-play of its era and that, carrying *Richard III*, *Richard II*, *Henry IV*, and *Henry VIII* amongst its paradigms, it deliberately refreshes that august inheritance. That, too, is an exceptional thing, though of a rather different sort. Henry and James and such lessons in kingship as they may be thought to administer are vital to the whole. *Perkin* does affirm the 'Truth and State' of which the prologue boasts. In an age too late and a cold climate, Ford learned to rehandle that topic with astonishing, if soberly deployed, competence. But he qualified it with the fervour of new interests and with the elegance and purity of his own manners. There are complex relations, which include some hint of an arrangement of counter-truths, between various elements in the play. In that line in the epilogue—'The threats of majesty, the strength of passion'—Ford, with an objectivity characteristic of his basic design, blends some of them together, softly cradled in an antithesis.

6. BIOGRAPHICAL INDEX OF HISTORICAL CHARACTERS

Nicholas Astley. His name is variously spelled (Ashley, Askeley, etc.). Nothing is recorded of him except that he was a scrivener (a clerk, copyist, or kind of banker). After he took sanctuary with Warbeck in 1497 (see v. ii. 40), he was, according to Bacon (p. 178), left unmolested.

John a-Water. Also known as John Walters. He was twice mayor of Cork: in 1494–95, when he helped to protect Warbeck from the citizens of Waterford, and in 1499, the year in which he and his son (?Thomas: see note on I. iii. 59–61) were hanged at Tyburn for their part in Warbeck's undertaking. They were the only ones of his counsellors to be executed with him.

Sir Robert Clifford. The youngest son of Sir Thomas Clifford, he began his career under Henry VII as chamberlain of Berwick upon Tweed. He was the brother of the Lancastrian leader John, lord Clifford, sheriff of Westmoreland, whose estates were confiscated after his death at the battle of Towton (1461); and he was the uncle of Henry, lord Clifford (b. about 1564), who was said to have been brought up as a shepherd to conceal him from proscription but was restored to his lands and title by Henry VII and fought at Flodden (see Wordsworth's 'Song at the Feast of Brougham Castle' and *The White Doe of Rylstone*). Sir William Stanley [q.v.] temporarily obtained the forfeited lands, and this may have been a motive for Clifford's denunciation of him; he also received a gratuity of £500.

Countess of Crawford. See below under 'Crawford'. If she is to be thought of as the wife of the fifth earl, she was Elizabeth, daughter of James, first lord Hamilton; her marriage was dissolved in the 1480's after she had borne four children to the earl. If the wife of the sixth earl, she was Mariota, daughter of Alexander, second lord Home; she bore him no children but survived his death at Flodden.

Crawford. The character in the play may be either David Lindsay, fifth earl of Crawford, or his second son John Lindsay, sixth earl. David (d. 1495) was created duke of Montrose by James III in 1488 and fought at the battle of Sauchieburn. His son did not assert a claim to the dukedom; he was suspected of conspiring with his sister-in-law Janet Gordon, daughter of the second earl of Huntly [q.v.], to murder his elder brother who died in 1492; he fell at Flodden.

Dalyell. The character is probably an invention of Ford's, and no one corresponding to him appears in the sources. The Quarto spells the name Daliell; but all editors except Anderson have adopted Dalyell, as used by Weber, which is an acceptable modern spelling (another current spelling is Dalzell).

Daubeney. Giles, first baron Daubeney (d. 1508). This is the spelling adopted by many modern historians of the name ordinarily spelled Dawbney in the Quarto (others use D'Aubigny). He served under Edward IV, and during Richard III's reign conspired for the Lancastrians, was attainted, and fled into exile. After Bosworth Henry VII made him a privy councillor and throughout his reign assigned to him a number of civil, military, and diplomatic tasks, appointed him lord chamberlain (1495), and engaged him against the Scots and the Cornish rebels (1497). He held extensive lands in Somerset and Dorset. There is an elaborate effigy of him in Westminster Abbey.

Durham. Richard Fox(e), bishop of Durham (1448 ?–1528). An early adherent of Henry Tudor, he became secretary of state, lord privy seal, and bishop of Exeter after Henry's accession, bishop of Durham in 1494, and of Winchester in 1501. His diplomatic skills were often in demand in foreign and Anglo-Scottish affairs. He was also, in company with Wolsey, one of Henry VIII's chief counsellors, but gradually withdrew into ecclesiastical life. He founded Corpus Christi College, Oxford, and schools at Taunton and Grantham.

Frion. Stephen Frion was appointed Henry's French secretary and clerk of the signet in 1485, and was one of the commissioners chosen to treat of peace with France in 1488. About 1489 he deserted Henry's service for that of Charles VIII of France, who made him Warbeck's principal aide.

Henry. Henry VII (1457–1509). Henry Tudor, as head of the house of Lancaster since the death in 1471 of Henry VI, invaded England with French and English troops and became king after the defeat of Richard III at the battle of Bosworth in 1485. His reign up to the time of the play had seen measures taken to defend the duchy of Brittany against the attacks of Charles VIII of France, and his marriage to the princess Elizabeth, eldest daughter of Edward IV (signalizing the union of the Yorkist and Lancastrian factions).

John Heron. Also called 'Herne', a bankrupt London merchant who had fled to Ireland to avoid his creditors. He took sanctuary with Warbeck after the collapse of the invasion in 1497 and seems to have escaped further attention.

Hialas. Don Pedro de Ayala was sent by Ferdinand and Isabella of Spain to conduct negotiations about the marriage between Henry's son Arthur and their daughter Catherine of Aragon. When Anglo-Scottish relations deteriorated in 1496, Ferdinand instructed him to proceed to Scotland in order to reconcile James and Henry so that they might both turn together against France. Hialas succeeded in bringing about the negotiations at Norham and Jedburgh as depicted in the play. Bacon reckoned him 'a man of great wisdom'.

Huntly. George [not Alexander] Gordon, second earl of Huntly, succeeded to the title in 1470 and died about 1502. He attempted without success to mediate between James III of Scotland and his turbulent nobles, was made a privy councillor by James IV, and in

1498 appointed lord high chancellor, an office which he lost shortly before his death. By his second marriage (subsequently dissolved) in or about 1459 he became the husband of the princess Annabella Stewart, youngest daughter of James I, but it is not certain whether Lady Katherine Gordon was a child of this marriage: 'The second Earl of Huntly had a considerable family, but it is not easy to say who were their mothers' (Paul, *The Scots Peerage*, IV. 529). Byron was one of his descendants.

James. James IV (1473–1513) was only a boy when he participated in the rebellion that overthrew his father, 1488. He strengthened Scotland militarily and renewed the 'auld alliance' with France, but after a firm peace with England in 1502 he married princess Margaret, daughter of Henry VII. Hostility between England and Scotland intensified after the accession of Henry VIII, and when Henry attacked France James invaded England and perished with his nobles at Flodden in Northumberland.

Jane Douglas. Archibald Douglas, fifth earl of Angus (1449–? 1513) had a daughter named Janet, who married Andrew Herries in 1495. She was the younger sister of Gavin Douglas the poet. She may be the Jane Douglas of the play. Her father had at one time (in 1461) been contracted to marry Lady Katherine Gordon [q.v.].

Katherine. Lady Katherine Gordon (d. 1537), eldest daughter of the second earl of Huntly [q.v.]. After Warbeck's death she remained, with a pension and other emoluments, at the English court, and was granted lands in Berkshire by Henry VIII. She subsequently married: before 1512, James Strangeways, one of the king's gentlemen-ushers (d. 1515); then in 1517 (Sir) Mathias Cradocke, a gentleman of Glamorganshire (d. 1531); and finally Christopher Ashton, another royal gentleman-usher. She died at Fyfield in Berkshire where there is a tomb called 'Lady Gordon's monument'; but there is also a tomb and effigy at Swansea.

Oxford. John de Vere, thirteenth earl of Oxford (1443–1513). He played an active military and conspiratorial part on the Lancastrian side in the Wars of the Roses (his father had been executed by Edward IV) and was attainted and imprisoned under Richard III.

He landed at Milford with Henry Tudor in 1485 as captain-general of his army, and was rewarded with many high and lucrative offices.

Lambert Simnel (d. ?1534). His origin is not known for certain. He personated Edward, earl of Warwick, Edward IV's nephew, at the instigation of Richard Simon, a priest, and other Yorkist leaders. Simon took him to Ireland in 1486, where the eighth earl of Kildare and others recognized his claims; Margaret of Burgundy [see under 'Warbeck'] also acknowledged him as her nephew. Henry VII caused the real earl of Warwick to be brought out of the Tower and paraded through London, but Lambert was none the less crowned as Edward VI a few weeks later in Dublin cathedral. In June 1487 he landed in Lancashire with an army and was defeated and taken prisoner at a battle at Stoke, near Newark.

Skelton. Denominated Edward Skelton by Gairdner and Mackie, Richard Skelton by Hall and Gainsford; his surname is spelled Sketon in the Quarto but Skelton in all the historical sources except Gainsford (sig. O2). He was a tailor. He took sanctuary in 1497 with Warbeck, and was left unmolested like Astley and Heron.

Stanley. Sir William Stanley (1435?–95). He early became a Yorkist partisan, and obtained various grants and appointments from Edward IV. Richard III retained his support for a time by means of handsome gifts; but when Henry Tudor invaded, Stanley and his elder brother came to an understanding with him; by bringing his troops into action at a decisive moment he saved the day at Bosworth for Henry, who appointed him lord chamberlain. It is uncertain how deeply he involved himself ten years later in the Warbeck affair, but Henry was probably suspicious of a very wealthy man who had changed sides before.

Surrey. Thomas Howard, earl of Surrey and duke of Norfolk (1443–1524). He fought on Edward IV's side and became one of his privy councillors; he was with Richard III at the battle of Bosworth (where his father was killed). He consequently forfeited his estates and was imprisoned in the Tower, but Henry VII released him and restored his earldom in 1489, and used him to subdue various insurgents. He became chiefly responsible for guarding the

Scottish borders, and gradually won his way deeper into Henry's employments and favour. He was privy councillor to Henry VIII and held other high offices, and in 1513, after he had defeated James IV at Flodden, was created (second) duke of Norfolk.

Christopher Urswick (1448–1522). A Cambridge man, originally from Furness in Lancashire, he became attached, through the Stanleys, to the service of Margaret Beaufort, mother of Henry Tudor, and was involved in the Lancastrian schemes for invasion during Richard III's reign. He accompanied Henry at Bosworth, and consequently obtained numerous ecclesiastical appointments and was sent on diplomatic missions to Rome, Spain, France, and Scotland. He was dean of York (1488) and dean of Windsor (1495); he became a friend of More and of Erasmus, who visited and corresponded with him. He is a minor character in Shakespeare's *Richard III*.

Perkin Warbeck (1474?–99). It is conceivable but not probable that he was an illegitimate scion of the house of York (Mackie, p. 120). A letter attributed to him, written in French, is signed 'Perrequin Werbecque'. According to his own confession, made under duress in 1497, he was the son of John Osbe[c]k, comptroller of Tournay, of whose name his is a variant. He stated that after spending some time in the Netherlands he travelled to Portugal and after about a year entered the service of a Breton merchant with whom he came to Cork in 1491, where he learnt to speak English. He was probably already a centre for Yorkist plots before he went to Ireland, where he first assumed the rôle of Richard, duke of York, second son of Edward IV, one of the two 'princes in the Tower' supposed to have been murdered by Richard III. In 1492 he was invited to France by Charles VIII and by him, after his treaty with Henry at Étaples in the same year, dismissed to Flanders to Margaret of York, duchess of Burgundy, whose court had become a refuge for disaffected Yorkists and who was continually plotting against Henry VII. She accepted Warbeck as her nephew and instructed him further in his rôle of duke of York. In November 1493 he arrived at Vienna and was recognized as king of England by the emperor Maximilian I of Habsburg, archduke of Austria, in 1494, who gave financial backing to his abortive attempt to land at Deal on 3 July 1495. From off Deal Warbeck sailed to Ireland and for eleven days laid unsuccessful siege to Waterford; from there he took his small fleet to Scotland. At about this point (November 1495) the main action of the play begins, but some of the early scenes deal with incidents (such as Clifford's confession and Stanley's execution) which took place during the preceding winter.

[NOTE: The standard modern account of Warbeck's career is that by Gairdner and of the Cornish rebellions of 1497 and Warbeck's involvement in them that by Rowse: see list of Abbreviations.]

THE CHRONICLE HISTORY OF
PERKIN WARBECK

A STRANGE TRUTH

THE
CHRONICLE
HISTORIE
OF
PERKIN WARBECK.

A Strange Truth.

Acted (some-times) by the Queenes
MAIESTIES Servants at the
Phænix in *Drurie* lane.

Fide Honor.

LONDON,
Printed by *T. P.* for *Hugh Beeston,* and are to
be sold at his Shop, neere the *Castle* in
Cornehill. 1 6 3 4.

Title-page of the Quarto of 1634

[DRAMATIS PERSONAE

HENRY: Henry VII, *King of England.*

DURHAM: Richard Fox, *Bishop of Durham.*

OXFORD: John de Vere, *Earl of Oxford.*

SURREY: Thomas Howard, *Earl of Surrey.*

STANLEY: Sir William Stanley, *King's Chamberlain.*

DAUBENEY: Giles, *Lord Daubeney.*

URSWICK: Christopher Urswick, *chaplain to Henry VII.*

HUNTLY: George Gordon, *second Earl of Huntly.*

DALYELL: *Lord Dalyell.*

KATHERINE: Lady Katherine Gordon, *Huntly's daughter.*

JANE: Jane Douglas, *maid-in-waiting to Lady Katherine Gordon.*

CRAWFORD: *The Earl of Crawford.*

CLIFFORD: Sir Robert Clifford.

The Countess of CRAWFORD.

JAMES: James IV, *King of Scotland.*

PERKIN WARBECK.

FRION: Stephen Frion.

HERON: John Heron, *a merchant of London.*

SKELTON: Richard, or Edward, Skelton, *a tailor.*

ASTLEY: Nicholas Astley, *a scrivener.*

A-WATER: John a-Water, *Mayor of Cork.*

⎫
⎬ Perkin Warbeck's chief counsellors.
⎭

HIALAS: Don Pedro de Ayala, *ambassador from Ferdinand and Isabella of Spain.*

MARCHMOUNT: *a herald.*

The Post: *a courier to Henry VII.*

A Servant: *groom to Lady Katherine Gordon.*

A Constable.

LAMBERT SIMNEL.

Dramatis Personae] *The Quarto supplies a list of 'The Persons presented', divided into English characters, Scottish characters, Perkin and his counsellors, and Women. For spellings and other details see the 'Biographical Index to the Historical Characters', pp. lxxxiii–lxxxix.*

In addition, the text calls for numerous non-speaking extras, as follows: A Confessor, an Executioner, eight Maskers (four Scotch Antics and four wild Irish), an additional Herald, the Sheriff and his Officers, the Constable's Officers, Ladies, Attendants, Guards, and Soldiers.]

The Scene: The Continent of Great Britain.

The Scene . . . Britain] from Q. Continent means 'mainland' (as distinct from islands, etc.): see *O.E.D.*, 4.

[Dedicatory Epistle]

To the rightly honourable William Cavendish, Earl of Newcastle,
Viscount Mansfield, Lord Bolsover and Ogle.

My Lord,

Out of the darkness of a former age (enlightened by a late
both learned and an honourable pen) I have endeavoured to
personate a great attempt, and in it a greater danger. In other
labours you may read actions of antiquity discoursed; in this   5
abridgement, find the actors themselves discoursing: in some
kind, practised as well what to speak, as speaking why to do.
Your Lordship is a most competent judge in expressions of
such credit, commissioned by your known ability in examining and enabled by your knowledge in determining the monu-   10
ments of time. Eminent titles may indeed inform who their
owners are, not often what. To yours the addition of that in-

---

Dedicatory Epistle. Heading. Bolsover] *Boulfouer Q.*

Dedicatory Epistle. Heading. *William Cavendish*] first earl (1628) of
Newcastle (1592–1676). He was a poet and patron of Ben Jonson, from
whom in 1633–34 he commissioned two entertainments for Charles I's visit
to his great Nottinghamshire houses of Welbeck and Bolsover. An unsuccessful leader of the royalist armies in the North, he went into exile after the
royalist defeat at Marston Moor (1644), and in the following year married,
as his second wife, the eccentric authoress Margaret Lucas, whose *Life* of
him is her best-known work. Created a duke in 1665, he retired with the
duchess to Welbeck to a life of literary and philosophical study.

2–3. *a late . . . pen*] presumably a reference to Bacon's *Henry VII*, 1622.
Bacon died in 1626.

4. *personate*] represent, describe (*O.E.D.*, 5).

6. *actors*] the participants in the historical action, with a quibble on
'stage-actors'.

6–7. *in some . . . do*] naturally as experienced in what to say as in saying
why something is done.

8–9. *in expressions . . . credit*] of representations of such matters of (historical) reputation.

9. *commissioned*] authorized.

10. *determining*] deciding what [the monuments] are.

12–14. *To . . . Truth*] i.e., it cannot possibly be called flattery to regard as

5

formation in Both cannot in any application be observed
flattery, the authority being established by Truth. I can only
acknowledge the errors in writing mine own, the worthiness   15
of the subject written being a perfection in the story, and of
it. The custom of your Lordship's entertainments, even to
strangers, is rather an example than a fashion: in which consideration I dare not profess a curiosity, but am only studious
that your Lordship will please, amongst such as best honour   20
your goodness, to admit into your noble construction

John Ford.

---

13. Both] BOTH Q.   14. Truth] TRVTH Q.

---

an addition to your great title the fact that it not only describes who you are
but what kind of man you are (one as eminent in person as in name), for the
'addition' is warranted by its being true.

    17. *entertainments*] takings into favour or service (*O.E.D.*, 2).

    19. *curiosity*] skill, cleverness (*O.E.D.*, 3).

    21. *construction*] interpretation of conduct, i.e., enrol me amongst those
upon whose conduct you put your usual generous interpretation.

[Commendatory Verses]

[i] To my own friend, master John Ford, on his justifiable
poem of *Perkin Warbeck*, this Ode.

They who do know me know that I,
    Unskilled to flatter,
Dare speak this piece in words, in matter,
A work, without the danger of the lie.
Believe me, friend, the name of this and thee   5
    Will live, your story.
Books may want faith, or merit glory;
This neither, without judgement's lethargy.

When the arts dote, then some sick poet may
    Hope that his pen   10
In new-stained paper can find men
To roar, 'He is The Wit; his Noise doth sway.'
But such an age cannot be known; for all,
    Ere that time be,
Must prove such truth mortality.   15
So, friend, thy honour stands too fixed to fall.

George Donne.

---

i. 4. A work,] A WORKE: *Q*.   12. He . . . sway] *This ed.; HE is* THE WIT'S;
His NOYSE doth sway. *Q;* "He is the wit;" his noise doth sway: *D*.

---

i. 0.1. *justifiable*] worthy of justification, defensible.
4. *work*] i.e., a true work of art, an *opus*.
the lie] being told I am lying.
11. *new-stained*] newly-inked (?).
13–15.] The general meaning may possibly be: 'but we shall never experience such an age; for, before it can come, this true work (Ford's play)
must turn out to be perishable (which, it is implied, is impossible—see
ll. 5–6 above.)'
17. George Donne] A son (b. 1605) of John Donne, he also prefixed
verses to Ford's *The Lover's Melancholy*, 1629; he and Ford both wrote
commendatory poems for Massinger's *The Great Duke of Florence*, 1636,
and contributed to the collection of elegies for Jonson, *Jonsonus Virbius*,
1638.

7

[ii] To his worthy friend, master John Ford, upon his
Perkin Warbeck.

Let men who are writ poets lay a claim
To the Phoebean hill, I have no name
Nor art in verse; true, I have heard some tell
Of Aganippe, but ne'er knew the well.
Therefore have no ambition with the times   5
To be in print for making of ill rhymes;
But love of thee and justice to thy pen
Hath drawn me to this bar with other men
To justify, though against double laws,
(Waiving the subtle bus'ness of his cause)   10
The Glorious Perkin and thy poet's art,
Equal with his, in playing the King's Part.

Ra. Eure,
Baronis Primogenitus.

ii. 11. Glorious Perkin] GLORIOVS PERKIN *Q*.   12. King's Part] KINGS
PART *Q*.   14. Primogenitus] *Primogen: Q*.

ii. 1. *writ poets*] acknowledged as, or claiming to be, poets.
2. *Phoebean hill*] Mount Helicon, sacred to Phoebus Apollo and the
Muses.
4. *Aganippe*] a spring on Helicon.
13. Ra. Eure] presumably a descendant of Sir Ralph Eure, the English
military leader on the Scottish Border who was killed at the battle of An-
crum Moor in 1545 (see Ridpath, *The Border-History of England and
Scotland* [Berwick, 1848], p. 381).

[iii] To my faithful, no less deserving, friend, the
author, this indebted oblation.

Perkin is redivived by thy strong hand
And crowned a king of new; the vengeful wand
Of greatness is forgot. His execution
May rest unmentioned; and His birth's collusion
Lie buried in the story: but His fame   5
Thou hast eternized; made a crown His game.
His lofty spirit soars yet. Had He been
Base in his enterprise, as was His sin
Conceived, His Title, doubtless proved unjust,
Had but for thee been silenced in his dust.   10

George Crymes, miles.

[iv] To the author, his friend, upon his Chronicle History.

These are not to express thy wit,
But to pronounce thy judgement fit
In full-filed phrase those times to raise
When Perkin ran his wily ways.
Still let the method of thy brain   5
From error's touch and envy's stain

iii. 3, 4, 5, 6, 8. His] HIS *Q.*   7. He] HE *Q.*   9. His Title] HIS TITLE *Q.*

iii. 1. *redivived*] the first appearance of the word in *O.E.D.*, meaning
'brought to life again'.
  2. *of new*] anew.
  wand] sceptre, or wand of office, as a synecdoche for 'rule'.
  4. *birth's collusion*] the fraudulent story about his birth.
  7–9. *Had . . . Conceived*] i.e., had he been, in the execution of his enterprise, base, like the sin which he committed in conceiving it.
  9. *Title*] the justification which he advanced for his claims.
  11. George Crymes] unidentified.

iv. 1. *These*] these verses.
  3. *full-filed*] fully polished.

Preserve thee free, that e'er thy quill
Fair truth may whet and fancy fill.
Thus graces are with muses met,
And practic critics on may fret: 10
For here thou hast produced a story
Which shall eclipse their future glory.

John Brograve, Armiger.

[v] To my friend and kinsman master John Ford, the author.

Dramatic poets, as the times go now,
Can hardly write what others will allow;
The cynic snarls; the critic howls and barks;
And ravens croak to drown the voice of larks.
Scorn those Stage-Harpies! This I'll boldly say: 5
Many may imitate, few match thy play.

John Ford, Graiensis.

iv. 8. whet] wett *Q.*   13. Armiger] Ar: *Q.*

v. 5. Stage-Harpies] STAGE-HARPYES *Q.*

---

8. *whet*] sharpen.

10. *practic*] practising or practical, applied (in a pejorative sense—unenlightened by knowledge of theory), or possibly even 'artful, cunning' (*O.E.D.*, 4).

13. John Brograve] a son of Sir John Brograve (d. 1613—he was attorney to the duchy of Lancaster and knighted by James I), of Gray's Inn.

v. 2. *allow*] sanction, approve of.

7. John Ford] the playwright's cousin, older than he, of Gray's Inn. The playwright's epistle to him, prefixed to *Love's Sacrifice*, 1633, expresses warm affection. This cousin was also one of four Gray's Inn friends to whom Ford dedicated *The Lover's Melancholy*, 1629.

Prologue

Studies have of this nature been of late
So out of fashion, so unfollowed, that
It is become more justice to revive
The antic follies of the times than strive
To countenance wise industry. No want   5
Of art doth render wit or lame or scant
Or slothful in the purchase of fresh bays,
But want of truth in them who give the praise
To their self-love, presuming to out-do
The writer, or, for need, the actors too.   10
But such This Author's silence best befits,
Who bids them be in love with their own wits.
From him to clearer judgements we can say
He shows a history couched in a play,
A history of noble mention, known,   15
Famous, and true: most noble, 'cause our own;
Not forged from Italy, from France, from Spain,

Prol. 11. This Author's] THIS AVTHOVR'S *Q;* the author's *G*.

---

2. *out of fashion*] After *Henry VIII* (1613) less than a dozen English history plays are recorded.

3. *more justice*] more sensible; *justice* is 'judiciousness'.

4. *antic*] absurd, grotesque.

5. *countenance*] look with favour on.

5–10. *No . . . too*] a contrast between the readiness of good writers and players ('wit') to do good work and the bad judgement and conceit of certain sections of the audience who imagine that they can do better than either.

10. *for need*] if necessary.

14. *couched*] expressed (*O.E.D.*, 15).

15. *mention*] record (*O.E.D.*, 3); cf. I. ii. 155, V. iii. 206.

15–16. *known, Famous*] Pickburn drops the comma and interprets 'known to be famous', which is a tautology.

17. *forged*] fashioned, devised.

But chronicled at home; as rich in strain
Of brave attempts as ever fertile rage
In action could beget to grace the stage.   20
We cannot limit scenes, for the whole land
Itself appeared too narrow to withstand
Competitors for kingdoms; nor is here
Unnecessary mirth forced, to endear
A multitude; on these two rests the fate   25
Of worthy expectation: Truth and State.

26. Truth and State] TRVTH *and* STATE *Q*.

---

18. *strain*] stock, ancestral line; the genetic metaphor continues with *fertile, beget*.

19–20. *rage In action*] 'furor', height of feeling as expressed in the 'action' of a play or in the mode of acting it (*O.E.D.*, *s.vv.* rage 6, action 4, 6).

21. *limit scenes*] i.e., to any particular place; an apology for the absence of 'unity of place'.

24. *endear*] attract, conciliate (*O.E.D.*, 6).

25–6. *the fate . . . expectation*] the outcome of what may be justifiably expected.

26. *State*] matter of state, concerning ruling power (*O.E.D.*, 32), or 'stateliness, dignity' (*O.E.D.*, 17, 18).

The Chronicle History of
Perkin Warbeck

A Strange Truth

Act I

Enter King HENRY, DURHAM, OXFORD, SURREY, Sir WILLIAM
STANLEY (*Lord Chamberlain*), Lord DAUBENEY. *The King supported to his throne by* STANLEY *and* DURHAM. *A Guard.*

Hen. Still to be haunted, still to be pursued,
    Still to be frighted with false apparitions
    Of pageant majesty and new-coined greatness,
    As if we were a mockery-king in state,
    Only ordained to lavish sweat and blood   5

Heading. A Strange Truth] *not in Q.*   Act I] *Actus primus, Scæna prima.*
Q.   0.2. STANLEY (*Lord Chamberlain*)] Stanly, *Lord Chamberlaine, Q.*
5. blood] *W;* blond *Q.*

---

1. i. Location] Westminster (see I. i. 136–7), the king's palace.
Historical Time] 7 January 1495.
    0.2. Lord Chamberlain] Stanley *was* Lord Chamberlain, and the
Quarto's S.D., although it omits the brackets, does not indicate an additional character. Stanley's office is mentioned perhaps because he was to
be singled out by a special gown or staff.
    0.2–3. supported] formally escorted on their arms (*O.E.D.*, 6 c).
    1–7.] reminiscent of Henry IV's speech and situation at the beginning
of *1 Henry IV.* The imagery of haunting derives from Bacon (p. 104), a
passage which also introduces the Warbeck affair.
    4. *mockery-king*] counterfeit king; cf. *Richard II*, IV. i. 260, where the
mockery-king is a snowman; 'sweat and blood' (l. 5) alludes to the mal-
treatment of sacrificial kings, especially Jesus as Rex Iudaeorum.

In scorn and laughter to the ghosts of York,
Is all below our merits; yet, my lords,
My friends and counsellors, yet we sit fast
In our own royal birthright; the rent face
And bleeding wounds of England's slaughtered people   10
Have been by us, as by the best physician,
At last both throughly cured and set in safety;
And yet for all this glorious work of peace
Ourself is scarce secure.

Dur.   The rage of malice
Conjures fresh spirits with the spells of York;   15
For ninety years ten English kings and princes,
Threescore great dukes and earls, a thousand lords
And valiant knights, two hundred fifty thousand
Of English subjects have in civil wars
Been sacrificed to an uncivil thirst   20
Of discord and ambition. This hot vengeance
Of the just powers above to utter ruin
And desolation had rained on, but that
Mercy did gently sheathe the sword of Justice
In lending to this blood-shrunk commonwealth   25
A new soul, new birth, in your sacred person.

Dau. Edward the Fourth, after a doubtful fortune,
Yielded to nature, leaving to his sons,
Edward and Richard, the inheritance

---

23. rained] *D;* raign'd *Q;* reign'd *W.*

---

6. *ghosts*] Henry thinks of the Yorkist pretenders as ghostly manifestations of the dead house of York or of the dead Richard duke of York, Edward IV's second son, one of the 'princes in the Tower'.

11. *physician*] The king/physician metaphor is traditional and frequent; cf. *Richard II*, I. i. 152–5; and below, v. iii. 218–19.

16. *ninety years*] This rough computation from the accession of Henry IV, 1399, and the statistics about kings, subjects, etc. in ll. 16–19 below are taken, not quite accurately, from Gainsford, sig. B4.

18. *two . . . thousand*] '150000 Soldiers and people' (Gainsford, sig. B4).

23. *rained*] continued to rain down; the biblical and Shakespearian echoes (Ps. xi. 7, Job xx. 23, *Richard II*, I. ii. 8, etc.) support Dyce's reading.

25. *blood-shrunk*] shrunk by loss of blood in war.

Of a most bloody purchase; these young princes   30
Richard the tyrant, their unnatural uncle,
Forced to a violent grave; so just is heaven,
Him hath your majesty by your own arm,
Divinely strengthened, pulled from his boar's sty
And struck the black usurper to a carcass.   35
Nor doth the house of York decay in honours,
Though Lancaster doth repossess his right.
For Edward's daughter is king Henry's queen—.
A blessed union, and a lasting blessing
For this poor panting island, if some shreds,   40
Some useless remnant of the house of York,
Grudge not at this content.

Oxf.   Margaret of Burgundy
Blows fresh coals of division.

Sur.   Painted fires,
Without or heat to scorch or light to cherish.

Dau. York's headless trunk, her father; Edward's fate, 45
Her brother-king; the smothering of her nephews
By tyrant Gloucester, brother to her nature;
Nor Gloucester's own confusion—all decrees

---

32. heaven,] *D;* Heauen. *Q;* Heaven! *G.*   44. or heat to] *W;* to heate or *Q.*

---

30. *purchase*] legally, a *purchase* is something acquired other than by inheritance; Edward IV took the crown by force from Henry VI (Pickburn).

32. *so . . . heaven*] The phrase obviously goes with the sentence about the
'divinely strengthened' arm, so Q's punctuation (*graue, so just is Heauen*)
is wrong.

33–4.] Cf. Gainsford, sig. B4: 'King *Henry* . . . had obtained the Crowne
by a strong hand; and as we say, *diuinitùs præmunitus*'.

34. *boar's sty*] an allusion to the armorial bearings of Richard III.

38.] The marriage took place in 1486, in the year following that of the
battle of Bosworth.

42. *Margaret*] the younger daughter of Richard, duke of York, and sister
of Edward IV. She was the second wife of Charles the Bold, duke of Burgundy (d. 1477). All the sources lay great stress on her malice.

45.] Richard, duke of York, was killed at the battle of Wakefield (1460),
but Edward IV died in his bed.

47. *Gloucester*] later Richard III.

48. *confusion*] destruction (*O.E.D.*, 1).

Sacred in heaven—can move this woman-monster
But that she still from the unbottomed mine   50
Of devilish policies doth vent the ore
Of troubles and sedition.

Oxf.   In her age—
Great sir, observe the wonder—she grows fruitful,
Who in her strength of youth was always barren,
Nor are her births as other mothers' are,   55
At nine or ten months' end—she has been with child
Eight or seven years at least; whose twins being born
—A prodigy in nature—even the youngest
Is fifteen years of age at his first entrance,
As soon as known i' th' world, tall striplings, strong,   60
And able to give battle unto kings.
Idols of Yorkish malice!

Dau.   And but idols;
A steely hammer crushes 'em to pieces.

Hen. Lambert the eldest, lords, is in our service,
Preferred by an officious care of duty   65
From the scullery to a falc'ner; strange example!
Which shows the difference between noble natures

62. *Dau.*] *G; Ox: Q; Dur. W.*

---

50. *unbottomed*] bottomless.
52–62.] Oxford's speech is very closely modelled on the speech of pro-
test made by Henry's ambassador Sir William Warham at the court of the
archduke Philip of Burgundy (the young son of Warbeck's principal sup-
porter at this time, Emperor Maximilian I) in the summer of 1494, as it is
reported by Hol., 777/2/1 ff., Hall, p. 466, Gainsford, sigs. H–H2, Bacon,
pp. 117 ff. Ford is closest to Bacon, who alone uses the phrase 'tall striplings'; but Bacon does not, as do the others, mention that the pretenders
were 'fifteen years of age'.
57. *twins*] Lambert Simnel and Warbeck.
64. *Lambert*] see Biographical Index. All sources report that he was a
turnspit and then a falconer; but the phraseology clearly echoes Bacon
(p. 38) 'preferred to be one of the king's falconers' and Hall (p. 435), the
latter being the only source to mention the scullery.
65. *Preferred*] promoted (*O.E.D.*, 1).
officious] dutiful (*O.E.D.*, 2).
67–8. *Which . . . born*] Henry no doubt intends some general reflection
such as 'Lambert has shown himself fit only to be a servant, as one might

And the base born. But for the upstart duke,
The new-revivèd York, Edward's second son,
Murdered long since i' th' Tower—he lives again   70
And vows to be your king.
Stan.   The throne is filled, sir.
Hen. True, Stanley, and the lawful heir sits on it;
A guard of angels and the holy prayers
Of loyal subjects are a sure defence
Against all force and counsel of intrusion.   75
But now, my lords, put case some of our nobles,
Our 'great ones', should give countenance and courage
To trim duke Perkin, you will all confess
Our bounties have unthriftily been scattered
Amongst unthankful men.
Dau.   Unthankful beasts,   80
Dogs, villains, traitors!
Hen.   Daubeney, let the guilty
Keep silence. I accuse none, though I know
Foreign attempts against a state and kingdom
Are seldom without some great friends at home.
Stan. Sir, if no other abler reasons else   85
Of duty or allegiance could divert
A headstrong resolution, yet the dangers

---

69. revivèd] *this ed.;* reviu'd *Q.*   77. 'great ones'] GREAT ONES *Q.*

---

expect of the base-born'; but it is phrased so badly that it looks as if Henry were saying that Lambert's *ability* (to rise from scullion to falconer) was a proof of his base birth—not a likely sentiment from a Tudor monarch.

68. *for*] regarding.

75. *force . . . intrusion*] invasion by open force and secret plan (*O.E.D.*, *s.v.* counsel 5).

77. *'great ones'*] an ironical and meaningful use of a phrase (meaning 'statesmen') commonly used in a pejorative sense in seventeenth-century political writing: see Samuel Daniel's view, as expressed in *Philotas* (1604), that there are two sorts of 'great men'—the cunning politician and the ambitious favourite; both can be suspected of making a party in the state by wooing the people: see *Philotas* (ed. L. Michel, New Haven, 1949), ll. 91 ff., 350 ff., 1110 ff., etc.

78. *trim*] neat and pretty (ironical use: see *O.E.D.*, 3).

So lately passed by men of blood and fortunes
In Lambert Simnel's party must command
More than a fear, a terror to conspiracy.   90
The high-born Lincoln, son to De la Pole,
The earl of Kildare, lord Geraldine,
Francis, lord Lovell, and the German baron,
Bold Martin Swart, with Broughton and the rest—
Most spectacles of ruin, some of mercy—   95
Are precedents sufficient to forewarn
The present times, or any that live in them,
What folly, nay, what madness 'twere to lift
A finger up in all defence but yours,
Which can be but impostorous in a title.   100
Hen. Stanley, we know thou lovest us, and thy heart

---

88. *passed*] undergone (*O.E.D.*, *v.*, 32).

89–90. *command . . . conspiracy*] The abstractions cause awkwardness;
the nearest analogue (from which the line might derive) is a phrase like
'command [i.e., enjoin] fear to the conspirators', a usage of *command* where
the customary infinitive with the direct object is replaced by a substantive
with *to*: see *O.E.D.*, *s.v.* command 1 d, and cf. Guildenstern's commanding
harmony to his pipe in *Hamlet*, III. ii. 352.

91–5.] All these persons supported Simnel's invasion from Ireland,
which was defeated at Stoke near Newark in 1487. Gerald Fitzgerald, 8th
earl of Kildare, was Henry's lord deputy in Ireland, but Simnel's chief
backer. The others (who all fell at Stoke) were his brother Thomas, lord
Geraldine; John De la Pole, the young earl of Lincoln (Richard III's
cousin) and Francis, 1st viscount Lovell (both fought for Richard at Bosworth); Sir Thomas Broughton, an important Yorkist from Lancashire;
and Swart, a 'nobleman of Germany', the courageous leader of 2,000 mer-
cenaries at Stoke. It is not clear whether Ford thought Kildare and Geraldine were one person, as Bacon and Gainsford did. Kildare renewed his oath
and retained his deputyship (and was again pardoned and reinstated in
1496 after he had shown interest in Warbeck). If he is the 'spectacle of
mercy' (l. 95), the source of Ford's information is puzzling, for Bacon and
Gainsford thought that he was killed at Stoke and neither Hall nor Holinshed mentions him in this connexion. 'Mercy' may be a reference to Henry's
(thwarted) *intention* of pardoning Lincoln, reported by the sources.

99. *defence*] almost in the sense of 'cause'.

100.] *Which* refers to a 'defence' other than one pertaining to Henry; its
justification or claim (*O.E.D.*, *s.v.* title 6, 7 c) can only be fraudulent (for
impostorous, a word used in Chapman's Homer, cf. Ford, *Lover's Melancholy*, I. ii, 'impostorous empiric').

Is figured on thy tongue; nor think we less
Of any's here. How closely we have hunted
This cub, since he unlodged, from hole to hole,
Your knowledge is our chronicle: first Ireland,   105
The common stage of novelty, presented
This gewgaw to oppose us; there the Geraldines
And Butlers once again stood in support
Of this colossic statue; Charles of France
Thence called him into his protection,   110
Dissembled him the lawful heir of England;
Yet this was all but French dissimulation,
Aiming at peace with us, which being granted
On honourable terms on our part, suddenly
This smoke of straw was packed from France again   115
T' infect some grosser air; and now we learn,
Maugre the malice of the bastard Neville,

---

102. *figured*] portrayed (*O.E.D.*, *v.*, 4).

104. *unlodged*] When used as a hunting term or metaphor (as here), normally transitive and equivalent to 'dislodge' (see *O.E.D.*, 1, 2).

107–8. *Geraldines And Butlers*] The great Anglo-Norman families in Ireland, the Geraldines (earls of Kildare and of Desmond, powerful in northern and central Ireland) and the Butlers (earls of Ormond, in the south-east), were rivals; the Butlers were less implicated in Yorkist intrigues than were the Geraldines, and there had been Butler opposition to Simnel; but Henry could trust neither group.

109. *colossic statue*] The point of Henry's metaphor is that the colossi were hollow pretences. This is explicit in the passage from which Ford was probably borrowing, Chapman, *Bussy d'Ambois*, I. i. 15–17, 'those colossic statues, / Which with heroic forms without o'erspread, / Within are nought but mortar, flint and lead'; Chapman's own lines derive from Plutarch's *Moralia*, *Ad Principem ineruditum*.

Charles] Charles VIII, reigned 1483–98, concluded the treaty of Étaples with Henry in November 1492.

111. *Dissembled*] pretended that he was (*O.E.D.*, 5 c).

115. *smoke*] 'Upon the first grain of incense, that was sacrificed upon the altar of peace . . . Perkin was smoked away' (Bacon, p. 110); 'all these [the rebels mentioned in ll. 117–18] were but smoaking illusions' (Gainsford, sig. G1ᵛ).

117. *Maugre*] in spite of.

117–18.] 'Hither also repaired vnto him, especially while he lay in *Paris Sir George Neuil* the Bastard: Sir *Iohn Tailor* . . . and a hundred English

  Sir Taylor and a hundred English rebels,
  They're all retired to Flanders, to the dam
  That nursed this eager whelp, Margaret of Burgundy. 120
  But we will hunt him there too, we will hunt him,
  Hunt him to death even in the beldam's closet,
  Though the archduke were his buckler.
Sur. She has styled him 'the fair white rose of England'.
Dau. Jolly gentleman! more fit to be a swabber 125
  To the Flemish after a drunken surfeit.

Enter URSWICK.

Urs. Gracious sovereign, please you peruse this paper.
Dur. The king's countenance gathers a sprightly blood.
Dau. Good news, believe it.
Hen.   Urswick, thine ear—
  Thou 'st lodged him?
Urs.   Strongly safe, sir. 130
Hen. Enough—is Barley come too?
Urs.   No, my lord.
Hen. No matter—phew, he's but a running weed,
  At pleasure to be plucked up by the roots.
  But more of this anon. I have bethought me.
  My lords, for reasons which you shall partake, 135
  It is our pleasure to remove our court
  From Westminster to th' Tower. We will lodge

Rebels' (Gainsford, sig. G1ᵛ, copying almost verbatim from Hall, p. 463).
Bacon's wording is less close. Henry says 'Sir Taylor' in scorn.

 122. *beldam*] witch, virago (*O.E.D.*, 3).

 123. *archduke*] Maximilian I; see Biographical Index, *s.v.* Warbeck,
IV. iii. 1–7 and note.

 124.] All sources record Margaret's bestowal of this Yorkist title.

 125–6.] *Swabber* was a word for 'ship's cleaner' recently introduced from
Dutch—hence a special appropriateness in its being here connected with
the reputation of Dutchmen for drunkenness.

 131. *Barley*] William Barley, a Hertfordshire gentleman who had joined
Warbeck in Flanders in company with Clifford, but, unlike him, remained
loyal to the pretender for several years; he was eventually pardoned. The
name is not, as Miss Crum (*Notes and Queries*, March 1965, p. 104) states,
a misprint for 'Barcley'.

This very night there; give, lord chamberlain,
A present order for it.
Stan. [*Aside*]   The Tower! [*Aloud*] I shall, sir.
Hen. Come, my true, best, fast friends, these clouds will vanish,
The sun will shine at full; the heavens are clearing.   141
                                        Flourish. Exeunt.

[I. ii]
                Enter HUNTLY *and* DALYELL.

Hunt. You trifle time, sir.
Dal.   O my noble lord,
You construe my griefs to so hard a sense
That where the text is argument of pity,
Matter of earnest love, your gloss corrupts it
With too much ill-placed mirth.
Hunt.   Much mirth, lord Dalyell?
Not so, I vow. Observe me, sprightly gallant: 6
I know thou art a noble lad, a handsome,
Descended from an honourable ancestry,
Forward and active, dost resolve to wrestle
And ruffle in the world by noble actions   10
For a brave mention to posterity.
I scorn not thy affection to my daughter,
Not I, by good St. Andrew; but this bugbear,
This whoreson tale of honour—honour, Dalyell—
So hourly chats and tattles in mine ear   15

139. *Aside*] G; *not in* Q.   *Aloud*] *this ed.; not in* Q.   141. *Flourish*]
centred after end of scene in Q.

I. ii. 2. construe] conster Q.   14. whoreson] W; whoresome Q.

I. ii. Location] Edinburgh, Huntly's house.
Historical Time] November 1495.
3–4. *argument . . . Matter*] a distinction similar to that between the
'theme' and the 'subject-matter' of a book.
10. *ruffle*] do battle; cf. v. iii. 35.
14. *whoreson*] wretched, bothersome.
15. *chats and tattles*] For the use of these words without a preposition
following, cf. *Coriolanus*, II. i. 198, *Titus Andronicus*, IV. ii. 169, and see
Abbott § 200.

    The piece of royalty that is stitched up
    In my Kate's blood, that 'tis as dangerous
    For thee, young lord, to perch so near an eaglet
    As foolish for my gravity to admit it.
    I have spoke all at once.
Dal.   Sir, with this truth   20
    You mix such wormwood that you leave no hope
    For my disordered palate e'er to relish
    A wholesome taste again; alas, I know, sir,
    What an unequal distance lies between
    Great Huntly's daughter's birth and Dalyell's fortunes.   25
    She's the king's kinswoman, placed near the crown,
    A princess of the blood, and I a subject.
Hunt. Right; but a noble subject—put in that too.
Dal. I could add more; and in the rightest line
    Derive my pedigree from Adam Mure,   30
    A Scottish knight, whose daughter was the mother
    To him that first begot the race of Jameses
    That sway the sceptre to this very day.
    But kindreds are not ours when once the date
    Of many years have swallowed up the memory   35
    Of their originals: so pasture fields,
    Neighbouring too near the ocean, are sooped up

37. sooped up] *Q;* supp'd up *W;* swoop'd-up *D.*

---

   19. *admit*] allow (*O.E.D.*, 2).

   26. *king's kinswoman*] All the sources say this, but none is more specific; see Biographical Index, *s.v.* Huntly.

   32. *him*] Robert III, who succeeded his father Robert II (the first Stuart king of Scotland) in 1390. His mother Elizabeth was the daughter of Sir Adam Mure of Rowallan, Ayrshire, a knight of Robert I, the Bruce. He married, *c.* 1367, Annabella Drummond, daughter of Sir John Drummond of Stobhall; his third-born but only surviving son succeeded to the throne as James I in 1406, and from him came 'the race of Jameses'. (I owe this information to Professor G. W. S. Barrow.)

   34. *kindreds . . . ours*] kinship (or pedigree) is no longer recognized.

   date] period (*O.E.D.*, 4).

   37. *sooped up*] The word, in the sense of 'sweep up' (*O.E.D.*, *s.v.* swoop 2; see also *s.v.* soop), is obsolete in both its spellings, *swoop* and *soop*. Q's form is retained in preference to modernizing to *swept*.

And known no more; for, stood I in my first
And native greatness, if my princely mistress
Vouchsafed me not her servant, 'twere as good   40
I were reduced to clownery, to nothing,
As to a throne of wonder.

Hunt. [*Aside*]   Now, by St. Andrew,
A spark of mettle, a' has a brave fire in him,
I would a' had my daughter so I knew 't not.
But 't must not be so, must not. [*To him*] Well, young lord, 45
This will not do yet; if the girl be headstrong
And will not hearken to good counsel, steal her
And run away with her, dance galliards, do,
And frisk about the world to learn the languages.
'Twill be a thriving trade; you may set up by 't.   50

Dal. With pardon, noble Gordon, this disdain
Suits not your daughter's virtue or my constancy.

Hunt. You are angry. [*Aside*] Would a' would beat me, I deserve it.
[*To him*] Dalyell, thy hand, we're friends; follow thy courtship,
Take thine own time and speak; if thou prevail'st   55
With passion more than I can with my counsel,
She's thine—nay, she is thine, 'tis a fair match,
Free and allowed; I'll only use my tongue
Without a father's power, use thou thine.
Self do self have, no more words, win and wear her.   60

Dal. You bless me; I am now too poor in thanks
To pay the debt I owe you.

Hunt.   Nay, thou'rt poor

42. *Aside*] G; *apart W; not in Q.*   45. 't] *W; not in Q.*   *To him*] *this ed.; not in Q.*   53. *Aside*] *W; not in Q.*   54. *To him*] *this ed.; not in Q.*
62–3. Nay . . . infinitely] *so D; one line in Q.*

41. *clownery*] i.e., the condition of a rustic or peasant.
42. *As to*] There is ellipsis of a word such as 'raised'; see Abbott § 382.
48. *galliards*] lively dances of various types: see *Shakespeare's England*, II. 443 ff.
50. *set up*] begin housekeeping (*O.E.D., s.v.* set 154 aa).
60.] See Tilley S 217, W 248.
62. *poor*] implying that poverty is 'one of the main objections to thy suit' (Pickburn).

H

Enough. [*Aside*] I love his spirit infinitely.

[*To him*] Look ye, she comes, to her now, to her, to her.

Enter KATHERINE *and* JANE.

Kath. The king commands your presence, sir.

Hunt.   The gallant—   65

This, this, this lord, this servant, Kate, of yours

Desires to be your master.

Kath.   I acknowledge him

A worthy friend of mine.

Dal.   Your humblest creature.

Hunt. [*Aside*] So, so, the game's afoot; I'm in cold hunting;

The hare and hounds are parties.

Dal.   Princely lady,   70

How most unworthy I am to employ

My services in honour of your virtues,

How hopeless my desires are to enjoy

Your fair opinion, and much more your love,

Are only matter of despair, unless   75

Your goodness give large warrant to my boldness,

My feeble-winged ambition.

Hunt. [*Aside*]   This is scurvy.

Kath. My lord, I interrupt you not.

Hunt. [*Aside*]   Indeed?

Now, on my life, she'll court him. [*To him*] Nay, nay, on, sir.

Dal. Oft have I tuned the lesson of my sorrows   80

To sweeten discord and enrich your pity,

---

63. *Aside*] W; *not in* Q.   64. *To him*] *this ed.; not in* Q.   65–7. The gallant . . . master] *so* W; *two lines in* Q *ending* Lord, this *and* Maister. 67–8. I . . . mine] *so* W; *one line in* Q.   69. *Aside*] W; *not in* Q.   70–1. Princely . . . employ] *so* W; *one line in* Q.   77, 78, 85. *Aside*] W; *not in* Q. 79. *To him*] *this ed.; not in* Q.

69–70.] These are hunting-metaphors, not very successfully managed: 'The hare and the hounds have got together, and I'm left out in the cold, have lost the scent'. For *parties*, 'partners', see *O.E.D.*, 13.

80. *tuned the lesson*] a difficult musical metaphor: 'modulated the performance [of my sorrows]' (*O.E.D.*, s.vv. tune 1 b, lesson 5 b).

But all in vain. Here had my comforts sunk
And never ris'n again to tell a story
Of the despairing lover, had not now,
Even now, the earl your father—
Hunt. [*Aside*]   A' means me, sure.   85
Dal. After some fit disputes of your condition,
    Your highness and my lowness, giv'n a licence
    Which did not more embolden than encourage
    My faulting tongue.
Hunt.   How, how? how's that? Embolden?
    Encourage? I encourage ye? d'ye hear, sir?   90
    A subtle trick, a quaint one—will you hear, man?
    What did I say to you? Come, come, to th' point.
Kath. It shall not need, my lord.
Hunt.   Then hear me, Kate.
    Keep you on that hand of her; I on this:
    Thou stand'st between a father and a suitor,   95
    Both striving for an interest in thy heart.
    He courts thee for affection, I for duty;
    He as a servant pleads, but by the privilege
    Of nature though I might command, my care
    Shall only counsel what it shall not force.   100
    Thou canst but make one choice; the ties of marriage
    Are tenures not at will but during life.
    Consider whose thou art, and who: a princess,
    A princess of the royal blood of Scotland,
    In the full spring of youth and fresh in beauty.   105
    The king that sits upon the throne is young
    And yet unmarried, forward in attempts

89–90.] *so W; Q divides the lines at* that.

___

86. *disputes*] not 'quarrels', but 'statements of the case'.
91. *quaint*] crafty.
98–9. *privilege . . . nature*] goes with *command*.
102. *tenures . . . will*] property-holdings which can be terminated at the will of the person leasing them.
107. *attempts*] endeavours, enterprises, presumably of a military nature; cf. II. i. 113.

On any least occasion to endanger
His person. Wherefore, Kate, as I am confident
Thou darest not wrong thy birth and education   110
By yielding to a common servile rage
Of female wantonness, so I am confident
Thou wilt proportion all thy thoughts to side
Thy equals, if not equal thy superiors.
My lord of Dalyell, young in years, is old   115
In honours, but nor eminent in titles
Or in estate, that may support or add to
The expectation of thy fortunes. Settle
Thy will and reason by a strength of judgement;
For, in a word, I give thee freedom; take it.   120
If equal fates have not ordained to pitch
Thy hopes above my height, let not thy passion
Lead thee to shrink mine honour in oblivion.
Thou art thine own; I have done.

Dal.   O, you're all oracle,
The living stock and root of truth and wisdom!   125
Kath. My worthiest lord and father, the indulgence
Of your sweet composition thus commands
The lowest of obedience; you have granted
A liberty so large that I want skill
To choose without direction of Example: 130
From which I daily learn, by how much more
You take off from the roughness of a father,
By so much more I am engaged to tender
The duty of a daughter. For respects

123. shrink] *Q;* sink *D conj.*   130. Example] EXAMPLE *Q.*

---

111. *servile rage*] slave-like passion; cf. Prologue 19.
113. *side*] rival, keep up with (*O.E.D.*, 2 d).
121. *equal*] impartial.
126–7. *indulgence . . . composition*] kindness of your sweet nature.
130. *Example*] Emphasized by Q, *Example* is perhaps equivalent to 'the whole body of moral *exempla*'; so Milton in *The Reason of Church Government* speaks of 'Teaching . . . through all the instances of example' (*Complete Poems and Major Prose*, ed. M. Y. Hughes, p. 670).
134. *respects*] considerations (*O.E.D.*, 14).

Of birth, degrees of title, and advancement,   135
I nor admire nor slight them; all my studies
Shall ever aim at this perfection only,
To live and die so that you may not blush
In any course of mine to own me yours.

Hunt. Kate, Kate, thou grow'st upon my heart like peace,   140
Creating every other hour a jubilee.

Kath. To you, my lord of Dalyell, I address
Some few remaining words: the general fame
That speaks your merit, even in vulgar tongues
Proclaims it clear; but in the best, a precedent.   145

Hunt. Good wench, good girl, i' faith!

Kath.   For my part, trust me,
I value mine own worth at higher rate
'Cause you are pleased to prize it; if the stream
Of your protested service, as you term it,
Run in a constancy more than a compliment,   150
It shall be my delight that worthy love
Leads you to worthy actions, and these guide ye
Richly to wed an honourable name;
So every virtuous praise in after-ages
Shall be your heir, and I in your brave mention   155
Be chronicled the Mother of that issue,
That glorious issue.

Hunt.   O that I were young again!

156. Mother] MOTHER *Q.*

---

141. *jubilee*] occasion for rejoicing.

144-5. *even . . . precedent*] Even when the people's tongues spread your fame they proclaim that your merit is stainless; but when the better sort do so, they proclaim it an example others should follow.

149. *protested*] solemnly affirmed (*O.E.D., s.v.* protested 1).

150. *Run in*] i.e., 'is composed of'; but the attempt to continue the metaphor from *stream* gives an unintended ambiguity to the line as a whole.

153-7.] Whatever Katherine is hinting at, the passage uses marriage and procreation metaphors which must not be taken literally; Dalyell will achieve a reputation for honour (*wed an honourable name*), inspired by love for her, and so in that sense she will be the *Mother* of his *issue* and of his *heir*, namely, the praise accorded to him by posterity.

155. *brave mention*] record of your brave deeds; cf. Prologue 15.

    She'd make me court proud danger and suck spirit
    From reputation.
Kath.   To the present motion
    Here's all that I dare answer: when a ripeness   160
    Of more experience and some use of time
    Resolves to treat the freedom of my youth
    Upon exchange of troths, I shall desire
    No surer credit of a match with virtue
    Than such as lives in you; meantime my hopes are   165
    Preserved secure in having you a friend.
Dal. You are a blessed lady, and instruct
    Ambition not to soar a farther flight
    Than in the perfumed air of your soft voice.
    My noble lord of Huntly, you have lent   170
    A full extent of bounty to this parley,
    And for it shall command your humblest servant.
Hunt. Enough; we are still friends and will continue
    A hearty love. O Kate, thou art mine own—
    No more: my lord of Crawford.

                 Enter CRAWFORD.

Craw.   From the king   175
    I come, my lord of Huntly, who in council
    Requires your present aid.
Hunt.   Some weighty business?
Craw. A secretary from a duke of York,
    The second son to the late English Edward,
    Concealed I know not where these fourteen years,   180
    Craves audience from our master: and 'tis said
    The duke himself is following to the court.
Hunt. Duke upon duke; 'tis well, 'tis well; here's bustling

175–7. From . . . aid] *so W; two lines divided at 'Huntley' in Q.*

---

   159. *motion*] proposal (*O.E.D.*, 7).
   162. *treat*] bargain away (Pickburn).
   163. *Upon*] upon the occasion of.
   183. *bustling*] contending (*O.E.D.*, 3).

For majesty. My lord, I will along with ye.

Craw. My service, noble lady.

Kath.   Please ye walk, sir ?   185

Dal. [*Aside*] Times have their changes, sorrow makes men wise,
    The sun itself must set as well as rise;
    Then why not I ? [*To her*] Fair madam, I wait on ye.

                                Exeunt omnes.

[I. iii]

Enter DURHAM, Sir ROBERT CLIFFORD, *and* URSWICK. *Lights.*

Dur. You find, Sir Robert Clifford, how securely
    King Henry our great master doth commit
    His person to your loyalty; you taste
    His bounty and his mercy even in this,
    That at a time of night so late, a place   5
    So private as his closet, he is pleased
    To admit you to his favour; do not falter
    In your discovery, but as you covet
    A liberal grace, and pardon for your follies,
    So labour to deserve it by laying open   10
    All plots, all persons, that contrive against it.

Urs. Remember not the witchcraft or the magic,
    The charms and incantations, which the sorceress
    Of Burgundy hath cast upon your reason!
    Sir Robert, be your own friend now, discharge   15

---

186. *Aside*] D; *not in* Q.   Times] "Times Q.   187. The] "The Q.
188. *To her*] *this ed.; not in* Q.

186–7.] These sound like proverbs, but are not recorded as such. Except
possibly the first, they all seem inappropriate to a man with Dalyell's am-
bitions, though Ford may mean us to understand that Dalyell suspects
already that he will never win Katherine.

I. iii. Location] The Tower of London: see I. i. 135–8.
Historical Time] January 1495 (Clifford's betrayal of Stanley, etc.), but
with references to events of July 1495 (Warbeck's assault at Deal) and
June 1497 (the first Cornish rising).
  1. *securely*] confidently.
  8. *discovery*] disclosure.

Your conscience freely; all of such as love you
Stand sureties for your honesty and truth.
Take heed you do not dally with the king,
He is wise as he is gentle.

Cliff.   I am miserable
If Henry be not merciful.

Urs.   The king comes.   20

Enter King HENRY.

Hen. Clifford!

Cliff.   Let my weak knees rot on the earth
If I appear as leprous in my treacheries
Before your royal eyes, as to mine own
I seem a monster by my breach of truth.

Hen. Clifford, stand up; for instance of thy safety,   25
I offer thee my hand.

Cliff.   A sovereign balm
For my bruised soul, I kiss it with a greediness.
Sir, you are a just master, but I—

Hen.   Tell me,
Is every circumstance thou hast set down
With thine own hand within this paper true?   30
Is it a sure intelligence of all
The progress of our enemies' intents
Without corruption?

Cliff.   True, as I wish heaven,
Or my infected honour white again.

Hen. We know all, Clifford, fully, since this meteor,   35

21. rot on] *Q;* rot to *W;* root on *D.*   28–9. Tell . . . down] *so W; one line
in Q.*

21.] Clifford's kneeling and abject humility derive from the sources;
Ford does not seem to have been specially influenced by Gainsford's feeble
attempts to amplify and dramatize the episode.

25. *for instance*] as a proof, token (*O.E.D.*, 7).

27. *with a greediness*] analogous to 'in a readiness', 'with an appetite', etc.

31. *intelligence*] information.

35–80.] Ford incorporates all this historical information (derived from
various places in his sources) into the scene about Stanley's treason and

This airy apparition, first discradled
From Tournay into Portugal, and thence
Advanced his fiery blaze for adoration
To th' superstitious Irish; since the beard
Of this wild comet, conjured into France,   40
Sparkled in antic flames in Charles his court;
But shrunk again from thence, and, hid in darkness,
Stole into Flanders, flourishing the rags
Of painted power on the shore of Kent,
Whence he was beaten back with shame and scorn,   45
Contempt, and slaughter of some naked outlaws.
But tell me, what new course now shapes Duke Perkin?

Cliff. For Ireland, mighty Henry; so instructed
By Stephen Frion, sometimes secretary

43. into] *Q; out of B (Struble conj.).*   Flanders] *G adds asterisks for
missing words.*

Clifford's informing on him; it is the treason only that the sources represent as being reported by Clifford.

35. *meteor*] The astronomical metaphors derive from Bacon (p. 108), whose influence over this speech is paramount. Hall calls Warbeck Margaret of Burgundy's 'new inuented Mawmet' (p. 462), Gainsford, sig. F3ᵛ, 'Idol and puppet ... made of straw and painted cloth'.

36. *discradled*] left the cradle; the only example of this word cited in *O.E.D.*

37. *Tournay ... Portugal*] See Biographical Index, *s.v.* Warbeck.

39. *since*] thereupon.
beard] tail (*O.E.D.*, 7).

41. *antic*] absurd, grotesque.
Charles] Charles VIII of France.

43–5.] About two and a half years separated Warbeck's retreat from the French court to Flanders and his abortive attempt to land at Deal, which was eventually launched from Flanders. This account is meant to be highly compressed; there is no need to accept Dyce's theory of a lacuna. The attempt occurred in July 1495, so what is being described has not yet happened: on the dramatic treatment of time, see Introduction, p. xxxvii.

44. *painted*] Cf. I. i. 43.

46. *naked outlaws*] Struble suggests that the reference is especially to Warbeck's Irish adherents; when Warbeck retreated to Ireland after Deal he despaired of getting help from the Irish because they were 'naked people, without furniture of armour or weapon' (Hol., 780/1/25; cf. Hall, p. 473).

49. *Frion.*] See Biographical Index. The main reference to him (and this spelling of his name) is in Bacon (pp. 109, 110), where he is described as

In the French tongue unto your sacred excellence,   50
But Perkin's tutor now.

Hen.   A subtle villain,
That Frion! Frion—you, my lord of Durham,
Knew well the man.

Dur.   French both in heart and actions!

Hen. Some Irish heads work in this mine of treason;
Speak 'em.

Cliff.   Not any of the best; your fortune   55
Hath dulled their spleens; never had counterfeit
Such a confused rabble of lost bankrupts
For counsellors: first Heron, a broken mercer,
Then John a-Water sometimes mayor of Cork,
Skelton a tailor, and a scrivener   60
Called Astley; and whate'er these list to treat of,
Perkin must hearken to; but Frion, cunning
Above these dull capacities, still prompts him
To fly to Scotland to young James the Fourth,
And sue for aid to him; this is the latest   65
Of all their resolutions.

Hen.   Still more Frion!

60. Skelton] *D; Sketon Q.*

Warbeck's 'principal counsellor'; the other sources merely list him as a
name in Warbeck's confession after his final capture.

sometimes] formerly.

59–61.] Spellings here afford clear proof of Ford's debt to Gainsford.
None of the sources mentions any of these names until it reaches the ac-
count of Warbeck's invasion of Cornwall in September 1497; none, except
Gainsford (sig. O2; see also sig. O4ᵛ), mentions John a-Water at all until
it reaches the account of the execution of John and of his son (perhaps the
Thomas a-Water mentioned by Gainsford, sig. O4ᵛ) in 1499. Bacon alone
does not even then give the name a-Water, referring only to 'the mayor of
Cork and his son' (p. 178). Gainsford's first mention uses the form 'John of
Water' but elsewhere he has the form found in Q, a Water; Hall (p. 491)
and Hol. (782/2/29) both have Awater. The sources vary amongst themselves and with Q in the spellings of the other names, but yield no clear
conclusion about indebtedness. All except Gainsford have Skelton (Hall,
'Scelton'), not Q's form Sketon, which derives from Gainsford (sig. O2).
Dyce was the first to introduce the historical spelling of the name into the
play.

Pestilent adder, he will hiss out poison
As dang'rous as infectious: we must match him.
Clifford, thou hast spoke home; we give thee life.
But Clifford, there are people of our own   70
Remain behind untold; who are they, Clifford?
Name those and we are friends, and will to rest;
'Tis thy last task.

Cliff.   O sir, here I must break
A most unlawful oath to keep a just one.

Hen. Well, well, be brief, be brief.

Cliff.   The first in rank   75
Shall be John Ratcliffe, lord Fitzwater, then
Sir Simon Mountford and Sir Thomas Thwaites,
With William Daubeney, Cressoner, Astwood,
Worsley the dean of Paul's, two other friars,
And Robert Ratcliffe.

Hen.   Churchmen are turned devils.   80
These are the principal?

Cliff.   One more remains
Unnamed, whom I could willingly forget.

Hen. Ha, Clifford! one more?

Cliff.   Great sir, do not hear him:
For when Sir William Stanley your lord chamberlain

---

68. infectious: we] *D;* infections—we *Q.*   him] *D;* 'em *Q.*   78. Cressoner] *B; Chessoner Q.*   81. principal?] *W;* principall. *Q.*

---

68. *infectious . . . him*] Dyce's readings. The line in Q is unsatisfactory because Henry would not talk about 'matching' (i.e., 'being a match for') *infections*; this might be overcome merely by altering *'em* to *him,* but *infectious* (first suggested by Weber) yields a very characteristic locution and a big improvement in sense. The alteration of *'em* to *him* is justified because, once it is granted that Henry is not matching 'infections', it is plain that he is considering not the entire group of conspirators but the *one,* Frion, who of them all is really dangerous; for Q's mistaking of *him* for *'em,* cf. II. ii. 33.

74.] The two oaths are the conspiratorial one and his oath of allegiance.

75–80.] This list probably derives from Bacon (p. 120), with slight alterations in the order of names; the other sources supply longer lists. Q's *Chessoner* is a mistake for Cressoner or Cressenor, which could easily have occurred in transmission if Ford wrote *Chressoner.* The mistake was first corrected in Pickburn, then in Baskervill and in Anderson.

83. *do . . . him*] i.e., don't listen to his name (Stanley's).

Shall come into the list, as he is chief,   85
I shall lose credit with ye; yet this lord,
Last named, is first against you.
Hen.   Urswick, the light!
View well my face, sirs; is there blood left in it?
Dur. You alter strangely, sir.
Hen.   Alter, lord bishop?
Why, Clifford stabbed me, or I dreamed a' stabbed me.   90
Sirrah, it is a custom with the guilty
To think they set their own stains off by laying
Aspersions on some nobler than themselves.
Lies wait on treasons, as I find it here.
Thy life again is forfeit; I recall   95
My word of mercy, for I know thou darest
Repeat the name no more.
Cliff.   I dare, and once more
Upon my knowledge name Sir William Stanley
Both in his counsel and his purse the chief
Assistant to the feignèd duke of York.   100
Dur. Most strange!
Urs.   Most wicked!
Hen.   Yet again, once more.
Cliff. Sir William Stanley is your secret enemy,
And if time fit will openly profess it.
Hen. Sir William Stanley! Who? Sir William Stanley,

87–9.] *so W; four lines in Q divided at* you, Sirs, You alter, Bishop.
100–1.] *so W; two lines in Q divided at* strange, more.   100. feignèd]
fain'd *Q*.

88.] See below, note on ll. 104–19.
94. *wait on*] attend upon.
95. *recall*] take back.
101.] 'Clifford was required to say over again and again the particulars
of his accusation' (Bacon, p. 122).
104–19.] All the sources emphasize Henry's shock and distress; but
Gainsford (sigs. I–I^v) seems to have left special traces on ll. 105–8 in the
phrases *bosom friend, the love, pleasure of my court* ('the loue and fauour of
our Court'), *keys . . . of my treasury*. Henry's debt to Stanley at Bosworth
(ll. 114–17) is not, however, mentioned in the Gainsford passage; it is only
Bacon (p. 122, pp. 124–5) who stresses the crown itself. There is disagree-

My chamberlain, my counsellor, the love,   105
The pleasure of my court, my bosom friend,
The charge and the controlment of my person,
The keys and secrets of my treasury,
The all of all I am! I am unhappy.
Misery of confidence—let me turn traitor   110
To mine own person, yield my sceptre up
To Edward's sister and her bastard duke!

Dur. You lose your constant temper.

Hen.   Sir William Stanley!
O do not blame me; he, 'twas only he
Who having rescued me in Bosworth field   115
From Richard's bloody sword, snatched from his head
The kingly crown, and placed it first on mine.
He never failed me; what have I deserved
To lose this good man's heart, or he his own?

Urs. The night doth waste, this passion ill becomes ye;   120
Provide against your danger.

Hen.   Let it be so.
Urswick, command straight Stanley to his chamber.
'Tis well we are i' th' Tower; set a guard on him;
Clifford, to bed; you must lodge here tonight,
We'll talk with you tomorrow. My sad soul   125
Divines strange troubles.

Dau. [*Within*]   Ho, the king, the king!
I must have entrance.

---

126. *Within*] *W; not in Q.*

ment amongst modern historians as to whether it was William or his
brother Thomas who placed the crown on Henry's head after Bosworth
(see Gairdner, p. 244). The episode neatly exemplifies some differences of
style and handling between the sources most accessible to Ford: see Bacon,
pp. 121–2, 124–5; Hall, pp. 468–9; Gainsford, sigs. I–I2; Hol., pp. 778–9;
and see Mackie, pp. 54, 122–3.

107. *charge and controlment*] Both Hall and Gainsford have this: 'charge
and controlment of all that are next my person' (Gainsford, sig. I^v; 'next
to his bodye', Hall). Ford alters the phrase somewhat, but perhaps both
he and the chroniclers mean that Stanley was responsible for Henry's
personal security.

112. *Edward's sister*] Margaret of Burgundy; see I, i, 120.

Hen.   Daubeney's voice; admit him.
What new combustions huddle next to keep
Our eyes from rest?

Enter DAUBENEY.

The news?
Dau.   Ten thousand Cornish,
Grudging to pay your subsidies, have gathered   130
A head; led by a blacksmith and a lawyer,
They make for London, and to them is joined
Lord Audley; as they march, their number daily
Increases; they are—
Hen.   Rascals! Talk no more;
Such are not worthy of my thoughts tonight.   135
To bed; and if I cannot sleep, I'll wake.
When counsels fail, and there's in man no trust,
Even then an arm from heaven fights for the just.   *Exeunt.*

---

129. S.D.] *after* newes? *in Q.*   129–34.] *so W; seven lines in Q divided at*
newes, your, by a, *London,* march, are, more.   136.] *G;* And if I cannot
sleepe, Ile wake:—to bed. *Q.*   138. *Exeunt*] Exeunt./*Finis Actus primi Q.*

129–34.] This rebellion, the first Cornish rising, did not occur until the
summer of 1497: see note on Historical Time and note on ll. 43–5. The
subsidies (special taxes levied on the entire kingdom by the parliament of
1496–7: see Bacon, p. 147), resented by the Cornish, were raised to repel
the Scots *after* Warbeck's attempted invasion at Deal.

130–1. *gathered A head*] raised a force: see *O.E.D., s.v.* head; and *Titus
Andronicus*, IV. iv. 63: 'The Goths have gathered head'.

131. *blacksmith . . . lawyer*] Michael Joseph of St Keverne and Thomas
Flammock (or Flamank) of Bodmin, both hanged at Tyburn in June 1497
(see III. i. 75 ff.). They were joined by a number of the lesser Cornish
gentry: see Rowse, pp. 121–2. This rebellion is the subject of a tragedy in
The Mirror for Magistrates, 'The wilful fall of Blacke Smyth and the
foolish ende of the Lord Awdeley' (L. B. Campbell's edition of *The Mirror*,
pp. 402–18). There is little evidence that Ford knew this tragedy, but see
note on III. i. 51.

133. *Audley*] James Touchet, 14th Lord Audley, beheaded on Tower
Hill, 1497: see III. i. 94 ff. and Rowse, p. 123.

Act II

Enter above [the] Countess of CRAWFORD, KATHERINE, JANE, *with other Ladies.*

Countess. Come, ladies, here's a solemn preparation
    For entertainment of this English prince;
    The king intends grace more than ordinary;
    'Twere pity now if a' should prove a counterfeit.
Kath. Bless the young man, our nation would be laughed at   5
    For honest souls through Christendom. My father
    Hath a weak stomach to the business, madam,
    But that the king must not be crossed.
Countess.   A' brings
    A goodly troop, they say, of gallants with him;
    But very modest people, for they strive not   10
    To fame their names too much; their godfathers
    May be beholding to them, but their fathers
    Scarce owe them thanks. They are disguisèd princes,
    Brought up, it seems, to honest trades; no matter;
    They will break forth in season.

Act II] *Actus Secundus: Scæna prima. Q.*

II. i. Location] Scotland, either Edinburgh or Stirling, which latter was the historical location (Gairdner, pp. 300–1) but is not mentioned by Ford's sources.

Historical Time] November 1495.

6. *honest*] ingenuous (first citation in *O.E.D.*, 3 d).

7. *weak stomach*] disinclination.

11–13. *their godfathers . . . thanks*] i.e., because they have taken false names; their godfathers are beholden to them because therefore they are no longer associated with such rascals, but their fathers are displeased because the sons consider their fathers' names no longer good enough for them.

37

Jane.   Or break out,   15
For most of 'em are broken by report.   *Flourish.*
The king!
Kath.   Let us observe 'em and be silent.

Enter King JAMES, HUNTLY, CRAWFORD, *and* DALYELL.

Ja.   The right of kings, my lords, extends not only
To the safe conservation of their own,
But also to the aid of such allies   20
As change of time and state hath oftentimes
Hurled down from careful crowns, to undergo
An exercise of sufferance in both fortunes:
So English Richard surnamed Coeur-de-Lion,
So Robert Bruce our royal ancestor,   25
Forced by the trial of the wrongs they felt,
Both sought, and found, supplies from foreign kings
To repossess their own. Then grudge not, lords,
A much distressèd prince; king Charles of France
And Maximilian of Bohemia both   30
Have ratified his credit by their letters.
Shall we then be distrustful? No; compassion

16–17. For . . . king] *so W; one line in Q.*   16. *Flourish*] *after l. 17 in Q.*

15–16.] The countess's primary meaning is simply that there true names
and identities will eventually be revealed; it is uncertain whether she is
quibbling, although *in season* may suggest a horticultural metaphor. *Break
forth* and *break out* are nearly synonymous in senses of 'burst out', 'break
loose'. But Jane's utterance entails an obvious quibble, first probably
medical (as of skin-diseases, boils, etc.) and then financial: *broken*, 'bankrupt'.

16. *by*] according to.
22. *careful*] full of care.
23. *sufferance*] endurance.
both fortunes] i.e., those of time and state.
26. *trial*] undergoing.
24–8. *English . . . own*] Richard was aided by Philip Augustus of France,
Robert Bruce by Philip IV the Fair of France. These two historical examples seem to be original to Ford, not drawn from the sources.
28. *grudge*] 'complain against', or 'grudge help to'.
29–30.] See Biographical Index, *s.v.* Warbeck.

Is one rich jewel that shines in our crown,
And we will have it shine there.

Hunt.   Do your will, sir.

Ja. The young duke is at hand; Dalyell, from us   35
First greet him, and conduct him on; then Crawford
Shall meet him next, and Huntly last of all
Present him to our arms; sound sprightly music,
Whilst majesty encounters majesty.   *Hautboys.*

DALYELL *goes out, brings in* PERKIN [WARBECK] *at the door where*
CRAWFORD *entertains him, and from* CRAWFORD, HUNTLY *salutes*
him and presents him to the King. *They embrace.* PERKIN *in state*
retires some few paces back. During which ceremony the Noblemen
slightly salute FRION, HERON *a mercer,* SKELTON *a tailor,* ASTLEY
a scrivener, with JOHN A-WATER, *all Perkin's followers. Salutations*
ended, cease music.

War. Most high, most mighty king! that now there stands   40
Before your eyes, in presence of your peers,
A subject of the rarest kind of pity
That hath in any age touched noble hearts,
The vulgar story of a prince's ruin
Hath made it too apparent. Europe knows,   45

39.5. SKELTON] *D;* Sketon *Q.*   39.6. WATER] *W;* Watring *Q.*   45.
Europe] EVROPE *Q.*

39.2. entertains] receives (*O.E.D.*, 12)
39.7. music] Since the ladies are watching from 'above' in the balcony
(see 0.1), the musicians may have been somewhere else, although the
Phoenix theatre may have had a 'penthouse' for the musicians which was
structurally part of the balcony, as perhaps the Blackfriars theatre did: see
I. A. Shapiro, *Shakespeare Studies*, II (1966), 204.
40–79.] This speech is closely modelled on the first half of the similar
speech made by Warbeck on his arrival at the Scottish court in Bacon, pp.
136–8, which itself derives in part from Hall; cf. notes on l. 69, ll. 85–102
below.
44. *vulgar*] widespread.
45. *it*] a redundant pronoun.
Europe] The word and its derivatives are only just coming into common
usage about this time (see D. Hay, *Europe: the Emergence of an Idea* [1957]);
hence perhaps the emphatic capitals in Q; used by Gainsford, sig. L^v.

I

And all the western world, what persecution
Hath raged in malice against us, sole heir
To the great throne of old Plantagenets.
How from our nursery we have been hurried
Unto the sanctuary, from the sanctuary   50
Forced to the prison, from the prison haled
By cruel hands to the tormentor's fury,
Is registered already in the volume
Of all men's tongues; whose true relation draws
Compassion, melted into weeping eyes   55
And bleeding souls. But our misfortunes since
Have ranged a larger progress through strange lands,
Protected in our innocence by heaven.
Edward the Fifth, our brother, in his tragedy
Quenched their hot thirst of blood, whose hire to murder   60
Paid them their wages of despair and horror;
The softness of my childhood smiled upon
The roughness of their task, and robbed them farther
Of hearts to dare or hands to execute.
Great king, they spared my life, the butchers spared it;   65
Returned the tyrant, my unnatural uncle,
A truth of my dispatch; I was conveyed
With secrecy and speed to Tournay; fostered
By obscure means, taught to unlearn myself.

48. old] *Q;* th'old *G.*   54. tongues;] *G;* tongues, *Q.*

---

53. *volume*] book; no quibble on 'book/sound' is likely.
54. *whose . . . relation*] the true narration of which [volume].
57. *ranged . . . progress*] made a larger journey, or wandered on a larger journey. An unusual transitive use of *ranged.*
60. *hire to murder*] i.e., hired engagement to, the fact of being hired to; *murder* is a personified abstract noun.
62.] Warbeck drops the royal 'we', and resumes it at l. 99.
66. *Returned*] reported to.
67. *A truth*] i.e., an (allegedly) true report. Cf. III. ii. 151.
68. *Tournay*] not mentioned by Bacon at this point, but in Gainsford, sig. K4.
69. *taught . . . myself*] This constitutes one of the rare direct links with Hall (p. 473): 'so that I thus escapynge, by reason of my tendre infancy,

But as I grew in years I grew in sense   70
Of fear and of disdain: fear of the tyrant
Whose power swayed the throne then; when disdain
Of living so unknown, in such a servile
And abject lowness, prompted me to thoughts
Of recollecting who I was, I shook off   75
My bondage, and made haste to let my aunt
Of Burgundy acknowledge me her kinsman,
Heir to the crown of England snatched by Henry
From Richard's head, a thing scarce known i' th' world.

Ja.   My lord, it stands not with your counsel now   80
To fly upon invectives; if you can
Make this apparent what you have discoursed
In every circumstance, we will not study
An answer, but are ready in your cause.

War.   You are a wise and just king, by the powers   85
Above reserved beyond all other aids
To plant me in mine own inheritance;
To marry these two kingdoms in a love
Never to be divorced while time is time.
As for the manner, first of my escape,   90
Of my conveyance next, of my life since,
The means and persons who were instruments,
Great sir, 'tis fit I overpass in silence;
Reserving the relation to the secrecy
Of your own princely ear, since it concerns   95
Some great ones living yet, and others dead,

75. was,] *G;* was; *Q;* was. *B.*

---

forgate almost myself and knewe not wel what I was'—an element not
represented in the other sources.
    80. *stands . . . counsel*] It doesn't accord with your plans, or purposes:
'there's no point in . . .'
    81. *fly upon*] resort to.
    83. *study*] meditate at length upon.
    85–102.] This speech comes from three places in Bacon's version of
Warbeck's speech at Stirling: cf. note on ll. 40–79 above.
    86. *reserved*] set apart.
    91. *my conveyance*] how I was transported, where I was taken to.

      Whose issue might be questioned. For your bounty,
      Royal magnificence, to him that seeks it,
      We vow hereafter to demean ourself
      As if we were your own and natural brother,   100
      Omitting no occasion in our person
      To express a gratitude beyond example.
Ja. He must be more than subject who can utter
      The language of a king, and such is thine.
      Take this for answer: be whate'er thou art,   105
      Thou never shalt repent that thou hast put
      Thy cause and person into my protection.
      Cousin of York, thus once more we embrace thee;
      Welcome to James of Scotland! for thy safety,
      Know, such as love thee not shall never wrong thee.   110
      Come, we will taste a while our court delights,
      Dream hence afflictions past, and then proceed
      To high attempts of honour. On, lead on;
      Both thou and thine are ours, and we will guard ye.
      Lead on.   *Exeunt all but the Ladies above.*
Countess.   I have not seen a gentleman   115
      Of a more brave aspect or goodlier carriage;
      His fortunes move not him—madam, you're passionate.
Kath. Beshrew me, but his words have touched me home

---

98. magnificence,] *this ed.;* magnificence *Q.*   99. We] WEE *Q.*   115.
S.D.] *W*; *Exeunt, Manent Ladies aboue Q.*

---

    97. *issue*] descendants.
    98. *Royal magnificence*] sovereign munificence (*O.E.D.*, 2).
    99. *We*] Q emphasizes the resumption of the royal plural by capitals.
    demean] conduct (*O.E.D.*, v¹ 6).
    100.] i.e., as if we were your brother by blood as well as by our shared
kingship.
    109. *for*] as regards.
    112. *Dream . . . past*] The most likely of several possible meanings is
'dream away past afflictions', i.e., drive out the memory and effects of past
afflictions by means of the dream-like delights of the court. James is not
suggesting that the process is unreal or foolish, merely that it is as soothing-
ly pleasurable as (pleasant) dreams.
    113. *attempts*] military enterprises; cf. I. ii. 107.
    117. *passionate*] moved with pity (*O.E.D.*, 5).

As if his cause concerned me; I should pity him
If a' should prove another than he seems.   120

Enter CRAWFORD [*above*].

Craw. Ladies, the king commands your presence instantly
For entertainment of the duke.
Kath.   The duke
Must then be entertained, the king obeyed.
It is our duty.
Countess.   We will all wait on him.   *Exeunt.*

[II. ii]

Flourish. Enter King HENRY, OXFORD, DURHAM, SURREY.

Hen. Have ye condemned my chamberlain?
Dur.   His treasons
Condemned him, sir, which were as clear and manifest
As foul and dangerous. Besides, the guilt
Of his conspiracy pressed him so nearly
That it drew from him free confession   5
Without an importunity.
Hen.   O lord bishop,

II. ii. I–6.] *so W; seven lines in Q ending* Chamberlaine, were as, dangerous,
prest him, free, importunitie, Bishop.

119–20. *I should . . . should*] The modern locution would be 'I would (or
should) pity him if he were to.'

II. ii. Location] The Tower of London.
Historical Time] February 1495 (Stanley was executed on 16 February),
with events of November 1495 and the summer of 1497 treated as though
occurring simultaneously.
4. *nearly*] closely.
6–17.] Six weeks passed between the confession and the trial and execution of Stanley, before 'seueritee tooke place, and mercy was put backe'
(Hall, p. 469). Bacon (p. 123) says this was partly in order that Henry might
'shew to the world that he had a conflict with himself what he should do.'
Ford improves on this in order to render Henry's behaviour closer to the
behaviour attributed to the merciful monarch of royalist doctrine of his
own day. His discussion with his advisers is invented.

This argued shame and sorrow for his folly,
And must not stand in evidence against
Our mercy and the softness of our nature;
The rigour and extremity of law   10
Is sometimes too, too bitter, but we carry
A chancery of pity in our bosom.
I hope we may reprieve him from the sentence
Of death; I hope we may.

Dur.   You may, you may;
And so persuade your subjects that the title   15
Of York is better, nay, more just and lawful
Than yours of Lancaster; so Stanley holds:
Which if it be not treason in the highest,
Then we are traitors all, perjured and false,
Who have took oath to Henry and the justice   20
Of Henry's title—Oxford, Surrey, Daubeney,
With all your other peers of state and church,
Forsworn, and Stanley true alone to heaven
And England's lawful heir.

Oxf.   By Vere's old honours,
I'll cut his throat dares speak it.

Sur.   'Tis a quarrel   25
T' engage a soul in.

Hen.   What a coil is here
To keep my gratitude sincere and perfect!
Stanley was once my friend and came in time
To save my life; yet to say truth, my lords,

26. T'] To' *Q.*

7.] Stanley 'not very wisely, thinking to make his offence less by confession, . . . made it enough for condemnation' (Bacon, p. 122).

12. *chancery*] i.e., a court of equity, of appeal: see *O.E.D.*, 2.

18. *highest*] highest degree.

24. *Vere*] the family name of the earls of Oxford.

26. *engage*] pledge (*O.E.D.*, 2).

coil] fuss (*O.E.D.*, 3).

28–30.] 'The King's wit began now to suggest unto his passion, that
Stanley at Bosworth-field, though he came time enough to save his life, yet
he stayed long enough to endanger it' (Bacon, p. 125).

The man stayed long enough t' endanger it.   30
But I could see no more into his heart
Than what his outward actions did present;
And for 'em have rewarded him so fully,
As that there wanted nothing in our gift
To gratify his merit, as I thought,   35
Unless I should divide my crown with him
And give him half; though now I well perceive
'Twould scarce have served his turn without the whole.
But I am charitable, lords; let justice
Proceed in execution, whiles I mourn   40
The loss of one whom I esteemed a friend.

Dur. Sir, he is coming this way.

Hen.   If a' speak to me
I could deny him nothing; to prevent it,
I must withdraw. Pray, lords, commend my favours
To his last peace, which I with him will pray for.   45
That done, it doth concern us to consult
Of other following troubles.   *Exit.*

Oxf.   I am glad
He's gone; upon my life, he would have pardoned
The traitor, had a' seen him.

Sur.   'Tis a king
Composed of gentleness.

Dur.   Rare and unheard of;   50
But every man is nearest to himself,
And that the king observes; 'tis fit a' should.

33. him] *W;* 'em *Q.*   45. I . . . him] *Q;* with him, I *W.*   47. S.D.] *G;*
Exeunt. Q.   47–50.] *so W; five lines in Q ending* troubles, would, him,
gentlenesse, vnheard of.

---

34. *As that*] See Abbott §§ 108, 109; cf. l. 79 below.
wanted] lacked.
38. *served his turn*] answered his requirements.
40. *Proceed in*] continue on in; not the same meaning as *proceed to*; cf.
Coriolanus, III. i. 333–4.
44–5. *commend . . . To*] give him my good wishes for (Pickburn).
52. *And . . . observes*] And that's a rule the king obeys, i.e., he's well
aware that self-preservation is the important thing.

Enter STANLEY, Executioner, [Confessor], URSWICK *and*
DAUBENEY.

Stan. May I not speak with Clifford ere I shake
 This piece of frailty off?
Dau.   You shall, he's sent for.
Stan. I must not see the king?
Dur.   From him, Sir William, 55
 These lords and I am sent; he bade us say
 That he commends his mercy to your thoughts,
 Wishing the laws of England could remit
 The forfeit of your life as willingly
 As he would in the sweetness of his nature 60
 Forget your trespass; but howe'er your body
 Fall into dust, he vows, the king himself
 Doth vow, to keep a requiem for your soul,
 As for a friend close treasured in his bosom.
Oxf. Without remembrance of your errors past, 65
 I come to take my leave and wish you heaven.
Sur. And I; good angels guard ye.
Stan.   O, the king,
 Next to my soul, shall be the nearest subject
 Of my last prayers. My grave lord of Durham,
 My lords of Oxford, Surrey, Daubeney, all, 70
 Accept from a poor dying man a farewell.
 I was as you are once—great, and stood hopeful
 Of many flourishing years; but fate and time
 Have wheeled about, to turn me into nothing.

Enter CLIFFORD.

Dau. Sir Robert Clifford comes—the man, Sir William, 75
 You so desire to speak with.

 53–110.] This dramatization of Stanley's execution owes nothing to the
known sources: see Introduction, p. xliv.
 57. *mercy*] in the sense of 'compassion' rather than 'leniency'.
 68. *nearest*] most immediate.
 74. *wheeled about*] revolved. The metaphor derives from Fortune's
wheel.

Dur.   Mark their meeting.

Cliff. Sir William Stanley, I am glad your conscience
     Before your end hath emptied every burden
     Which charged it, as that you can clearly witness
     How far I have proceeded in a duty   80
     That both concerned my truth and the state's safety.

Stan. Mercy, how dear is life to such as hug it!
     Come hither; by this token think on me—
                    Makes a cross on Clifford's face with his finger.

Cliff. This token! What! I am abused?

Stan.   You are not.
     I wet upon your cheeks a holy sign,   85
     The cross, the Christian's badge, the traitor's infamy.
     Wear, Clifford, to thy grave this painted emblem.
     Water shall never wash it off, all eyes
     That gaze upon thy face shall read there written
     A state-informer's character, more ugly   90
     Stamped on a noble name than on a base.
     The heavens forgive thee; pray, my lords, no change
     Of words; this man and I have used too many.

Cliff. Shall I be disgraced
     Without reply?

Dur.   Give losers leave to talk;   95
     His loss is irrecoverable.

Stan.   Once more
     To all a long farewell; the best of greatness
     Preserve the king. My next suit is, my lords,

84. I am] *Q;* am I *G.*   94–6.] *so W; two lines in Q ending* loosers, more.

---

79. *as that*] probably the same usage as that in l. 34 above, understanding *so* before *emptied.*

86. *Christian's . . . infamy*] i.e., the cross was both the symbol of Christ and the Roman punishment for treason.

90. *state-informer*] '. . . Clifford, who now was become the state informer' (Bacon, p. 125).

92. *change*] exchange.

95. *Give . . . talk*] a proverbial sentiment; cf. *'Tis Pity She's a Whore* (ed. Bawcutt, 1966), I. ii. 55.

97. *best of greatness*] i.e., God, who transcends even 'greatness' in its sense of 'exalted rank, kingly power'.

> To be remembered to my noble brother,
> Derby, my much grieved brother. O, persuade him   100
> That I shall stand no blemish to his house
> In chronicles writ in another age.
> My heart doth bleed for him and for his sighs;
> Tell him he must not think the style of Derby,
> Nor being husband to king Henry's mother,   105
> The league with peers, the smiles of fortune, can
> Secure his peace above the state of man.
> I take my leave, to travel to my dust:
> Subjects deserve their deaths whose kings are just.
> Come, confessor; on with thy axe, friend, on.   110
>   [*He is led off to execution.*]

Cliff. Was I called hither by a traitor's breath
          To be upbraided? Lords, the king shall know it.

          Enter King HENRY *with a white staff.*

Hen. The king doth know it, sir; the king hath heard
          What he or you could say. We have given credit
          To every point of Clifford's information,   115
          The only evidence 'gainst Stanley's head.
          A' dies for 't; are you pleased?
Cliff.   I pleased, my lord!
Hen. No echoes. For your service, we dismiss
          Your more attendance on the court; take ease

---

103. him] *D;* him; *Q;* him, *W.*   sighs;] *this ed.;* sighes, *Q;* sighs: *D.*
109. Subjects] "Subjects *Q.*   110.1.] *W; Exeunt. Q.*

---

100. *Derby*] Thomas Stanley (1435?–1504), created 1st earl of Derby after Bosworth, 1485, third husband of Henry's mother, Margaret Beaufort: see l. 105 below.

101–2.] Perhaps Stanley means that, when all the facts are known, his conduct will be justified by later chroniclers.

103. *him . . . sighs*] Q's punctuation would alter the sense to something like: 'as a consolation for him in his grief, tell him . . .'

104. *style*] title.

107. *above . . . man*] i.e., more than mankind's (naturally unpeaceful) condition and mode of existence allow of.

109.] Stanley may be cryptically implying that *his* death at least is undeserved.

And live at home; but, as you love your life,   120
Stir not from London without leave from us.
We'll think on your reward; away!

Cliff.   I go, sir.   *Exit.*

Hen. Die all our griefs with Stanley! Take this staff
Of office, Daubeney; henceforth be our chamberlain.

Dau. I am your humblest servant.

Hen.   We are followed   125
By enemies at home that will not cease
To seek their own confusion; 'tis most true
The Cornish under Audley are marched on
As far as Winchester. But let them come,
Our forces are in readiness; we'll catch 'em   130
In their own toils.

Dau.   Your army, being mustered,
Consist in all, of horse and foot, at least
In number six and twenty thousand; men
Daring and able, resolute to fight,
And loyal in their truths.

Hen.   We know it, Daubeney.   135
For them we order thus: Oxford in chief,

---

132. Consist] *Q;* Consists *W.*

---

122. *reward*] Clifford got £500, but this is not mentioned in Ford's sources.

124. *Daubeney*] His appointment is recorded by all the sources.

127. *confusion*] ruin: cf. I. i. 48.

128. *The Cornish*] See notes on I. iii. 129–34 and Historical Time (this scene); 'the lord Audley led them on from Wells to Salisbury and from Salisbury to Winchester' (Bacon, p. 150; cf. Hall, p. 478).

131. *toils*] traps, nets; Bacon (p. 153) speaks of the plans to 'have these wild beasts [the Cornishmen], as it were, in a toil'.

133. *six . . . thousand*] The figure seems to be invented; Hall (p. 481) and Gainsford (sig. N2) give 20,000 as the size of the earl of Surrey's army gathered in the North to repel the Scots and occupy Norham (see below ll. 154–5). This occurred at the same period as the Cornish rising (summer of 1497) and the account of it comes next to the rising in the sources. Bacon gives no figures.

136–8.] 'the first was led by the earl of Oxford in chief [i.e., as commander-in-chief, *O.E.D.*, 11 b], assisted by the earls of Essex and Suffolk', Bacon (p. 152). Other sources differ in their treatment of this episode, but see note on III. i. 5.

Assisted by bold Essex and the earl
Of Suffolk, shall lead on the first battalia;
Be that your charge.

Oxf.   I humbly thank your majesty.

Hen. The next division we assign to Daubeney: 140
These must be men of action, for on those
The fortune of our fortunes must rely.
The last and main ourself commands in person,
As ready to restore the fight at all times
As to consummate an assurèd victory.   145

Dau. The king is still oraculous.

Hen.   But, Surrey,
We have employment of more toil for thee!
For our intelligence comes swiftly to us
That James of Scotland late hath entertained
Perkin the counterfeit with more than common   150
Grace and respect, nay, courts him with rare favours;
The Scot is young and forward, we must look for
A sudden storm to England from the North:
Which to withstand, Durham shall post to Norham
To fortify the castle and secure   155
The frontiers against an invasion there.

---

138. *battalia*] battalion; not a plural, but derived from *battaglia*.

141. *action*] great activity and daring.

144. *restore the fight*] turn the tide of battle in case of impending defeat (Pickburn).

146. *oraculous*] divinely inspired; cf. *Broken Heart* (ed. Morris, 1965), I. iii. 11: 'oraculous lectures'.

148. *intelligence*] information.

149–59.] See note on Historical Time. Warbeck arrived in Scotland in November 1495; Henry's preparations for war on the Border, which included sending the earl of Surrey up to collect troops in the Northern counties, did not take place until the summer of 1497 (simultaneously with the first Cornish rising).

154. *Durham . . . Norham*] See Biographical Index, *s.v.* Durham, and, for Norham, below, III. iv, note on location. Ford represents the strengthening of Norham as though it originated from a direct order by Henry; but all the sources attribute it to Bishop Fox's own foresight and vigilance.

156.] The line scans badly unless the first syllable of *against* is elided in pronunciation.

Surrey shall follow soon, with such an army
As may relieve the bishop and encounter
On all occasions the death-daring Scots.
You know your charges all; 'tis now a time   160
To execute, not talk. Heaven is our guard still.
War must breed peace; such is the fate of kings.   *Exeunt.*

[II. iii]

Enter CRAWFORD *and* DALYELL.

Craw. 'Tis more than strange; my reason cannot answer
Such argument of fine imposture, couched
In witchcraft of persuasion, that it fashions
Impossibilities, as if appearance
Could cozen truth itself; this dukeling mushroom   5
Hath doubtless charmed the king.
Dal.   A' courts the ladies,
As if his strength of language chained attention
By power of prerogative.
Craw.   It madded
My very soul to hear our master's motion:
What surety both of amity and honour   10
Must of necessity ensue upon
A match betwixt some noble of our nation
And this brave prince, forsooth.
Dal.   'Twill prove too fatal;
Wise Huntly fears the threat'ning. Bless the lady
From such a ruin!
Craw.   How the council privy   15

---

162. *War . . . peace*] Clifford Leech compares *Timon of Athens*, v. iv. 83.

II. iii. Location] Edinburgh.
Historical Time] January 1496 (Warbeck's marriage).
2. *couched*] expressed; cf. Prologue 14.
3. *that*] correlative of *Such*; see Abbott § 279.
6. *charmed*] put a spell upon.
8. *prerogative*] sovereign right.
9. *motion*] proposal: cf. I. ii. 159
14. *Bless*] May God protect (*O.E.D.*, 3).

Of this young Phaëthon do screw their faces
Into a gravity their trades, good people,
Were never guilty of! the meanest of 'em
Dreams of at least an office in the state.

Dal. Sure, not the hangman's—'tis bespoke already   20
For service to their rogueships. Silence!

Enter King JAMES *and* HUNTLY.

Ja.   Do not
Argue against our will; we have descended
Somewhat, as we may term it, too familiarly
From justice of our birthright, to examine
The force of your allegiance—sir, we have;   25
But find it short of duty.

Hunt.   Break my heart,
Do, do, king; have my services, my loyalty—
Heaven knows, untainted ever—drawn upon me
Contempt now in mine age? when I but wanted
A minute of a peace not to be troubled?   30
My last, my long one? Let me be a dotard,
A bedlam, a poor sot, or what you please
To have me, so you will not stain your blood,
Your own blood, royal sir, though mixed with mine,
By marriage of this girl to a straggler!   35
Take, take my head, sir; whilst my tongue can wag
It cannot name him other.

Ja.   Kings are counterfeits
In your repute, grave oracle, not presently

16. Phaëthon] *Phueton Q.*   21. rogueships. Silence!] *W;* rogueshippes
—silence. *Q.*

---

16. *Phaëthon*] He mismanaged the chariot of the Sun and was destroyed
by Zeus.
23. *familiarly*] unceremoniously, condescendingly (*O.E.D.*, 4).
29–30. *wanted A minute*] was but a minute short of.
35. *girl*] disyllabic, as customarily in Ford; cf. l. 54.
straggler] vagabond (*O.E.D.*, 1).
38. *repute*] opinion (*O.E.D.*, 1).
not presently] i.e., if they are not here and now (or actually).

Set on their thrones with sceptres in their fists.
But use your own detraction. 'Tis our pleasure   40
To give our cousin York for wife our kinswoman,
The lady Katherine. Instinct of sovereignty
Designs the honour, though her peevish father
Usurps our resolution.

Hunt.   O, 'tis well,
Exceeding well. I never was ambitious   45
Of using congees to my daughter-queen:
A queen, perhaps a quean! Forgive me, Dalyell,
Thou honourable gentleman; none here
Dare speak one word of comfort?

Dal.   Cruel misery!

Craw. The lady, gracious prince, maybe hath settled   50
Affection on some former choice.

Dal.   Enforcement
Would prove but tyranny.

Hunt.   I thank 'ee heartily.
Let any yeoman of our nation challenge
An interest in the girl, then the king
May add a jointure of ascent in titles,   55

---

47. quean!] *W; Queene?* Q.   51–2. Enforcement . . . tyranny] *so W; one
line in* Q.

---

40. *use . . . detraction*] make free with your calumnies.

42. *Instinct of sovereignty*] prompting, innate impulse (*O.E.D., s.v.*
instinct 1, 2) coming from my sovereignty; or, conceivably, as Pickburn
thinks, 'my instinctive perception of Warbeck's royal birth'.

44. *Usurps our resolution*] 'encroaches upon our fixed determination', or
'arrogates to himself our power of decision'.

46. *congees*] obeisances (Pickburn).

47. *queen . . . quean*] The words were normally distinguished in spelling
then as now; but the likelihood of confusion and the apology Huntly makes
to Dalyell (for defaming his mistress) strongly support Weber's alteration
of Q. *Quean* is 'harlot', which Katherine may prove to be because her
'vagabond' husband may turn out to have a wife already. Compare the
tale/tayle pun in *'Tis Pity* (De Vocht's facsimile edition, ll. 2025–6).

53. *challenge*] lay claim to.

55. *jointure . . . titles*] dowry consisting of a backdated set of titles. For
jointure meaning 'dowry' see *O.E.D.*, 4 b; *ascent* here means one single step
back in a genealogy (*O.E.D.*, 3). What Huntly is suggesting is that if
Katherine were to marry a yeoman, her dowry from the king could be her

    Worthy a free consent; now a' pulls down
    What old desert hath builded.

Ja.   Cease persuasions.
    I violate no pawns of faiths, intrude not
    On private loves; that I have played the orator
    For kingly York to virtuous Kate, her grant   60
    Can justify, referring her contents
    To our provision. The Welsh Harry henceforth
    Shall therefore know, and tremble to acknowledge,
    That not the painted idol of his policy
    Shall fright the lawful owner from a kingdom.   65
    We are resolved.

Hunt.   Some of thy subjects' hearts,
    King James, will bleed for this!

Ja.   Then shall their bloods
    Be nobly spent. No more disputes; he is not
    Our friend who contradicts us.

Hunt.   Farewell, daughter!
    My care by one is lessened; thank the king for 't,   70
    I and my griefs will dance now.

Enter [PERKIN] WARBECK *leading* KATHERINE, *complimenting;*
Countess *of* CRAWFORD, JANE, FRION, [JOHN A-WATER] Mayor *of*
           CORK, ASTLEY, HERON *and* SKELTON.

                           Look, lords, look,

70.] *Q adds 'Enter.' at end of line.*   71.1–3.] *after l. 72 in Q.*   71.3.
SKELTON] *D; Sketon Q.*

---

bridegroom's ennoblement prior to the marriage, i.e., the opposite of
marrying someone (Warbeck) who claims to be noble before marriage but
turns out afterwards not to be.

    56. *Worthy . . . consent*] goes with 'jointure', not 'titles'.

    58. *pawns of faiths*] The phrase means 'interchange of plighted troths';
either 'faith' is a *pledge* in the hands of the other. *O.E.D.* gives no exact
parallels. Since the Hartley Coleridge edition (1839 and many later reprints) is normally a faithful reprint of Gifford, its reading (*pawns of faith*)
must be a misprint not an emendation; Pickburn also reads *faith*.

    61–2. *referring . . . provision*] indicating her satisfaction and acquiescence
in whatever we may provide. A pompous way of saying that Katherine has
promised to accept whatever the king arranges for her.

Here's hand in hand already!

Ja.   Peace, old frenzy.
How like a king a' looks! Lords, but observe
The confidence of his aspect! Dross cannot
Cleave to so pure a metal; royal youth!   75
Plantagenet undoubted!

Hunt. [*Aside*]   Ho, brave! Youth,
But no Plantagenet, by'r lady, yet,
By red rose or by white.

War.   An union this way
Settles possession in a monarchy
Established rightly as is my inheritance.   80
Acknowledge me but sovereign of this kingdom,
Your heart, fair princess, and the hand of providence
Shall crown you queen of me and my best fortunes.

Kath. Where my obedience is, my lord, a duty,
Love owes true service.

War.   Shall I ?—

Ja.   Cousin, yes,   85
Enjoy her; from my hand accept your bride;
And may they live at enmity with comfort
Who grieve at such an equal pledge of troths.
You're the prince's wife now.

Kath.   By your gift, sir.

War. Thus I take seizure of mine own.

Kath.   I miss yet   90

76. Ho, brave! Youth,] *G;* Ho braue Lady! *Q;* Ho, brave youth! *W.*

---

76. *Youth*] The compositor of Q picked up 'Lady' from l. 77.

78. *By . . . white*] by kinship with either Lancaster or York (Pickburn).

78–80. *An union . . . inheritance*] A union of this kind establishes our possession of a monarchy [of love], which [possession] is as well grounded as my right of inheritance [to the monarchy of England]. The conceit is continued in the next lines.

86–90.] James's words constitute the actual marriage-ceremony, which we are not to think of as having been already performed off stage. It is a stage marriage, hardly a representation of any kind of legal one, even for royal persons. Gifford supplied a stage-direction at l. 86, *He joins their hands*, but Ford appears to have imagined them as hand in hand since their entry at l. 71. They embrace at l. 90.

K

A father's blessing. Let me find it. Humbly
Upon my knees I seek it.

Hunt.   I am Huntly,
Old Alexander Gordon, a plain subject,
Nor more nor less; and, lady, if you wish for
A blessing, you must bend your knees to heaven,   95
For heaven did give me you. Alas, alas,
What would you have me say? May all the happiness
My prayers ever sued to fall upon you
Preserve you in your virtues! Prithee, Dalyell,
Come with me; for I feel thy griefs as full   100
As mine; let's steal away and cry together.

Dal. My hopes are in their ruins. *Exeunt* HUNTLY *and* DALYELL.
Ja.   Good kind Huntly
Is overjoyed; a fit solemnity
Shall perfect these delights. Crawford, attend   104
Our order for the preparation.   *Exeunt all but* FRION,
                JOHN A-WATER, ASTLEY, HERON, *and* SKELTON.

Fri. Now, worthy gentlemen, have I not followed
My undertakings with success? Here's entrance
Into a certainty above a hope.

Her. Hopes are but hopes; I was ever confident, when I
traded but in remnants, that my stars had reserved me   110
to the title of a viscount at least: honour is honour,
though cut out of any stuffs.

Skel. My brother Heron hath right wisely delivered his
opinion; for he that threads his needle with the sharp
eyes of industry shall in time go through-stitch with the 115
new suit of preferment.

102. S.D.] *opposite ll. 101–2 in Q.*   105. S.D.–105.1.] *Exeunt, manent,
Frion, Major, Astley, Heron, & Sketon. Q.*

---

93. *Alexander*] His name was George; Ford derived the mistake from his
sources (other than Bacon, who does not mention Huntly's baptismal
name).

103. *solemnity*] the festival gambols of III. ii; cf. l. 141 below.

115. *go through-stitch with*] carry out completely, go through with
(*O.E.D., s.v.* through-stitch B).

116. *suit*] with a quibble.

Ast. Spoken to the purpose, my fine-witted brother Skelton;
    for as no indenture but has its counterpawn, no noverint
    but his condition or defeasance, so no right but may have
    claim, no claim but may have possession, any act of par-   120
    liament to the contrary notwithstanding.

Fri. You are all read in mysteries of state,
    And quick of apprehension, deep in judgement,
    Active in resolution; and 'tis pity
    Such counsel should lie buried in obscurity.   125
    But why in such a time and cause of triumph
    Stands the judicious mayor of Cork so silent?
    Believe it, sir, as English Richard prospers
    You must not miss employment of high nature.

a-Wat. If men may be credited in their mortality, which I   130
    dare not peremptorily aver but they may or not be, pre-
    sumptions by this marriage are then, in sooth, of fruitful
    expectation. Or else I must not justify other men's be-
    lief more than other should rely on mine.

Fri. Pith of experience! Those that have borne office   135
    Weigh every word before it can drop from them.
    But, noble counsellors, since now the present
    Requires in point of honour—pray mistake not—

117. Skelton] *D; Sketon Q.*   118. counterpawn] *Q;* counterpane *W.*
128. English Richard] ENGLISH RICHARD *Q.*

---

118. *indenture*] deed between two or more parties.

counterpawn] more common in the form *counterpane*, both words being
obsolete in this sense. The modern form is *counterpart.* The different
copies of an indenture were written on the same parchment and then cut
jaggedly apart to form the counterparts, which could be identified by fitting
the indented edges together.

noverint] bond (from its opening words *noverint universi*, 'let everybody
know').

119. *condition or defeasance*] condition on performance of which the bond
takes effect or is rendered void.

130. *If . . . mortality*] if men merely mortal may be believed.

133. *justify*] uphold.

134. *other*] others; see Abbott § 12.

137. *present*] present circumstances.

138. *honour . . . not*] Frion covertly mocks their lack of 'honour' (i.e.,
noble rank) by ironically apologizing for using the word.

Some service to our lord, 'tis fit the Scots
Should not engross all glory to themselves   140
At this so grand and eminent solemnity.

Skel. The Scots! the motion is defied. I had rather, for my
  part, without trial of my country, suffer persecution
  under the pressing-iron of reproach; or let my skin be
  punched full of eyelet-holes with the bodkin of derision. 145

Ast. I will sooner lose both my ears on the pillory of forgery.

Her. Let me first live a bankrupt, and die in the lousy Hole
  of hunger, without compounding for sixpence in the
  pound.

a-Wat. If men fail not in their expectations, there may be 150
  spirits also that digest no rude affronts, master secretary
  Frion, or I am cozened: which is possible, I grant.

Fri. Resolved like men of knowledge; at this feast, then,
  In honour of the bride, the Scots, I know,
  Will in some show, some masque, or some device,   155
  Prefer their duties. Now it were uncomely
  That we be found less forward for our prince
  Than they are for their lady: and by how much
  We outshine them in persons of account,
  By so much more will our endeavours meet with   160
  A livelier applause. Great emperors
  Have for their recreations undertook

145. punched] *G;* pincht *Q;* pinch'd *W.*   eyelet] oylett *Q.*   151. digest]
disgest *Q.*

---

142. *motion*] i.e., the suggestion that the Scots may get all the glory.

143. *trial . . . country*] trial by jury (*O.E.D., s.v.* country 7).

144. *pressing-iron*] iron, smoothing-iron; a possible allusion to pressing
an accused person to death with weights (*peine forte et dure*).

145. *eyelet-holes*] It is arguable that Q's words (*oylett holes*) should be
modernized as *oillet-holes*; see *O.E.D., s.v.* oillet 4).

147. *Hole*] a name for the worst part of certain debtors' prisons in London
and elsewhere.

148–9. *compounding . . . pound*] i.e., settling to pay his creditors according
to this proportion.

151. *digest*] Q's *disgest* was an alternative form.

155. *device*] entertainment.

156. *Prefer . . . duties*] offer their homage.

159. *in*] i.e., 'in the eyes of' (?).

Such kind of pastimes; as for the conceit,
Refer it to my study; the performance
You all shall share a thanks in—'twill be grateful.   165

Her. The motion is allowed: I have stole to a dancing-school
when I was a prentice.

Ast. There have been Irish hubbubs, when I have made one
too.

Skel. For fashioning of shapes and cutting a cross-caper,   170
turn me off to my trade again.

a-Wat. Surely there is, if I be not deceived, a kind of gravity
in merriment; as there is, or perhaps ought to be, respect
of persons in the quality of carriage, which is, as it is
construed, either *so,* or *so.*   175

Fri. Still you come home to me; upon occasion
I find you relish courtship with discretion.
And such are fit for statesmen of your merits.
Pray 'ee wait the prince, and in his ear acquaint him
With this design; I'll follow and direct 'ee.   180

Exeunt all but FRION.

180.1.] *Exeunt, mane Frion. Q.*

---

163. *conceit*] idea, general plan (*O.E.D.,* 1), contrasted with *performance* (l. 164).

166. *motion*] proposal.

168. *hubbubs*] noisy entertainments, though *O.E.D.* does not support Gifford's 'tumultuous merry-meetings at wakes and fairs'; often associated with Irish (and Welsh) and perhaps an Irish word; cf. *Faerie Queene,* III. x. 43: 'a noyse of many bagpipes shrill, / And shrieking Hububs'.

made one] i.e., of the company present.

170. *shapes . . . cross-caper*] *Shapes* can mean 'stage-costumes' as well as an attitude in dancing (*O.E.D.,* 8, 12, citing this instance). Presumably there is a similar pun in *cutting a cross-caper,* a kind of caper in dancing, perhaps thought specially appropriate to tailors because they worked with crossed legs (but see *O.E.D.,* s.v. cross-caper); cf. Massinger, *Virgin Martyr,* IV. i (Mermaid Massinger, II. 350).

173–5. *respect . . . or* so] It is hard to make out the exact meaning of this, and perhaps little is intended.

176. *come . . . me*] understand my meaning.

upon occasion] as opportunity arises.

177. *relish courtship*] 'flavour (or taste) courtly behaviour'; or *relish* might mean 'appreciate, understand' (*O.E.D.,* 1, 2, 3).

178. *such*] i.e., courtship and discretion.

O, the toil
Of humouring this abject scum of mankind!
Muddy-brained peasants! Princes feel a misery
Beyond impartial sufferance, whose extremes
Must yield to such abettors; yet our tide   185
Runs smoothly without adverse winds; run on!
Flow to a full sea! time alone debates
Quarrels forewritten in the book of fates.   *Exit.*

181–3.] There is no historical warrant for Frion's attitude to Warbeck's other supporters or for the depiction of them as clowns: see Introduction, pp. xliii–xliv, lxiv.

184. *Beyond . . . sufferance*] beyond being impartially endured—whether by us or 'princes' is not clear; some extension of meaning in *impartial* seems likely: 'in which one cannot but take part' (Pickburn).

extremes] extreme necessities.

187. *debates*] reduces, abates (*O.E.D., v*² 1).

Act III

Enter King HENRY, *his gorget on, his sword, plume of feathers,*
leading-staff, and URSWICK.

Hen. How runs the time of day?
Urs.   Past ten, my lord.
Hen. A bloody hour will it prove to some,
     Whose disobedience, like the sons o' th' earth,
     Throw a defiance 'gainst the face of heaven.
     Oxford, with Essex and stout De la Pole,   5
     Have quieted the Londoners, I hope,
     And set them safe from fear?
Urs.   They are all silent.

Act III] *Actus Tertius: Scæna prima. Q.*   4. Throw] *Q;* Throws *G.*
7. fear?] *this ed.;* feare! *Q;* fear. *W.*

III. i. Location] Usually given as 'Westminster. The Palace'.

Historical Time] Saturday, 17 June 1497 (the battle at Blackheath, wrongly dated by Bacon as 22 June).

0.1. gorget] a piece of armour for the throat, in Elizabethan times frequently worn without other armour as a sign of military rank.

0.2. leading-staff] baton.

3. *sons o' th' earth*] the Titans, overthrown by Zeus.

5. *Oxford . . . De la Pole*] To the process of quieting the panic in London Bacon (p. 154) attaches the names 'Oxford, Essex, and Daubeney', whereas Hall (p. 479 and cf. Hol., 782/1/61) and Gainsford (sig. M4ᵛ) substitute 'Edmond de la Poole' for Daubeney. Although Bacon has already (p. 152) named 'the earl of Oxford, assisted by the earls of Essex and Suffolk' as Henry's commanders (and see II. ii. 136–8 and note), it seems probable that Ford consulted the other sources, although he may merely be reconciling an apparent contradiction in Bacon. Edmund De la Pole, earl of Suffolk (1472–1513), a Yorkist claimant, was the brother of the traitor-earl mentioned in I. i. 91, later conspired against Henry and was executed by Henry VIII. The earl of Essex was Henry Bourchier, 2nd earl (d. 1540). For Oxford, see Biographical Index.

Hen. From their own battlements they may behold
    Saint George's Fields o'erspread with armèd men;
    Amongst whom our own royal standard threatens   10
    Confusion to opposers; we must learn
    To practise war again in time of peace,
    Or lay our crown before our subjects' feet;
    Ha, Urswick, must we not?
Urs.   The powers who seated
    King Henry on his lawful throne will ever   15
    Rise up in his defence.
Hen.   Rage shall not fright
    The bosom of our confidence; in Kent
    Our Cornish rebels, cozened of their hopes,
    Met brave resistance by that country's earl,
    George Aberg'enny, Cobham, Poynings, Guildford,   20
    And other loyal hearts; now, if Blackheath
    Must be reserved the fatal tomb to swallow
    Such stiff-necked abjects as with weary marches
    Have travelled from their homes, their wives and children,
    To pay instead of subsidies their lives,   25
    We may continue sovereign. Yet, Urswick,

---

26. sovereign] *W* (sovereign!); Soveraigne ? *Q*.

---

9. *Saint George's Fields*] S.E., between Southwark and Lambeth, and mentioned by all the sources.

11. *Confusion*] ruin.

19–20.] The list comes from one of the sources other than Bacon (p. 150), who does not mention Aberg'enny's name George nor Poynings or Guildford in this connexion. Spellings of the names vary a great deal in the different sources and provide no assured clue. The earl was George Grey, 2nd earl (d. 1503); the others were: Aberg'enny: George Nevill (d. 1535), son of Lord Abergavenny; Cobham: John, 7th lord (d. 1512); Sir Edward Poynings (d. 1520?), one of Henry's more important servants and his deputy in Ireland (1494); and Sir Richard Guildford (1455?–1506), comptroller of the household from 1498.

21. *Blackheath*] about five miles from the city of London.

22. *reserved*] set apart as (*O.E.D.*, 3).

23. *abjects*] outcasts (*O.E.D.*, B).

25–7. *subsidies . . . parliament*] See I. iii. 129–34 and note. Struble points out that Henry used words like these in 1489 (Bacon, p. 65).

We'll not abate one penny what in parliament
Hath freely been contributed; we must not;
Money gives soul to action. Our competitor,
The Flemish counterfeit, with James of Scotland,   30
Will prove what courage, need, and want can nourish
Without the food of fit supplies; but, Urswick,
I have a charm in secret that shall loose
The witchcraft wherewith young king James is bound,
And free it at my pleasure without bloodshed.   35
Urs. Your majesty's a wise king, sent from heaven
Protector of the just.
Hen.   Let dinner cheerfully
Be served in. This day of the week is ours,
Our day of providence, for Saturday
Yet never failed in all my undertakings   40
To yield me rest at night.   *A flourish.*
                    What means this warning?
Good fate, speak peace to Henry!

Enter DAUBENEY, OXFORD, *and* Attendants.

Dau.   Live the king,
Triumphant in the ruin of his enemies!
Oxf. The head of strong rebellion is cut off,
The body hewed in pieces.
Hen.   Daubeney, Oxford,   45
Minions to noblest fortunes, how yet stands
The comfort of your wishes?
Dau.   Briefly thus:

---

31. *prove*] find out by experience. Henry is saying that Warbeck's
courage and necessities will get him nowhere unless he has money.

need, and want] compulsion and shortage.

39–41.] From an early page (p. 11) in Bacon, as Struble points out: 'He
entered the city [in 1485] upon a Saturday, as he had also obtained the victory [of Bosworth] upon a Saturday [not historically true]; which day of
the week, first upon an observation, and after upon memory and fancy, he
accounted and chose as a day prosperous to him'; and cf. Bacon, p. 154,
and note on Historical Time above.

46. *Minions*] favourites.

The Cornish under Audley, disappointed
Of flattered expectation from the Kentish,
Your majesty's right-trusty liegemen, flew,   50
Feathered by rage and heartened by presumption,
To take the field even at your palace-gates,
And face you in your chamber-royal. Arrogance
Improved their ignorance; for they, supposing,
Misled by rumour, that the day of battle   55
Should fall on Monday, rather braved your forces
Than doubted any onset; yet this morning,
When in the dawning I by your direction
Strove to get Deptford Strand Bridge, there I found
Such a resistance as might show what strength   60

---

49. expectation] *this ed.;* expectation, *Q.*   59. Deptford] *W; Dertford Q;*
Dartford *B.*

48–78.] This account is mainly a conflation of Bacon and Gainsford,
with the latter predominating: see Appendix I, pp. 160–1.

48–50. *disappointed . . . liegemen*] This allusion to the failure of the rebels'
hope that Kent would rise reads more meaningfully if the whole phrase up
to *liegemen* is taken as going with *disappointed Of;* Q's comma after *expectation* is misleading. *flattered,* 'exaggerated': cf. a 1665 example quoted by
O.E.D., s.v. flatter 10—'flattered conceit of himself'.

51. *Feathered*] propelled, winged; the word may have been suggested
by the remarkable Cornish arrows (ll. 61–2) which are prominent in the
sources; cf. also the phrase 'weare their fether braue' in the 'Blacksmith'
(Cornish revolt) tragedy in *The Mirror for Magistrates,* ed. Campbell, p.
407 (cf. note on I. iii. 131).

52–3.] derived from Gainsford's account of Michael Joseph's dying
speech: 'they were sure to be registred to eternity for daring to doe somewhat in behalfe of their Countries liberty, and bidding battaile to Kings
and Princes at their Pallace Gates, and before the Citie Wals, euen *London*
it selfe, that great Citie, the Chamber for their treasury, and strength of
their roialtie' (sig. N^v).

54. *Improved*] aggravated (*O.E.D.,* 4).

56. *Should*] was to: see Abbott § 325.

57. *doubted*] feared.

59. *Deptford . . . Bridge*] Q, Hol., 782/2/2, and Gainsford, sig. M4^v, have
the spelling *Dertford,* a form of the name Dartford (in Kent, seventeen
miles from London). This is probably a misprint originating with Holinshed, but Stow, 480/2/35, has *Dartford;* it is odd that Ford should have
perpetuated the error; he can hardly have supposed that the battle did take
place at Dartford and not Deptford.

Could make; here arrows hailed in showers upon us
A full yard long at least; but we prevailed.
My lord of Oxford with his fellow peers
Environing the hill fell fiercely on them
On the one side, I on the other, till—great sir,   65
Pardon the oversight—eager of doing
Some memorable act I was engaged
Almost a prisoner, but was freed as soon
As sensible of danger. Now the fight
Began in heat, which quenchèd in the blood of   70
Two thousand rebels, and as many more
Reserved to try your mercy, have returned
A victory with safety.

Hen.   Have we lost
An equal number with them?

Oxf.   In the total
Scarcely four hundred. Audley, Flammock, Joseph,   75
The ringleaders of this commotion,
Railèd in ropes, fit ornaments for traitors,
Wait your determinations.

Hen.   We must pay

---

66. *oversight*] It is Bacon who censures Daubeney for foolhardiness;
Gainsford glosses over his behaviour, but the phrases in the immediately
preceding line echo Gainsford.

67–8. *engaged . . . prisoner*] The phrase is awkward and unexampled; it
results from compression of Gainsford's 'engaged himselfe so farre, that
he was taken prisoner' (sig. N).

69. *sensible*] aware.

70. *quenchèd*] the intransitive form (*O.E.D.*, 6).

72. *Reserved*] set apart: cf. l. 22.

have returned] has brought back (*O.E.D.*, 13); the antecedent is *fight*.

75. *four hundred*] Gainsford's figure (the others, 300).

Audley . . . Joseph] See I. iii. 131, 133 and notes.

76. *commotion*] a word caught from Bacon: 'captains of commotions'
(p. 155).

77. *Railèd*] fastened in a row; the only two citations in *O.E.D.* in this
sense are this one and Bacon's account of the prisoners after the invasion
at Deal (see above I. iii. 43–6) in 1495: 'all railed in ropes like horses in a
cart' (p. 130), a phrase derived by Bacon from the corresponding context
in Hall (p. 472), and also used by Gainsford (sig. K2ᵛ) in the same context.

Our thanks where they are only due. O, lords,
Here is no victory, nor shall our people   80
Conceive that we can triumph in their falls.
Alas, poor souls! Let such as are escaped
Steal to the country back without pursuit.
There's not a drop of blood spilt but hath drawn
As much of mine; their swords could have wrought wonders
On their king's part, who faintly were unsheathed   86
Against their prince, but wounded their own breasts.
Lords, we are debtors to your care; our payment
Shall be both sure and fitting your deserts.

Dau. Sir, will you please to see those rebels, heads   90
Of this wild monster-multitude?

Hen.   Dear friend,
My faithful Daubeney, no; on them our justice
Must frown in terror; I will not vouchsafe
An eye of pity to them. Let false Audley
Be drawn upon an hurdle from the Newgate   95
To Tower Hill in his own coat of arms
Painted on paper, with the arms reversed,
Defaced and torn; there let him lose his head.
The lawyer and the blacksmith shall be hanged,
Quartered, their quarters into Cornwall sent,   100
Examples to the rest, whom we are pleased
To pardon and dismiss from further quest.

---

91. monster-multitude] *W; unhyphenated in Q.*

80–5.] Henry's clemency as depicted here is heightened from Bacon's
puzzled speculations on why only three men were executed—'whether it
were that the King put to account the men that were slain in the field, or
that he was not willing to be severe in a popular cause, or . . . the harmless
behaviour of the people . . . did somewhat mollify him, and move him to
compassion' (p. 156).

86. *who*] which: see Abbott § 264.

faintly] half-heartedly.

91. *monster-multitude*] *monster* is appositive to *multitude* and qualifies it
as both huge and monster-like.

95. *hurdle*] a kind of sledge.

Newgate] Newgate prison.

102. *quest*] inquiry, pursuit.

My lord of Oxford, see it done.
Oxf.   I shall, sir.
Hen. Urswick.
Urs.   My lord?
Hen.   To Dinham, our high-treasurer,
    Say we command commissions be new granted   105
    For the collection of our subsidies
    Through all the west, and that speedily.
    Lords, we acknowledge our engagements due
    For your most constant services.
Dau.   Your soldiers
    Have manfully and faithfully acquitted   110
    Their several duties.
Hen.   For it we will throw
    A largesse free amongst them, which shall hearten
    And cherish up their loyalties; more yet
    Remains of like employment; not a man
    Can be dismissed, till enemies abroad,   115
    More dangerous than these at home, have felt
    The puissance of our arms. O, happy kings,
    Whose thrones are raisèd in their subjects' hearts!
                                Exeunt omnes.

[III. ii]

Enter HUNTLY *and* DALYELL.

Hunt. Now, sir, a modest word with you, sad gentleman:
    Is not this fine, I trow, to see the gambols,

---

104. *Dinham*] That Dinham was 'high treasurer of England' is mentioned
by Gainsford, sig. M3 (and cf. Hall, p. 478, Hol., 781/2/72).

108. *engagements*] obligations (*O.E.D.*, 4).

112–13. *A . . . loyalties*] Bacon (p. 155) is the only source who mentions
any reward for Henry's men: 'And for matter of liberality, he did . . . give
the goods of all the prisoners unto those that had taken them'.

III. ii. Location] Edinburgh.
Historical Time] autumn and winter 1496, telescoped (see note on
ll. 131–2).

To hear the jigs, observe the frisks, b' enchanted
With the rare discord of bells, pipes and tabors,
Hotch-potch of Scotch and Irish twingle-twangles,   5
Like to so many quiristers of Bedlam,
Trolling a catch ? The feasts, the manly stomachs,
The healths in usquebaugh and bonny-clabber,
The ale in dishes never fetched from China,
The hundred thousand knacks not to be spoken of,   10
And all this for king Oberon and queen Mab,
Should put a soul int' ee. Look 'ee, good man,
How youthful I am grown; but, by your leave,
This new queen-bride must henceforth be no more
My daughter; no, by'r lady, 'tis unfit.   15
And yet you see how I do bear this change,
Methinks courageously: then shake off care
In such a time of jollity.

Dal.   Alas, sir,
How can you cast a mist upon your griefs ?
Which howsoe'er you shadow but present   20
To any judging eye the perfect substance

3. b'] *Q;* be *W.*   21. any] *Q (Bodleian Mal. 238 (5) omits).*

---

4. *rare*] fine.

4-5.] The musical accompaniment mingles the English morris (bells, pipes, tabors) and 'Celtic' music: *tabors,* drums; *twingle-twangles,* the first instance in *O.E.D.,* sounds made by the Gaelic harp, the only kind of harp familiar in England at the time; cf. ll. III.1-3 and note.

6. *quiristers*] choristers.

7. *Trolling a catch*] singing a (particular variety of) part-song.
stomachs] spirits.

8. *usquebaugh . . . bonny-clabber*] whisky, and buttermilk mixed with beer. Ford may have taken both the word 'bonny-clabber' and its associations from Jonson's *Irish Masque* (1613-14), ll. 87-8; it seems to have been served in cheap English taverns (Jonson's *New Inn,* I. ii. 25). The linking of this drink with whisky and the Irish is standard 'stage Irish' material of the period: see J. O. Bartley in *Modern Language Review,* 1942, p. 441.

10. *knacks*] delicacies, choice dishes (*O.E.D.,* 3 b).

19. *cast a mist*] i.e., blur the outlines of, conceal; the phrase has strong links with juggling and deceit (*O.E.D., s.v.* mist 2 b).

20-1. *shadow . . . substance*] *shadow* quibbles on 'conceal' and *shadow* as something unreal by comparison with *substance,* 'reality'. The passage is influenced by *Richard II,* II. ii. 14 ff. and IV. i. 292 ff.

Of which mine are but counterfeits.

Hunt.   Foh, Dalyell,
Thou interrupts the part I bear in music
To this rare bridal feast; let us be merry,
Whilst flattering calms secure us against storms.   25
Tempests, when they begin to roar, put out
The light of peace and cloud the sun's bright eye
In darkness of despair; yet we are safe.

Dal. I wish you could as easily forget
The justice of your sorrows as my hopes   30
Can yield to destiny.

Hunt.   Pish, then I see
Thou dost not know the flexible condition
Of my apt nature. I can laugh, laugh heartily
When the gout cramps my joints; let but the stone
Stop in my bladder, I am straight a-singing;   35
The quartan fever shrinking every limb
Sets me a-cap'ring straight; do but betray me,
And bind me a friend ever. What! I trust
The losing of a daughter, though I doted
On every hair that grew to trim her head,   40
Admits not any pain like one of these.
Come, thou'rt deceived in me: give me a blow,
A sound blow on the face, I'll thank thee for 't.
I love my wrongs; still thou'rt deceived in me.

Dal. Deceived? O noble Huntly, my few years   45

33. apt] *Q* (ap't); tough *G; Bodleian Mal. 238 (5) omits.*   35. Stop] *Q*
(Stoppe) (*Bodleian Mal. 238 (5) has* Stoppes).   37. but] *Q* (*Bodleian
Mal. 238 (5) omits*).   38. ever.] *Q* (*Bodleian Mal. 238 (5) has* ever,).

23. *interrupts*] A verb ending in -t often has this form of the 2nd pers.
sing.; 'for euphony', says Abbott § 340.

29–31.] Dalyell sees through Huntly's gaiety; out of friendship for him,
he wishes that Huntly could forget how justified are his sorrows as easily
as Dalyell's own hopes can admit defeat. This does not mean that Dalyell's
abandonment of hope is easy.

36. *quartan*] so called because the fever-fit was supposed to occur every
fourth day.

41. *Admits*] allows the presence of (*O.E.D.*, 6), entails.

45–7.] i.e., young though he is, he's sufficiently experienced not to forgo

Have learnt experience of too ripe an age
To forfeit fit credulity. Forgive
My rudeness, I am bold.
Hunt.   Forgive me first
A madness of ambition; by example
Teach me humility, for patience scorns   50
Lectures which schoolmen use to read to boys
Uncapable of injuries; though old,
I could grow tough in fury, and disclaim
Allegiance to my king; could fall at odds
With all my fellow peers that durst not stand   55
Defendants 'gainst the rape done on mine honour.
But kings are earthly gods, there is no meddling
With their anointed bodies; for their actions,
They only are accountable to heaven.
Yet in the puzzle of my troubled brain   60
One antidote's reserved against the poison
Of my distractions; 'tis in thee t' apply it.
Dal. Name it, O, name it quickly, sir!
Hunt.   A pardon
For my most foolish slighting thy deserts;
I have culled out this time to beg it: prithee   65
Be gentle; had I been so, thou hadst owned

---

the capacity for proper belief or disbelief. This is 'rude' and 'bold' because
he is accusing Huntly of lying.

49–52. *by . . . injuries*] The main contrast is between teaching *by example*
and giving *lectures*, mere expositions of theory which academics are accustomed (*schoolmen use*) to give to boys too young to have certain civil rights
capable of being injured (*Uncapable of injuries*; e.g., they are not fathers, as
Huntly is). *patience* in its recorded significations makes no sense because
Huntly is talking, with reference to his present state, about what *impatience*
does (i.e., 'scorns lectures', etc.). In the light of the main contrast noted
above I suggest that *patience* is here 'experience, endurance, in the sense of
having lived many years' (unlike the *boys* of l. 51): old men can't be expected to learn by academic means as boys do.

57–9. *kings . . . heaven*] These are commonplaces deployed (and disputed)
throughout Tudor and Stuart political thought.

58. *for*] as regards.

61. *reserved*] kept in reserve, apart.

66. *gentle*] generous.

A happy bride, but now a castaway,
And never child of mine more.
Dal.   Say not so, sir;
It is not fault in her.
Hunt.   The world would prate
How she was handsome; young I know she was,   70
Tender, and sweet in her obedience;
But lost now; what a bankrupt am I made
Of a full stock of blessings! Must I hope
A mercy from thy heart?
Dal.   A love, a service,
A friendship to posterity.
Hunt.   Good angels   75
Reward thy charity; I have no more
But prayers left me now.
Dal.   I'll lend you mirth, sir,
If you will be in consort.
Hunt.   Thank ye truly.
I must, yes, yes, I must; here's yet some ease,
A partner in affliction; look not angry.   80
Dal. Good noble sir.   *Flourish.*
Hunt.   O, hark! we may be quiet,
The king and all the others come: a meeting
Of gaudy sights; this day's the last of revels;
Tomorrow sounds of war; then new exchange:

68–9. Say . . . her] *so W; one line in Q.*   81. *Flourish] B; centred below
l. 85 in Q; in S.D. (l. 85.1) in W.*

75. *friendship . . . posterity*] *to* may be like *to* in 'an example to posterity';
or 'reaching as far as'.

78. *in consort*] *O.E.D.*, *s.v.* consort 2 b, glosses as 'in accord', presumably
'with me'; but it might mean 'with himself', i.e., in a state in which the
unbalanced passions which Huntly has earlier been showing are har-
moniously in accord with one another. Dalyell promises to lend him mirth
if only he'll control himself. In that case, Huntly's 'I must . . . ' (l. 79) would
mean 'must control myself'. This makes the sequence of this part of the
scene altogether more plausible, for whether the two men are in agreement
with one another ought, after the passionate professions of ll. 74–6, to
have ceased to be an issue.

84. *Tomorrow sounds*] punctuated as in Q; *sounds* may be a verb or a noun.

L

Fiddles must turn to swords. Unhappy marriage!   85

Enter King JAMES, [PERKIN] WARBECK *leading* KATHERINE,
CRAWFORD, Countess [*of* CRAWFORD], *and* JANE; *Huntly and
Dalyell fall among them.*

Ja. Cousin of York, you and your princely bride
  Have liberally enjoyed such soft delights
  As a new-married couple could forethink.
  Nor has our bounty shortened expectation;
  But after all those pleasures of repose,   90
  Or amorous safety, we must rouse the ease
  Of dalliance with achievements of more glory
  Than sloth and sleep can furnish. Yet, for farewell,
  Gladly we entertain a truce with time
  To grace the joint endeavours of our servants.   95
War. My royal cousin, in your princely favour
  The extent of bounty hath been so unlimited
  As only an acknowledgement in words
  Would breed suspicion in our state and quality.
  When we shall in the fulness of our fate—   100
  Whose minister, Necessity, will perfect—
  Sit on our own throne, then our arms, laid open
  To gratitude, in sacred memory
  Of these large benefits, shall twine them close
  Even to our thoughts and heart without distinction.   105

---

89. *shortened*] The natural meaning, preceding *expectation*, would be
'fallen short of'; but this meaning of *shorten* is not warranted by *O.E.D.*
 98. *As*] that; see Abbott § 109.
 99. *in*] in regard to.
 101. *perfect*] 'fate' (individual destiny) itself, perfected by its own minister, is the missing object of the verb.
 102–4.] The image is of the arms first held out for an embrace in the act
of expressing gratitude and then encircling *them* (presumably, the objects
of gratitude, the benefactors responsible for the *benefits* of l. 104, or even
perhaps the peoples of England and Scotland of l. 107). But the sentiments
are obscured by the bad syntax.
 105. *distinction*] discrimination, i.e., between 'them' (the benefactors,
or peoples).

Then James and Richard, being in effect
One person, shall unite and rule one people,
Divisible in titles only.

Ja.   Seat ye.
Are the presenters ready?

Craw.   All are ent'ring.

Hunt. Dainty sport toward, Dalyell; sit; come, sit,   110
Sit and be quiet; here are kingly bug's-words.

Enter at one door four Scotch Antics, *accordingly habited; enter at
another four wild* Irish *in trowses, long-haired, and accordingly
habited. Music. The Maskers dance.*

Ja. To all a general thanks.

War.   In the next room
Take your own shapes again; you shall receive
Particular acknowledgement.   [*Exeunt the Maskers.*]

Ja.   Enough
Of merriments. Crawford, how far's our army   115
Upon the march?

Craw.   At Heydonhall, great king;
Twelve thousand well prepared.

Ja.   Crawford, tonight

111. bug's-words] Q (buggs words); bug-words G.   114. S.D.] W; not
in Q.

___

109. *presenters*] actors (*O.E.D.*, 4).
110. *toward*] approaching.
111. *bug's-words*] swaggering language; alternative form, bug-words.
Presumably a comment on Warbeck's speech, ll. 96 ff.
111.1–3.] 'Celtic fringe' material is exploited in many plays and entertainments of the period (see J. O. Bartley, *Modern Language Review*, 1942,
and F. L. Scott, *ibid.*, 1947). The Irish *trowses* (close-fitting drawers) and
long hair are standard. The dance was presumably wild and comic; the
musical accompaniment may have included bagpipes and harps (see ll. 4–5
above) as in Jonson's *Irish Masque*. It is not clear whether the actors playing Skelton and his associates assumed the parts of three of the masquers
here, despite the preparations afoot in II. iii. 156–80. Struble calls attention
to the mention of 'shewes, masques, and sundry deuises' offered for Warbeck at James's court (Gainsford, sig. L^v).
116. *Heydonhall*] See IV. i. 5–7 and note.
117. *Twelve thousand*] probably an invented figure.

Post thither. We in person, with the prince,
By four o' clock tomorrow after dinner
Will be wi' ye; speed away!

Craw.   I fly, my lord.   [*Exit.*]   120

Ja.   Our business grows to head now; where's your secretary,
That he attends 'ee not to serve?

War.   With Marchmount,
Your herald.

Ja.   Good: the proclamation's ready;
By that it will appear how the English stand
Affected to your title. Huntly, comfort   125
Your daughter in her husband's absence; fight
With prayers at home for us, who for your honours
Must toil in fight abroad.

Hunt.   Prayers are the weapons
Which men so near their graves as I do use.
I've little else to do.

Ja.   To rest, young beauties!   130
We must be early stirring, quickly part;
A kingdom's rescue craves both speed and art.
Cousins, good-night.   *Flourish.*

War.   Rest to our cousin-king.

Kath. Your blessing, sir.

---

119. o'] a *Q.*   120. wi' ye] *D;* w'ee *Q;* wi' you *W.*   S.D.] *W; not in Q.*
121-3.] *so W; four lines in Q ending* your, serue, Herald, readie.   132. A]
"A *Q.*

---

118. *Post*] travel speedily.

122. *Marchmount*] mentioned by Hall (p. 411) and Gainsford (sig. N2ᵛ),
not by Bacon.

123. *proclamation*] Warbeck's proclamation to the English (autumn
1496), given in full by Bacon (pp. 140-4) from a document belonging to
Sir Robert Cotton; see Gairdner, p. 306.

124-5. *how . . . to*] how the English are disposed towards. 'Perkin's
proclamation did little edify the people of England' (Bacon); cf. III. iv.
24-5.

131-2.] The preparations here are for the Scottish raids of autumn 1496
and for the siege of Norham (and the subsequent English counter-attacks)
in July 1497: Ford treats them as a continuous unified episode in III. iv,
IV. i.

Hunt. Fair blessings on your highness; sure, you need 'em.   135
            Exeunt all but PERKIN WARBECK, KATHERINE [*and* JANE].
War. Jane, set the lights down, and from us return
            To those in the next room this little purse;
            Say we'll deserve their loves.
Jane.   It shall be done, sir.   [*Exit.*]
War. Now, dearest, ere sweet sleep shall seal those eyes,
            Love's precious tapers, give me leave to use   140
            A parting ceremony; for tomorrow
            It would be sacrilege to intrude upon
            The temple of thy peace. Swift as the morning
            Must I break from the down of thy embraces
            To put on steel, and trace the paths which lead   145
            Through various hazards to a careful throne.
Kath. My lord, I would fain go wi' ye; there's small fortune
            In staying here behind.
War.   The churlish brow
            Of war, fair dearest, is a sight of horror
            For ladies' entertainment. If thou hear'st   150
            A truth of my sad ending by the hand
            Of some unnatural subject, thou withal
            Shalt hear how I died worthy of my right
            By falling like a King; and in the close
            Which my last breath shall sound, thy name, thou fairest, 155
            Shall sing a requiem to my soul, unwilling

135.1. S.D.] *Exeunt omnes, Manent, Warb. & Katherine. Q.*   138. S.D.]
W; not in Q.   147. wi' ye] *D;* w'ee *Q;* wi' you *W;* with you *G.*   154.
King] KING *Q.*

---

136. *return*] give in recompense.
139–86.] After their marriage Gainsford's Warbeck and Katherine interchange long speeches of promise and affection, and Katherine is represented as a willing bride (sigs. L^v–L2^v); but the scene does not appear to have influenced Ford's; see Introduction, pp. xl–xli.
145. *trace*] tread.
146. *careful*] full of care.
150. *For . . . entertainment*] for ladies to occupy their attention with.
151. *A truth*] Cf. II. i. 67 and note.
154–6. *close . . . requiem*] a musical metaphor; *close*, 'cadence'.

> Only of greater glory 'cause divided
> From such a heaven on earth as life with thee.
> But these are chimes for funerals, my business
> Attends on fortune of a sprightlier triumph;   160
> For love and majesty are reconciled
> And vow to crown thee empress of the West.

Kath. You have a noble language, sir; your right
> In me is without question, and however
> Events of time may shorten my deserts   165
> In others' pity, yet it shall not stagger
> Or constancy or duty in a wife.
> You must be king of me, and my poor heart
> Is all I can call mine.

War.   But we will live,
> Live, beauteous virtue, by the lively test   170
> Of our own blood, to let the counterfeit
> Be known the world's contempt.

Kath.   Pray do not use
> That word; it carries fate in 't. The first suit
> I ever made I trust your love will grant?

War. Without denial, dearest.

Kath.   That hereafter,   175
> If you return with safety, no adventure
> May sever us in tasting any fortune:
> I ne'er can stay behind again.

War.   You're lady

---

174. grant?] graunt! *Q.*

165–6. *shorten . . . pity*] i.e., diminish my worth or merits by making me an object of other people's pity; or, possibly, 'cause me less to deserve the pity of others'; Pickburn's 'may cause others pityingly to hold me in less esteem' may give the general sense intended.

166. *stagger*] unsettle (*O.E.D.*, 6 d).

170–2.] Live so that we may cause the counterfeit to be known as the object of the world's contempt by the living proof of our own (royal) blood. It is not clear whether Warbeck is using the royal 'we' or speaking about Katherine and himself.

177. *tasting*] experiencing.

178–9. *lady . . . desires*] i.e., her 'ladyship' (specifically, her rank and its

Of your desires, and shall command your will.
Yet 'tis too hard a promise.

Kath.　　　　　　　　　What our destinies　　　180
Have ruled out in their books we must not search,
But kneel to.

War.　　　　　Then to fear when hope is fruitless
Were to be desperately miserable;
Which poverty our greatness dares not dream of,
And much more scorns to stoop to. Some few minutes　　185
Remain yet; let's be thrifty in our hopes.　　　　*Exeunt.*

[III. iii]

Enter King HENRY, HIALAS, *and* URSWICK.

Hen. Your name is Pedro Hialas, a Spaniard?
Hial. Sir, a Castilian born.
Hen.　　　　　　　　King Ferdinand,
With wise queen Isabel his royal consort,
Writes 'ee a man of worthy trust and candour.
Princes are dear to heaven who meet with subjects　　　5
Sincere in their employments; such I find

---

powers) is defined in terms of her desires alone and not of anything or anyone else—a way of acknowledging that what she wishes has complete authority over him.

179. *command your will*] ordain what pleases you.

181. *ruled out*] marked out; the only instance of this signification for
rule out in *O.E.D.* (*s.v.* rule *v* 11).

search] examine, scrutinize (*O.E.D.*, 5).

182–3. *Then . . . miserable*] To be afraid then, at a time when hoping is
useless, were to be both unfortunate and despairing, i.e., one ought to submit fearlessly to one's bad luck. Warbeck is expressing a general moral
sentiment complementary to Katherine's.

184. *poverty*] i.e., of spirit.

186. *thrifty*] thriving (*O.E.D.*, 1).

III. iii. Location] Usually given as 'Westminster. The Palace.'
Historical Time] summer of 1496.

1. *Pedro*] Peter in the sources; see Biographical Index.

2. *Castilian*] Spain was divided into Castile, Leon, and Aragon.

Your commendation, sir. Let me deliver
How joyful I repute the amity
With your most fortunate master, who almost
Comes near a miracle in his success   10
Against the Moors, who had devoured his country,
Entire now to his sceptre. We, for our part,
Will imitate his providence in hope
Of partage in the use on 't. We repute
The privacy of his advisement to us   15
By you, intended an ambassador
To Scotland, for a peace between our kingdoms,
A policy of love, which well becomes
His wisdom and our care.

Hial.   Your majesty
Doth understand him rightly.

Hen.   Else,   20
Your knowledge can instruct me; wherein, sir,
To fall on ceremony would seem useless,
Which shall not need; for I will be as studious
Of your concealment in our conference
As any counsel shall advise.

Hial.   Then, sir,   25

---

15. advisement] *Q;* advertisement *W.*   19. our] *Q;* your *W.*   20–1.
Else . . . sir] *so W; one line in Q.*

---

7. *commendation*] recommendation.
deliver] declare.
8, 14. *repute*] consider.
11. *the Moors*] The fall of Granada and the termination of Moorish
power in Spain occurred in 1492.
12. *Entire . . . sceptre*] which has now been brought completely under his
rule.
13. *providence*] foresight.
14. *partage . . . on 't*] share in the profit of it; cf. v. iii. 165.
15. *privacy . . . advisement*] his private advice (*O.E.D., s.v.* advisement 5).
20. *Else*] otherwise (*O.E.D.,* 4).
22. *fall on*] have recourse to; antedates earliest citation in *O.E.D., s.v.*
fall 64 d.
23–4. *as . . . conference*] as careful to conceal your part in our conference.
25–31.] According to Ford's sources, Hialas made this request from

My chief request is that on notice given
At my dispatch in Scotland you will send
Some learned man of power and experience
To join in treaty with me.

Hen.   I shall do it,
Being that way well provided by a servant   30
Which may attend 'ee ever.

Hial.   If king James
By any indirection should perceive
My coming near your court, I doubt the issue
Of my employment.

Hen.   Be not your own herald;
I learn sometimes without a teacher.

Hial.   Good days   35
Guard all your princely thoughts.

Hen.   Urswick, no further
Than the next open gallery attend him.
A hearty love go with you.

---

29. in treaty] *Q;* entreaty *G.*   35–6. Good . . . thoughts] *so W; one line
in Q.*

Scotland by letter to Henry, who sent bishop Fox to the conference at
Jedburgh. The meeting in this scene between Henry and Hialas is invented. See also below IV. i. 67–72 and note.

29. *join . . . me*] join in the negotiations alongside of me (see *O.E.D., s.v.*
treaty 2). Gifford's alteration of Q is due to a misunderstanding of *treaty*
and makes very poor historical sense.

30. *by a servant*] in respect of a servant (i.e., bishop Fox).

32. *indirection*] devious means.

34–5.] It seems that at some point here Henry either gives Hialas the
cash referred to in ll. 44–6 below or gives him a hint about it. 'Hialas seems
to be hinting that he deserves some reward for imperilling the success of
his mission to Scotland by this conference with Henry. The King sees his
meaning immediately, and lets him know that there is no necessity to say
any more' (Pickburn). *Be not your own herald* ('don't advertise yourself')
implies 'keep quiet about your visit to me yourself' and perhaps also 'don't
shout so loudly for your reward'. It is possible that Henry does not personally 'convey' (l. 45) the money to Hialas but that we are to suppose it
handed over off-stage. Both Hall and Gainsford (but not Bacon) say that
Hialas was liberally rewarded after the truce with Scotland, but neither
mentions a specific sum.

37. *open*] i.e., not private.

Hial.   Your vowed beadsman.

                    Exeunt URSWICK *and* HIALAS.

Hen. King Ferdinand is not so much a fox
    But that a cunning huntsman may in time   40
    Fall on the scent; in honourable actions
    Safe imitation best deserves a praise.

Enter URSWICK.

    What, the Castilian's passed away?

Urs.   He is,
    And undiscovered; the two hundred marks
    Your majesty conveyed a' gently pursed   45
    With a right modest gravity.

Hen.   What was 't
    A' muttered in the earnest of his wisdom?
    A' spoke not to be heard; 'twas about—

Urs.   Warbeck:
    How if king Henry were but sure of subjects,
    Such a wild runagate might soon be caged,   50
    No great ado withstanding.

Hen.   Nay, nay; something
    About my son prince Arthur's match!

Urs.   Right, right, sir.
    A' hummed it out, how that king Ferdinand

---

38. *beadsman*] 'humble servant' (*O.E.D.*, 5).

42. *Safe*] free from risk (*O.E.D.*, 9).

44–6.] See note on ll. 34–5 above.

47. *earnest*] seriousness (*O.E.D.*, sb^1 2).

49. *sure of subjects*] i.e., assured about the loyalty of his subjects.

50. *runagate*] vagabond (*O.E.D.*, 3); cf. V. iii. 24; Bacon (p. 145) calls Warbeck 'a runagate and citizen of the world'.

51. *No . . . withstanding*] and there'd be no great ado, which would offer opposition (to his being caged).

53–9.] Cf. IV. iii. 8–9 below. After recording the earl of Warwick's death (see below V. iii. 13–19 and note) all the sources state that it was one of Ferdinand's conditions for the marriage of Catherine of Aragon to the prince of Wales, Arthur. Negotiations for this marriage began in 1488; it took place in November 1501; Arthur died five months later, and Catherine was subsequently married to his brother (Henry VIII). Edward, earl of Warwick, was one of the last Yorkist claimants (nephew to Edward IV),

      Swore that the marriage 'twixt the lady Catherine
      His daughter and the prince of Wales your son   55
      Should never be consummated as long
      As any earl of Warwick lived in England,
      Except by new creation.
Hen.   I remember,
      'Twas so indeed; the king his master swore it?
Urs. Directly, as he said.
Hen.   An earl of Warwick!   60
      Provide a messenger for letters instantly
      To bishop Fox. Our news from Scotland creeps,
      It comes so slow; we must have airy spirits;
      Our time requires dispatch. The earl of Warwick!
      Let him be son to Clarence, younger brother   65
      To Edward! Edward's daughter is, I think,
      Mother to our prince Arthur. Get a messenger.   *Exeunt.*

[III. iv]

Enter King JAMES, [PERKIN] WARBECK, CRAWFORD, DALYELL,
    HERON, ASTLEY, JOHN A-WATER, SKELTON, *and* Soldiers.

Ja. We trifle time against these castle walls,
      The English prelate will not yield; once more

63. so] *Q (Bodleian Mal. 238 (5) has* too).

III. iv. 0.2. JOHN A-WATER, SKELTON] Major, Sketon *Q.*

1475–99; he was impersonated by Lambert Simnel in 1486–7 and had
been a prisoner in the Tower since 1486.
    58. *new creation*] revival of the title (after the extermination of the family).
    60. *Directly*] absolutely (*O.E.D.*, 4).
    63. *airy spirits*] i.e., messengers as fast as spirits of the air.
    65–7.] The lines are there partly to give the audience some dynastic in-
formation. Warwick was the son of George, duke of Clarence, who was the
brother of Edward IV (and see above note on ll. 53–9); Henry counter-
claims that his own wife (Elizabeth) is Edward's *daughter*.

    III. iv. Location] Norham Castle, on the Tweed, about seven miles S.W.
of Berwick. Although it is in Northumberland, it used to be administra-
tively part of the County Palatine of Durham and was therefore the bishop
of Durham's responsibility (and see II. ii. 154 and note).
    Historical Time] Warbeck was not present at the siege of Norham, which

Give him a summons.   [*A trumpet is sounded for a*] *parley.*

Enter above DURHAM *armed, a truncheon in his hand, and* Soldiers.

War.   See, the jolly clerk
Appears, trimmed like a ruffian.
Ja.   Bishop, yet
Set ope the ports, and to your lawful sovereign,   5
Richard of York, surrender up this castle,
And he will take thee to his grace; else Tweed
Shall overflow his banks with English blood,
And wash the sand that cements those hard stones
From their foundation.
Dur.   Warlike king of Scotland,   10
Vouchsafe a few words from a man enforced
To lay his book aside, and clap on arms
Unsuitable to my age or my profession.
Courageous prince, consider on what grounds
You rend the face of peace, and break a league   15
With a confederate king that courts your amity;
For whom too? for a vagabond, a straggler,
Not noted in the world by birth or name,
An obscure peasant, by the rage of hell
Loosed from his chains to set great kings at strife.   20

3. S.D.] *G (subs.); Parley Q.*

---

lasted a fortnight during July 1497 and coincided with the first Cornish
rising already treated in III. i (and see below ll. 84–7); but he raided
England in company with James in September 1496. The chief incident
in which he features in this scene (ll. 56 ff.) belongs to the latter occasion.
The notion of a parley between Fox and James at Norham is invented.
Ford conflates the two Scottish incursions of 1496 and '97 (which his
sources treat quite separately) and centres them both on Norham. On their
first incursion, the Scots, disappointed by the failure of the English to rise
for Warbeck, devastated Northumberland and went home after four days
(Gairdner, p. 306); after the second (Norham), they retreated in face of the
advance of Surrey's troops, who then invaded Scotland and destroyed
fortified places in Berwickshire (see below IV. i. 1–10).
　3.1. truncheon] i.e., a baton or staff of office.
　4. *trimmed . . . ruffian*] dressed up like a swaggering bully.
　5. *ports*] gates.

What nobleman, what common man of note,
What ordinary subject hath come in,
Since first you footed on our territories,
To only feign a welcome? Children laugh at
Your proclamations, and the wiser pity   25
So great a potentate's abuse by one
Who juggles merely with the fawns and youth
Of an instructed compliment; such spoils,
Such slaughters as the rapine of your soldiers
Already have committed, is enough   30
To show your zeal in a conceited justice.
Yet, great king, wake not yet my master's vengeance—
But shake that viper off which gnaws your entrails!
I and my fellow-subjects are resolved,
If you persist, to stand your utmost fury,   35
Till our last blood drop from us.

War.   O sir, lend
No ear to this traducer of my honour!
What shall I call thee, thou gray-bearded scandal,
That kick'st against the sovereignty to which
Thou owest allegiance? Treason is bold-faced   40

37. No] *W;* Me *Q.*   traducer] *G; seducer Q.*

---

22. *come in*] adhered (to you); *O.E.D., s.v.* come 59 f.
24–5.] See above III. ii. 124–5 and note.
27. *fawns*] flatteries.
28. *instructed compliment*] formal civility which has been taught (instead of being inborn); see *O.E.D., s.v.* complement [*sic*] 8–9). The use of an abstraction where we might expect a concrete is very characteristic of the style of this play.
30. *have . . . is*] *have* is attracted into the plural by *soldiers; is* has for its nominative the preceding noun-clause, *such spoils,* etc.: see Abbott § 337.
31. *a . . . justice*] what you imagine to be a (question of) justice.
33. *viper . . . entrails*] the viper was supposed to get born by gnawing through its dam's entrails; James is acting as the Pretender's 'parent'; see Tilley V 68.
37. *traducer*] There is no doubt that Gifford's emendation makes wholly appropriate sense, and the mistake could easily have occurred through the compositor's misreading a somewhat illegibly written first syllable; it is doubtful whether *seducer* can or could have been used simply in the sense of 'one who takes away [honour]'.

And eloquent in mischief; sacred king,
Be deaf to his known malice!
Dur.   Rather yield
Unto those holy motions which inspire
The sacred heart of an anointed body!
It is the surest policy in princes   45
To govern well their own than seek encroachment
Upon another's right.
Craw.   The king is serious,
Deep in his meditations.
Dal.   Lift them up
To heaven, his better genius!
War.   Can you study
While such a devil raves? O sir!
Ja.   Well... Bishop,   50
You'll not be drawn to mercy?
Dur.   Construe me
In like case by a subject of your own;
My resolution's fixed. King James, be counselled.
A greater fate waits on thee.   *Exit with his* Soldiers.
Ja.   Forage through
The country; spare no prey of life or goods.   55
War. O sir, then give me leave to yield to nature;

48. meditations] *G;* meditation *Q.*   49–50. Can . . . sir] *so W; one line
in Q.*   50. Well . . .] *this ed.;* Well,— *Q;* Well, *D.*   54. S.D.] *this ed.;
Exit Durham cum suis Q; Exit Durham and Soldiers from the Walls W.*

---

43. *motions*] inward promptings (*O.E.D.*, 9).

49. *study*] meditate.

51–2. *Construe . . . own*] Interpret me in the light of a similar case involving one of your own subjects, i.e., you'd expect him to do what I'm doing
now.

54. *A . . . thee*] i.e., you were intended for better things than helping
Warbeck.

Forage] plunder.

56–74.] The incident comes from the sources, but belongs to the first
Scottish raid not to Norham (see above, note on Historical Time).
Warbeck's speech and James's answer closely parallel Gainsford, sigs.
L3^v–L4; see Appendix, pp. 153–4.

56. *nature*] natural feelings (*O.E.D.*, 9 c). Anderson suggests that he
weeps.

I am most miserable: had I been
Born what this clergyman would by defame
Baffle belief with, I had never sought
The truth of mine inheritance with rapes   60
Of women, or of infants murdered, virgins
Deflowered, old men butchered, dwellings fired,
My land depopulated, and my people
Afflicted with a kingdom's devastation.
Show more remorse, great king, or I shall never   65
Endure to see such havoc with dry eyes.
Spare, spare, my dear, dear England.
Ja.   You fool your piety
Ridiculously, careful of an interest
Another man possesseth. Where's your faction ?
Shrewdly the bishop guessed of your adherents,   70
When not a petty burgess of some town,
No, not a villager hath yet appeared
In your assistance; that should make 'ee whine,
And not your country's sufferance, as you term it.
Dal. The king is angry.
Craw.   And the passionate duke   75
Effeminately dolent.
War.   The experience
In former trials, sir, both of mine own
Or other princes cast out of their thrones
Have so acquainted me how misery
Is destitute of friends or of relief,   80

67–8. piety Ridiculously,] *Q;* piety, Ridiculously *G.*   79. Have] *Q;*
Hath *G.*

---

58. *defame*] calumny.
60. *truth . . . inheritance*] Cf. II. i. 67, III. ii. 151.
65. *remorse*] pity (*O.E.D.*, 3).
67. *fool . . . piety*] make your piety a fool.
68. *Ridiculously, careful*] The echo of Gainsford's 'your Care is . . . ridiculous' might justify altering Q's punctuation to 'piety, Ridiculously careful'.
74. *sufferance*] suffering.
76. *dolent*] 'dolent for another mans possessions', says James in Gainsford (sig. L4); *dolent*, 'sorrowful'.

        That I can easily submit to taste
        Lowest reproof, without contempt or words.
Ja. An humble-minded man!

                 Enter FRION.

                     Now, what intelligence
        Speaks master secretary Frion ?
Fri.   Henry
        Of England hath in open field o'erthrown   85
        The armies who opposed him in the right
        Of this young prince.
Ja.   His subsidies, you mean.
        More, if you have it ?
Fri.   Howard, earl of Surrey,
        Backed by twelve earls and barons of the North,
        An hundred knights and gentlemen of name,   90
        And twenty thousand soldiers, is at hand
        To raise your siege. Brooke, with a goodly navy,
        Is admiral at sea; and Daubeney follows
        With an unbroken army for a second.
War. 'Tis false! they come to side with us.
Ja.   Retreat;   95
        We shall not find them stones and walls to cope with.

83.1.] *after l. 82 in* Q.   87–8. His . . . it] *so W; one line in* Q.

    82.] *Lowest* suggests that *reproof* here is primarily 'ignominy, disgrace'
(*O.E.D.*, 1). Possibly the rest of the line means 'silently and without scorn
or disdain (for those who wrong me)'.
    83. *intelligence*] news.
    87. *subsidies*] The reference must be to the 'subsidies' (taxes) of I. iii. 130
and III. i. 25, 106. James's interjection therefore means either (a) that it was
the subsidies which had overcome, not Henry; or (b) that when Frion talks
of Warbeck's 'right', James in his new mood of scepticism points to the true
cause of the first Cornish rising: Henry's demand for cash.
    88–94.] copied very closely from Gainsford, sig. N2, who summarizes
lists of names he found in Hall. Bacon does not supply these details.
    92. *Brooke*] Sir Robert Willoughby, 1st baron Willoughby de Broke
(1452–1502); he had been master of the household when Henry was
crowned; see V. ii. 20.
    94. *second*] support (*O.E.D.*, 8).

Yet, duke of York, for such thou sayest thou art,
I'll try thy fortune to the height: to Surrey
By Marchmount I will send a brave defiance
For single combat; once a king will venture   100
His person to an earl, with condition
Of spilling lesser blood; Surrey is bold,
And James resolved.
War.   O, rather, gracious sir,
Create me to this glory, since my cause
Doth interest this fair quarrel; valued least,   105
I am his equal.
Ja.   I will be the man.
March softly off; where victory can reap
A harvest crowned with triumph, toil is cheap. *Exeunt omnes.*

---

107. where] *Q;* "Where *B.*   108. A] "A *Q.*

98–103.] Bacon does not mention this challenge, and Ford's version derives mainly, perhaps entirely, from Gainsford; see also below, notes on
IV. i. 22–57, and Appendix, pp. 163–4.
    100. *once*] for once.
    101–2. *with . . . blood*] on condition that (thereby) less blood is spilled
(i.e., the armies themselves will not have to fight).
    104. *Create . . . glory*] i.e., 'invest me with this glory' (as though it were a
rank or title): see *O.E.D.*, *s.v.* create, 3.
    105. *Doth interest*] has a share in, is implicated in; there seem to be no
exact parallels, but see *O.E.D.*, *s.v.* interess.

M

Act IV

Enter SURREY, DURHAM, Soldiers, *with drums and colours.*

Sur. Are all our braving enemies shrunk back,
Hid in the fogs of their distempered climate,
Not daring to behold our colours wave
In spite of this infected air? Can they
Look on the strength of Cundrestine defaced,   5
The glory of Heydonhall devasted, that
Of Edington cast down, the pile of Foulden
O'erthrown? and this the strongest of their forts,
Old Ayton Castle, yielded and demolished,
And yet not peep abroad? The Scots are bold,   10
Hardy in battle; but it seems the cause
They undertake, consider̀d, appears
Unjointed in the frame on 't.
Dur.   Noble Surrey,
Our royal master's wisdom is at all times
His fortune's harbinger; for when he draws   15

Act IV] *Actus Quartus: Scæna prima. Q.*

IV. i. Location] Ayton, Berwickshire, about eight miles north of Berwick
upon Tweed.
   Historical Time] July 1497.
   2. *fogs . . . climate*] Bacon and Hall speak of rain, wind, and storms, but
Gainsford of 'distemperature of the Climate . . . mists and foggs' (sig.
N3).
   5–7.] Hall and Gainsford supply this list (not in Bacon). All these places
were small Border castles within the triangle formed by Norham, Berwick,
and Ayton; Heydonhall, probably the modern Hutton Hall, has already
been mentioned at III. ii. 116, and is spelled variously (Hedenhall, Heydonhall) in Q.
   9. *Ayton*] All sources say that it was one of the strongest places between
Berwick and Edinburgh.

His sword to threaten war, his providence
Settles on peace, the crowning of an empire.   *Trumpet.*

Sur. Rank all in order; 'tis a herald's sound,
Some message from king James; keep a fixed station.

Enter MARCHMOUNT *and another* Herald *in their coats.*

March. From Scotland's awful majesty we come   20
Unto the English general.

Sur.   To me?
Say on.

March.   Thus, then: the waste and prodigal
Effusion of so much guiltless blood
As in two potent armies of necessity
Must glut the earth's dry womb, his sweet compassion   25
Hath studied to prevent; for which to thee,
Great earl of Surrey, in a single fight
He offers his own royal person; fairly
Proposing these conditions only, that
If victory conclude our master's right,   30
The earl shall deliver for his ransom
The town of Berwick to him, with the fishgarths.
If Surrey shall prevail, the king will pay
A thousand pounds down present for his freedom,
And silence further arms. So speaks king James.   35

21-2. To . . . on] *so W; one line in Q.*

22-57.] The paramount and perhaps the only source for this passage is
Gainsford, who is himself copying from and amplifying Hall. Gainsford
(and not Hall) mentions the thousand pound ransom (l. 34) and has verbal
echoes with passages in the play that have no counterparts in Hall; cf. ll.
47-8, 50-1 with Appendix, pp. 163-4.
    24. *As . . . armies*] elliptically put—'as in the case of two potent armies
fighting'.
    26. *studied*] made it his aim (*O.E.D.*, 4).
    for which] for the which (i.e., preventing, etc.); see Abbott § 270.
    30. *conclude*] settle, establish by determining.
    31. *earl*] disyllabic; cf. 'girl', II. iii. 35, 54.
    32. *fishgarths*] enclosures for catching or preserving fish; the reference
is to salmon, which at Berwick are caught with boats and nets.
    34. *present*] immediately.

Sur. So speaks king James; so like a king a' speaks.
  Heralds, the English general returns
  A sensible devotion from his heart,
  His very soul, to this unfellowed grace.
  For let the king know, gentle heralds, truly,   40
  How his descent from his great throne to honour
  A stranger subject with so high a title
  As his compeer in arms, hath conquered more
  Than any sword could do. For which—my loyalty
  Respected—I will serve his virtues ever   45
  In all humility. But Berwick, say,
  Is none of mine to part with. In affairs
  Of princes, subjects cannot traffic rights
  Inherent to the crown. My life is mine,
  That I dare freely hazard; and—with pardon   50
  To some unbribed vainglory—if his majesty
  Shall taste a change of fate, his liberty
  Shall meet no articles. If I fall, falling
  So bravely, I refer me to his pleasure
  Without condition; and for this dear favour,   55
  Say, if not countermanded, I will cease
  Hostility, unless provoked.
March.   This answer
  We shall relate unpartially.
Dur.   With favour,
  Pray have a little patience. [*To Surrey*] Sir, you find

---

48. Of] "Of *Q.* 49. Inherent] "Inherent *Q.* 58. relate] *Q;* repeat *G.*
59. S.D.] *this ed.; not in Q; Apart to SURREY W.*

---

 38. *sensible*] deeply felt.
 44–5. *my . . . Respected*] provided my allegiance (to Henry) is unimpaired.
 50–1. *with . . . vainglory*] 'Surrey apologises for harbouring the possibly vainglorious thought that he may come off victor—a thought which even the honour done to him by the king cannot bribe to silence' (Pickburn); *unbribed* is Ford's addition to Gainsford's 'vaine-glory' (sig. N3).
 52. *Shall . . . fate*] is to (see Abbott § 315) experience an alteration in his fortunes.
 53. *Shall . . . articles*] shall not be subject to conditions.
 54. *bravely*] gloriously (because at a king's hand).

By these gay flourishes how wearied travail   60
Inclines to willing rest; here's but a prologue,
However confidently uttered, meant
For some ensuing acts of peace: consider
The time of year, unseasonableness of weather,
Charge, barrenness of profit; and occasion   65
Presents itself for honourable treaty,
Which we may make good use of. I will back,
As sent from you in point of noble gratitude
Unto king James, with these his heralds; you
Shall shortly hear from me, my lord, for order   70
Of breathing or proceeding; and king Henry,
Doubt not, will thank the service.

Sur.   To your wisdom,
Lord bishop, I refer it.

Dur.   Be it so then.

Sur. Heralds, accept this chain and these few crowns.

March. Our duty, noble general.

Dur.   In part   75
Of retribution for such princely love,
My lord the general is pleased to show
The king your master his sincerest zeal
By further treaty, by no common man:
I will myself return with you.

Sur.   Y' oblige   80
My faithfullest affections t' ee, lord bishop.

72–3. To . . . it] *so W; one line in Q.*

---

60. *gay flourishes*] 'meere flourishes' in Gainsford (sig. N3).

67–72.] Fox was sent by Henry early in July 1497 to confer with James at the suggestion of Hialas who was by now at the Scottish court (see III. iii. 25–31 and note); this way of arranging the meeting is the playwright's invention.

71. *breathing*] pausing.

74. *chain*] i.e., an ornamental chain of gold or silver, often used as cash: see *Comedy of Errors, passim.*

76. *retribution*] recompense (*O.E.D.*, 1).

79. *treaty*] negotiations; cf. III. iii. 29.

80. *oblige*] bind (*O.E.D.*, 1).

March. All happiness attend your lordship.

[*Exeunt* DURHAM *and* Heralds.]

Sur.   Come, friends
 And fellow-soldiers; we I doubt shall meet
 No enemies but woods and hills to fight with.
 Then 'twere as good to feed and sleep at home;   85
 We may be free from danger, not secure.   *Exeunt omnes.*

[IV. ii]

Enter [PERKIN] WARBECK *and* FRION.

War. Frion, O Frion, all my hopes of glory
 Are at a stand! the Scottish king grows dull,
 Frosty and wayward, since this Spanish agent
 Hath mixed discourses with him; they are private,
 I am not called to counsel now. Confusion   5
 On all his crafty shrugs! I feel the fabric
 Of my designs are tottering.
Fri.   Henry's policies
 Stir with too many engines.
War.   Let his mines,
 Shaped in the bowels of the earth, blow up
 Works raised for my defence, yet can they never   10
 Toss into air the freedom of my birth,
 Or disavow my blood Plantagenet's!
 I am my father's son still. But, O Frion,

82.1.] *D (subs.); not in Q.*

---

86. *secure*] carelessly over-confident (*O.E.D.*, 1).

IV. ii. Location] All edd. unwisely adopt Weber's 'the Scot[t]ish Camp'.
The conference to which bishop Fox was sent by Henry (see note on IV. i.
67–72), and which is a subject of this and the next scene, was at Jedburgh
(Hall's Iedwoorth, Gainsford's Jedworth).
Historical Time] July 1497.
4. *private*] alone by themselves.
8. *engines*] contrivances (*O.E.D.*, 3).
mines] underground passages filled with explosives (*O.E.D.*, 3).
12. *disavow*] deny (*O.E.D.*, 2).

When I bring into count with my disasters
My wife's compartnership, my Kate's, my life's,   15
Then, then my frailty feels an earthquake. Mischief
Damn Henry's plots, I will be England's king,
Or let my aunt of Burgundy report
My fall in the attempt deserved our ancestors!

Fri. You grow too wild in passion; if you will   20
Appear a prince indeed, confine your will
To moderation.

War.   What a saucy rudeness
Prompts this distrust! If, if I will appear!
Appear a prince! Death throttle such deceits
Even in their birth of utterance; cursed cozenage   25
Of trust! Ye make me mad; 'twere best, it seems,
That I should turn impostor to myself,
Be mine own counterfeit, belie the truth
Of my dear mother's womb, the sacred bed
Of a prince murdered and a living baffled!   30

Fri. Nay, if you have no ears to hear, I have
No breath to spend in vain.

War.   Sir, sir, take heed!
Gold, and the promise of promotion, rarely
Fail in temptation.

Fri.   Why to me this?

War.   Nothing.
Speak what you will; we are not sunk so low   35
But your advice may piece again the heart

---

15. *compartnership*] i.e., in the disasters.

19. *deserved*] was worthy of; *O.E.D.* gives no exact parallels.

21. *will*] passion, the opponent of Understanding in Elizabethan psychology.

25–6. *cursed . . . trust*] *cozenage* is here 'the fact of being deluded'; Warbeck curses the way we deceive ourselves by trusting others.

30.] i.e., '*one* prince murdered and *one* living one baffled'; *baffled*, 'disgraced, publicly humiliated' (*O.E.D.*, 1).

32–4.] On Frion, see IV. iii. 136–45 and note.

36. *piece*] repair (*O.E.D.*, 1).

                    Which many cares have broken. You were wont
                    In all extremities to talk of comfort:
                    Have ye none left now ? I'll not interrupt ye.
                    Good, bear with my distractions! If king James   40
                    Denies us dwelling here, next whither must I ?
                    I prithee be not angry.
Fri.   Sir, I told ye
                    Of letters come from Ireland, how the Cornish
                    Stomach their last defeat, and humbly sue
                    That with such forces as you could partake   45
                    You would in person land in Cornwall, where
                    Thousands will entertain your title gladly.
War. Let me embrace thee, hug thee! thou 'st revived
                    My comforts; if my cousin-king will fail,
                    Our cause will never.

               Enter JOHN A-WATER, HERON, ASTLEY, [*and*] SKELTON.

                                    Welcome, my tried friends.   50
                    You keep your brains awake in our defence.
                    Frion, advise with them of these affairs,
                    In which be wondrous secret; I will listen
                    What else concerns us here; be quick and wary.   *Exit.*
Ast. Ah, sweet young prince! Secretary, my fellow-councillors   55
                    and I have consulted, and jump all in one opinion directly,
                    that if these Scotch garboils do not fadge to our minds,

50.1.] *Enter Major, Heron, Astley, Sketon. Q (after l. 50).*   57. that] *Q;*
and *G;* an *D.*   these] *G;* this *Q.*

---

44. *Stomach*] resent.
44–7.] Bacon and Hall both mention a direct approach to Warbeck by
the still unpacified Cornishmen, but Gainsford does not.
45. *partake*] get, obtain a portion of; normally with *of* (*O.E.D.*, 4 b).
47. *entertain*] accept, receive (*O.E.D.*, 14).
50.] The sources mention Warbeck's counsellors for the first time at
about this point in his career.
56. *jump*] agree completely (*O.E.D.*, 5).
57.] Gifford, probably by mistake, printed *and* for *that*; Dyce 'modernized' the *and* to *an.*
garboils] tumults.
fadge . . . minds] thrive as we would wish; see *O.E.D.*, *s.v.* fadge 4.

we will pell-mell run amongst the Cornish choughs presently and in a trice.

Skel. 'Tis but going to sea and leaping ashore, cut ten or   60
twelve thousand unnecessary throats, fire seven or eight
towns, take half a dozen cities, get into the market-place,
crown him Richard the Fourth, and the business is
finished.

a-Wat. I grant ye, quoth I, so far forth as men may do, no   65
more than men may do; for it is good to consider, when
consideration may be to the purpose, otherwise still you
shall pardon me: little said is soon amended.

Fri. Then you conclude the Cornish action surest?

Her. We do so, and doubt not but to thrive abundantly. Ho,   70
my masters, had we known of the commotion when we
set sail out of Ireland, the land had been ours ere this time.

Skel. Pish, pish, 'tis but forbearing being an earl or a duke a
month or two longer; I say, and I say it again, if the work
go not on apace, let me never see new fashion more. I   75
warrant ye, I warrant ye; we will have it so, and so it shall
be.

Ast. This is but a cold phlegmatic country, not stirring enough
for men of spirit; give me the heart of England for my
money.   80

Skel. A man may batten there in a week only with hot loaves
and butter and a lusty cup of muscadine and sugar at
breakfast, though he make never a meal all the month
after.

63. Richard the Fourth] RICHARD THE FOVRTH *Q.*

---

58. *Cornish choughs*] Although these birds are a particular species
(*O.E.D.*, 2), a chough is a jackdaw or similar bird proverbial for its
gabble.

58–9. *presently*] immediately.

63. *Richard the Fourth*] Warbeck did assume this title at Bodmin, as the
sources report; cf. IV. v. 32 and note.

68. *little ... amended*] a proverb recorded from the mid-fifteenth century;
Tilley L 358.

81. *batten*] grow fat (*O.E.D.*, 1 a).

82. *muscadine*] muscatel.

a-Wat. Surely, when I bore office I found by experience that   85
        to be much troublesome was to be much wise and busy; I
        have observed how filching and bragging has been the
        best service in these last wars, and therefore conclude
        peremptorily on the design in England. If things and
        things may fall out, as who can tell what or how; but the   90
        end will show it.
Fri. Resolved like men of judgement! Here to linger
        More time is but to lose it. Cheer the prince
        And haste him on to this; on this depends
        Fame in success, or glory in our ends.   *Exeunt omnes.*   95

[IV. iii]

        Enter King JAMES; DURHAM *and* HIALAS *on either side.*

Hial. France, Spain, and Germany combine a league
        Of amity with England; nothing wants
        For settling peace through Christendom but love
        Between the British monarchs, James and Henry.

IV. iii. 0.1. JAMES;] *A; Iames, Q.*

85–6. *that to . . . busy*] i.e., that a way to be a nuisance to others is to do
too much work.

89–90. *things and things*] one thing and another (Pickburn); but there
are no obvious parallels.

IV. iii. Location] See note on Location for previous scene.
Historical Time] July–August 1497.
1–7.] Ford is copying from Gainsford's version (sig. N4ᵛ) of the pleas
made to James by Henry's commissioners Hialas and Fox, who argue that
'both Emperour, France and Spaine desireth a combination of amity with
England'. This is a confused reference to the Holy League for the defence
of Italy, which Henry entered into in July 1496 and which was organized
by Ferdinand and directed *against* Charles VIII of France (Mackie, pp.
115–16). Henry did in fact maintain good relations with France as well.
In Gainsford the commissioners next refer to the English merchants at
Antwerp, whereas the context of this reference in Hall (p. 483) and Bacon
(pp. 145–6) is different. English trade with Antwerp had been upset by
the quarrel with the 'emperor' (i.e., the archduke Maximilian I) about
Warbeck: see Biographical Index, *s.v.* Warbeck, I. i. 123, and Appendix,
p. 166.

2. *wants*] is lacking.

Dur. The English merchants, sir, have been received   5
    With general procession into Antwerp;
    The emperor confirms the combination.
Hial. The king of Spain resolves a marriage
    For Catherine his daughter with prince Arthur.
Dur. France courts this holy contract.
Hial.   What can hinder   10
    A quietness in England ?—
Dur.   But your suffrage
    To such a silly creature, mighty sir,
    As is but in effect an apparition,
    A shadow, a mere trifle ?
Hial.   To this union
    The good of both the church and commonwealth   15
    Invite 'ee.
Dur.   To this unity, a mystery
    Of providence points out a greater blessing
    For both these nations than our human reason
    Can search into. King Henry hath a daughter,
    The princess Margaret; I need not urge   20
    What honour, what felicity can follow
    On such affinity 'twixt two Christian kings

10–11. What . . . England] *so W; one line in Q.*

---

7. *combination*] treaty (*O.E.D.*, 4 c); Gainsford's word.
8–9.] See above III. iii. 53–9 and note.
11. *suffrage*] approval (*O.E.D.*, 5).
13. *apparition*] sham (*O.E.D.*, 10); another Gainsford word; cf. v. iii. 115.
16. *To*] in addition to, or in furtherance of, towards.
16–29.] Negotiations for James's marriage began long before this (in 1495) and it took place in 1502. Ford here deserts Gainsford (who does not mention the marriage) for Bacon (pp. 173–5). Hall has a similar passage (pp. 487–8); but the special link with Bacon is the reference to the 'mystery of providence' in ll. 16–19. A similar reflection opens the corresponding context in Bacon who meditates on the way in which a very minor Anglo-Scottish incident at Norham in 1498 (starting with a 'merry meeting' between some young Scottish gentlemen and their hosts in the English garrison) escalated until bishop Fox and James were involved; from *their* meeting arose the project for the marriage. Bacon's sequence of thought explains Ford's apparently rather arbitrary emphasis on its 'mysteriousness'.

        Inleagued by ties of blood; but sure I am,
        If you, sir, ratify the peace proposed,
        I dare both motion and effect this marriage   25
        For weal of both the kingdoms.
Ja.   Darest thou, lord bishop?
Dur. Put it to trial, royal James, by sending
        Some noble personage to the English court
        By way of embassy.
Hial.   Part of the business
        Shall suit my mediation.
Ja.   Well, what heaven   30
        Hath pointed out to be, must be; you two
        Are ministers, I hope, of blessed fate.
        But herein only I will stand acquitted:
        No blood of innocents shall buy my peace.
        For Warbeck, as you nick him, came to me   35
        Commended by the states of Christendom,
        A prince, though in distress; his fair demeanour,
        Lovely behaviour, unappallèd spirit,
        Spoke him not base in blood, however clouded.
        The brute beasts have both rocks and caves to fly to,   40
        And men the altars of the church; to us

---

40. both] *Q;* their *G.*

---

25. *motion*] propose.

29. *Part of*] a share in.

31. *pointed out*] ordained, fixed (*O.E.D.*, *s.v.* point *v²* 2); but a use with *out* is not recorded and perhaps there is some confusion with *point out* in the sense of 'indicate' (*O.E.D.*, *s.v.* appoint 10).

33. *acquitted*] i.e., delivered from any charge that I bartered Warbeck's life in exchange for peace.

34.] Ford goes back to Gainsford (sig. N4): 'the King . . . would not buy his peace with the bloud of Innocents', et seq.; see Appendix, p. 166.

35. *nick*] nickname (*O.E.D.*, 5 b).

38. *Lovely*] affectionate, friendly.

40–1.] Cf. Matthew viii. 20, but Ford is echoing Gainsford, including his quotation (in Latin) from Euripides' *Suppliant Women*; l. 41 echoes Euripides' *serui verò aras deorum*, but the line can also be taken (as by Struble) as a reference to the English right of sanctuary; see Appendix, pp. 166–7.

He came for refuge: kings come near in nature
Unto the gods in being touched with pity.
Yet, noble friends, his mixture with our blood,
Even with our own, shall no way interrupt   45
A general peace; only I will dismiss him
From my protection, throughout my dominions
In safety, but not ever to return.

Hial. You are a just king.

Dur.   Wise, and herein happy.

Ja. Nor will we dally in affairs of weight: 50
Huntly, lord bishop, shall with you to England,
Ambassador from us; we will throw down
Our weapons; peace on all sides now! Repair
Unto our council; we will soon be with you.

Hial. Delay shall question no dispatch; heaven crown it.   55

Exeunt DURHAM *and* HIALAS.

Ja. A league with Ferdinand, a marriage
With English Margaret, a free release
From restitution for the late affronts,
Cessation from hostility! and all
For Warbeck not delivered, but dismissed!   60
We could not wish it better. Dalyell!

Enter DALYELL.

Dal.   Here, sir.

42. kings] "Kings *Q.*   43. Unto] "Vnto *Q.*   53. sides . . . Repair] *W*
(*subs.*); sides now, repayre *Q;* sides! now, repair *G.*   55.] so *W;* . . . dispatch, / Heaven . . . *Q.*

44. *mixture . . . blood*] James means 'the fact that he is my kinswoman's
husband'; *mixture* (defined by *O.E.D.*, 1 e as 'sexual intercourse') must
bear a less specific sense here.

55. *question no dispatch*] not render prompt settlement doubtful.

58. *restitution . . . affronts*] Although Gainsford is very closely followed
in this scene, this element derives from Bacon, p. 160; 'The bishop . . .
demanded restitution of the spoils, taken by the Scottish, or damages for
the same. But the Scottish commissioners answered . . . that the King's
people were better able to bear the loss, than their master to repair it'; see
below, v. ii. 10–17.

Ja. Are Huntly and his daughter sent for?

Dal.   Sent for

And come, my lord.

Ja.   Say to the English prince,

We want his company.

Dal.   He is at hand, sir.

Enter [PERKIN] WARBECK, KATHERINE, JANE, FRION, HERON,
            SKELTON, JOHN A-WATER, ASTLEY.

Ja. Cousin, our bounty, favours, gentleness,   65
       Our benefits, the hazard of our person,
       Our people's lives, our land, hath evidenced
       How much we have engaged on your behalf.
       How trivial and how dangerous our hopes
       Appear, how fruitless our attempts in war,   70
       How windy, rather smoky, your assurance
       Of party shows, we might in vain repeat.
       But now obedience to the mother church,
       A father's care upon his country's weal,
       The dignity of state, directs our wisdom   75
       To seal an oath of peace through Christendom,
       To which we are sworn already. 'Tis you
       Must only seek new fortunes in the world,
       And find an harbour elsewhere. As I promised

62–3. Sent . . . lord] *so W; one line in Q.*   64.2. SKELTON, JOHN A-WATER]
Sketon, Major Q.   75. directs] *Q; direct D.*   77. 'Tis] *Q; it is W.*

65–108.] closely based on Gainsford (sigs. O–Oᵛ) with many verbal
correspondences; see Appendix, pp. 167–8. Bacon's similar account has
also left its traces (see below, ll. 79–81 and notes).

69.] Gainsford's 'dangerous hopes and triuiall aduentures' (sig. O).

71. *How . . . smoky*] Gainsford's 'all his promises winde and smoke'
(sig. O).

71–2. *assurance Of party*] promise that there was a body of adherents.
The word *party* is obscure; Pickburn's 'support' has no evidence. *party-
shows*, a possible emendment, does not remove all the difficulties.

73.] The phraseology is Gainsford's. The Borgia pope, Alexander VI,
was seeking adherents to the Holy League.

74.] Gainsford's 'fatherly regard of his Countrey' (sig. O).

79–81.] from Bacon (p. 161), not Gainsford: 'he [James] would make

On your arrival, you have met no usage   80
Deserves repentance in your being here;
But yet I must live master of mine own.
However, what is necessary for you
At your departure I am well content
You be accommodated with, provided   85
Delay prove not my enemy.

War.   It shall not,
Most glorious prince. The fame of my designs
Soars higher than report of ease and sloth
Can aim at; I acknowledge all your favours
Boundless and singular, am only wretched   90
In words as well as means to thank the grace
That flowed so liberally. Two empires firmly
You're lord of—Scotland and duke Richard's heart.
My claim to mine inheritance shall sooner
Fail than my life to serve you, best of kings.   95
And witness Edward's blood in me, I am
More loth to part with such a great example
Of virtue than all other mere respects.
But, sir, my last suit is, you will not force
From me what you have given: this chaste lady,   100
Resolved on all extremes.

Kath.   I am your wife;
No human power can or shall divorce
My faith from duty.

War.   Such another treasure
The earth is bankrupt of.

96. Edward's] EDVVARDS *Q.*

---

good what he said to him at his first receiving, which was that he should not repent him for putting himself into his hands.'

88. *report*] rumour, reputation (*O.E.D.*, 1); see below l. 145 and note.

96. *Edward's*] Edward IV's.

98. *than . . . respects*] than all other aspects whatsoever. An elliptical sentence; Warbeck is saying: 'I am so loth to part with such an example of virtue that it (the parting, etc.) overrides all other aspects of the situation'; for *respects* see *O.E.D.*, 8 a.

101. *Resolved . . . extremes*] determined in the face of all extremities.

Ja.   I gave her, cousin,
    And must avow the gift; will add withal   105
    A furniture becoming her high birth
    And unsuspected constancy; provide
    For your attendance. We will part good friends.
                          Exeunt King *and* DALYELL.
War. The Tudor hath been cunning in his plots:
    His Fox of Durham would not fail at last.   110
    But what? our cause and courage are our own.
    Be men, my friends, and let our cousin-king
    See how we follow fate as willingly
    As malice follows us. You're all resolved
    For the West parts of England?
All.   Cornwall, Cornwall!   115
Fri. The inhabitants expect you daily.
War.   Cheerfully,
    Draw all our ships out of the harbour, friends;
    Our time of stay doth seem too long, we must
    Prevent intelligence; about it suddenly.
All. A prince, a prince, a prince!   120
        Exeunt HERON, SKELTON, ASTLEY *and* JOHN A-WATER.
War. Dearest, admit not into thy pure thoughts
    The least of scruples, which may charge their softness
    With burden of distrust. Should I prove wanting
    To noblest courage now, here were the trial:
    But I am perfect, sweet; I fear no change,   125
    More than thy being partner in my sufferance.

108.1. *Exeunt] Exit Q.*   115. *All.] Omnes Q (in margin; partially cropped in some copies).*   120. *All.] Omnes Q (in margin; partially cropped in some copies).*   120.1.] *Exeunt Counsellors Q.*

---

   105. *avow*] acknowledge (*O.E.D.*, 5).
   106. *furniture*] equipment; Gainsford's word (sig. O[v]).
   107. *unsuspected*] that no one suspects (*O.E.D.*, 2).
   119. *Prevent intelligence*] forestall the news of our coming.
   125. *perfect*] complete, having all the necessary elements; cf. *Two Gentlemen of Verona*, I. iii. 20–1: 'he cannot be a perfect man, / Not being tried and tutor'd in the world'.
   126. *More than*] other than.
   sufferance] suffering.

Kath. My fortunes, sir, have armed me to encounter
  What chance soe'er they meet with. Jane, 'tis fit
  Thou stay behind, for whither wilt thou wander?
Jane. Never till death will I forsake my mistress,   130
  Nor then, in wishing to die with 'ee gladly.
Kath. Alas, good soul!
Fri.   Sir, to your aunt of Burgundy
  I will relate your present undertakings;
  From her expect on all occasions welcome.
  You cannot find me idle in your services.   135
War. Go, Frion, go! Wise men know how to soothe
  Adversity, not serve it; thou hast waited
  Too long on expectation; never yet
  Was any nation read of so besotted
  In reason as to adore the setting sun.   140
  Fly to the archduke's court; say to the duchess,
  Her nephew with fair Katherine his wife
  Are on their expectation to begin
  The raising of an empire. If they fail,
  Yet the report will never. Farewell, Frion. *Exit* FRION.
  This man, Kate, has been true, though now of late 146
  I fear too much familiar with the Fox.

---

138. never] "never *Q.* 139. Was] "Was *Q.* 140. In] "In *Q.* to] *Q;*
t' *D.*

136–45.] The desertion of Frion is developed from a hint in Bacon (p. 163), who, in listing Warbeck's council at the time of his invasion of Cornwall, mentions that 'secretary Frion was gone'; see also I. iii. 49 and note.

137. *Adversity*] misfortune, distress; abstract for personal. Warbeck says bitterly that wise men flatter the unfortunate but don't give any real help.

141.] This collocation of *archduke* and *duchess* (i.e., Margaret of York, duchess of Burgundy) suggests that Ford may be thinking of them as being in the same place; if so, it seems likely that *archduke* must refer not, as it normally does in this play, to the Emperor Maximilian I, archduke of Austria (cf. I. i. 123) but to his son Philip, the young archduke of Burgundy (cf. I. i. 52–62 and note).

145. *report*] reputation, fame (*O.E.D.*, 2); a slightly different signification from l. 88 above.

N

Enter HUNTLY *and* DALYELL.

Hunt. I come to take my leave. You need not doubt
    My interest in this sometime child of mine;
    She's all yours now, good sir. O poor lost creature,   150
    Heaven guard thee with much patience! If thou canst
    Forget thy title to old Huntly's family,
    As much of peace will settle in thy mind
    As thou canst wish to taste, but in thy grave.
    Accept my tears yet, prithee; they are tokens   155
    Of charity, as true as of affection.
Kath. This is the cruell'st farewell!
Hunt.   Love, young gentleman,
    This model of my griefs; she calls you husband;
    Then be not jealous of a parting kiss,
    It is a father's not a lover's off'ring;   160
    Take it, my last. [*Kisses her.*] I am too much a child.
    Exchange of passion is to little use,
    So I should grow too foolish. Goodness guide thee!   *Exit.*
Kath. Most miserable daughter! Have you aught
    To add, sir, to our sorrows?
Dal.   I resolve,   165
    Fair lady, with your leave, to wait on all
    Your fortunes in my person, if your lord
    Vouchsafe me entertainment.
War. We will be bosom-friends, most noble Dalyell;

161. S.D.] *W; not in Q.*   163. too] *Q.*

---

151. *guard . . . patience*] i.e., bestow upon you much patience as a
guard.

155–6. *they . . . affection*] i.e., my tears are as truly tokens of charity as
they are of affection.

158. *model . . . griefs*] i.e., likeness of me (*O.E.D., s.v.* model 2 b); *my griefs*
is abstract for personal: she is an image of him and he is just his griefs,
model being a word often used to express the child's relation to the father.
Alternatively, since they are both weeping, Huntly may be saying that she
is a model of his griefs in respect of being a reproduction of them.

163. *So I should*] if it be so that I should: see Abbott § 133; the modern
ocution would be 'If I'm going to'.

For I accept this tender of your love   170
Beyond ability of thanks to speak it.
Clear thy drowned eyes, my fairest: time and industry
Will show us better days, or end the worst.   *Exeunt omnes.*

[IV. iv]

Enter OXFORD *and* DAUBENEY.

Oxf. No news from Scotland yet, my lord?
Dau.   Not any
But what king Henry knows himself; I thought
Our armies should have marched that way; his mind,
It seems, is altered.
Oxf.   Victory attends
His standard everywhere.
Dau.   Wise princes, Oxford,   5
Fight not alone with forces. Providence
Directs and tutors strength; else elephants
And barbèd horses might as well prevail
As the most subtle stratagems of war.
Oxf. The Scottish king showed more than common bravery   10
In proffer of a combat hand to hand
With Surrey.
Dau.   And but showed it; Northern bloods
Are gallant being fired, but the cold climate,
Without good store of fuel, quickly freezeth
The glowing flames.
Oxf.   Surrey, upon my life,   15
Would not have shrunk an hair's-breadth.
Dau.   May a' forfeit

IV. iv. Location] Usually given as 'Westminster. The Palace'.
Historical Time] summer 1497.
3. *should*] were to have; see Abbott § 324.
6. *Providence*] foresight (*O.E.D.*, 2).
7. *elephants*] Their use in war would be well known from accounts of
Hannibal, e.g., Ralegh, *Historie of the World*, bk v, chap. 3.
8. *barbèd*] caparisoned.

The honour of an English name and nature
Who would not have embraced it with a greediness
As violent as hunger runs to food.
'Twas an addition any worthy spirit   20
Would covet next to immortality,
Above all joys of life. We all missed shares
In that great opportunity.

Enter King HENRY *and* URSWICK, *whispering.*

Oxf.   The king!
     See, a' comes smiling.
Dau.   O, the game runs smooth
     On his side, then, believe it; cards well shuffled   25
     And dealt with cunning bring some gamester thrift,
     But others must rise losers.
Hen.   The train takes?
Urs. Most prosperously.
Hen.   I knew it should not miss.
     He fondly angles who will hurl his bait
     Into the water 'cause the fish at first   30
     Plays round about the line and dares not bite.
     Lords, we may reign your king yet; Daubeney, Oxford,
     Urswick, must Perkin wear the crown?
Dau.   A slave!
Oxf. A vagabond!
Urs.   A glow-worm!

23–4. The ... smiling] *so W; one line in Q.*   28. should] *Q; could G.*
33–4. A slave ... Frion] *so W; two lines divided at* ... Vagabond. / A Glow-
worme ... *Q.*

20. *addition*] mark of honour; probably a heraldic metaphor (see *O.E.D.*,
5). Cf. v. ii. 165 below and *Troilus and Cressida*, IV. v. 141.
   26. *thrift*] success, good luck (*O.E.D.*, 1).
   27. *train takes*] lure takes effect. A metaphor from drag-hunting (*O.E.D.*,
s.v. train *sb*[1] 7).
   29. *fondly*] foolishly.
   29–30. *hurl ... water*] i.e., abandoning it in a fit of impatience.
   34. *glow-worm*] often applied contemptuously to persons: cf. Joseph
Hall, *Heaven upon Earth* (1606), Section III: 'These glow-wormes when a
night of sorow compasses them, make a lightsome and fierie show of ioy,

Hen.   Now, if Frion,
    His practised politician, wear a brain   35
    Of proof, king Perkin will in progress ride
    Through all his large dominions; let us meet him
    And tender homage; ha, sirs? Liegemen ought
    To pay their fealty.
Dau.   Would the rascal were,
    With all his rabble, within twenty miles   40
    Of London.
Hen.   Farther off is near enough
    To lodge him in his home; I'll wager odds
    Surrey and all his men are either idle
    Or hasting back; they have not work, I doubt,
    To keep them busy.
Dau.   'Tis a strange conceit, sir.   45
Hen. Such voluntary favours as our people
    In duty aid us with, we never scattered
    On cobweb parasites, or lavished out
    In riot or a needless hospitality.
    No undeserving favourite doth boast   50
    His issues from our treasury; our charge
    Flows through all Europe, proving us but steward
    Of every contribution which provides
    Against the creeping canker of disturbance.
    Is it not rare then, in this toil of state   55

---

when if thou presse them thou findest nothing but a cold & crude mois-
ture.'
    36. *Of proof*] of proved or tested power (*O.E.D.*, *s.v.* proof *sb* 10).
    42. *lodge*] discover; a metaphor from hunting, to lodge a buck being to
discover its lodge, or lair (*O.E.D.*, *s.v.* lodge *v* 4).
    44. *doubt*] fear.
    45. *'Tis . . . conceit*] Daubeney is referring to Warbeck's whole adventure,
not to what Henry has just said; *conceit*, 'fantasy'.
    46. *favours*] From the context this appears to refer to money.
    51. *issues*] proceeds (*O.E.D.*, 7).
    51-2. *our . . . Flows*] we have expenses to meet (Pickburn). Bacon (p. 216)
refers to Henry's secret 'spials . . . at home and abroad, by them to discover
what practices and conspiracies were against him'.
    55. *rare*] fine (ironic).

Wherein we are embarked, with breach of sleep,
Cares, and the noise of trouble, that our mercy
Returns nor thanks nor comfort ? Still the West
Murmur and threaten innovation,
Whisper our government tyrannical,   60
Deny us what is ours, nay, spurn their lives,
Of which they are but owners by our gift.
It must not be.

Oxf.   It must not, should not.

Enter a Post.

Hen.   So then.
          To whom ?
Post.   This packet to your sacred majesty.
Hen. Sirrah, attend without.   [*Exit the* Post.]   65
Oxf. News from the North, upon my life.
Dau.   Wise Henry
          Divines aforehand of events; with him
          Attempts and execution are one act.
Hen. Urswick, thine ear : Frion is caught, the man
          Of cunning is outreached; we must be safe.   70
          Should reverend Morton our archbishop move

63.1.] *after 'whom ?' (l. 64) Q.*   63–4. So . . . whom] *so W; one line in Q.*
65. S.D.] *W (Exit Post.); not in Q.*

---

59. *innovation*] revolution (*O.E.D.*, 1 b).
61–2. *spurn . . . gift*] 'the Cornish rebels stuck not to say . . . that the King did well to pardon them, for that he knew he should leave few subjects . . . if he hanged all that were of their mind' (Bacon, pp. 162–3).
63.1. *Post*] courier.
69. *Frion is caught*] There is no basis for this in the sources; it is the only new happening in the scene and has no sequel in the play. It is not the reason for the scene, which was written to prevent Henry slipping out of focus after a fairly long period off the stage (since the end of III. iii). This accounts for the relatively high proportion of invented 'historical' material: see notes on ll. 71, 83, 89–91.
70. *we must be*] we're bound to be.
71. *Morton*] the Morton famous for the fiscal device known as 'Morton's fork': Cardinal John Morton, archbishop of Canterbury 1486–1500, Henry's chancellor of the exchequer since 1487. Bacon mentions him many times and indicates (pp. 149–50) that he was one of the targets of the first

To a translation higher yet, I tell thee,
My Durham owns a brain deserves that see.
He's nimble in his industry, and mounting:
Thou hear'st me ?

Urs.   And conceive your highness fitly.   75

Hen. Daubeney and Oxford, since our army stands
Entire, it were a weakness to admit
The rust of laziness to eat amongst them.
Set forward toward Salisbury; the plains
Are most commodious for their exercise.   80
Ourself will take a muster of them there,
And or disband them with reward or else
Dispose as best concerns us.

Dau.   Salisbury ?
Sir, all is peace at Salisbury.

Hen.   Dear friend,
The charge must be our own; we would a little   85
Partake the pleasure with our subjects' ease.
Shall I entreat your loves ?

Oxf.   Command our lives.

Cornish rising, but this remark of Henry's about him is probably invented.

72. *translation . . . yet*] i.e., removal to a see in heaven (or to the papacy ?).

73.] See Biographical Index, *s.v.* Durham.

74. *mounting*] ambitious.

75. *conceive*] understand. Ford presumably thinks of Urswick (q.v. in Biographical Index) as Henry's channel to Rome when bishops were being appointed.

83. *Salisbury*] Its prominence in the scene and the troop-movements here have no basis in the sources, although Salisbury was the right direction in which to move in view of Warbeck's imminent invasion and his advance upon Exeter and Taunton. These have not yet happened. It may be historically true that Henry had advance knowledge of Warbeck's plans, but there is little reason to suppose that Ford was doing more than guessing intelligently. He invents in order to characterize Henry as a ruler whose foresight (cf. ll. 2–9 and 66–8 above, 88 below) can hardly be disentangled from the excellence of his intelligence-service (see ll. 89–91 below and note).

85. *charge*] responsibility.

86.] i.e., share the pleasure (of ease) with our easeful subjects; *subjects' ease* is abstract for personal, as in IV. iii. 137, 158.

Hen. You're men know how to do, not to forethink.
　　　My bishop is a jewel tried and perfect;
　　　A jewel, lords. The post who brought these letters　　　90
　　　Must speed another to the mayor of Exeter;
　　　Urswick, dismiss him not.
Urs.　　　　　　　　　　He waits your pleasure.
Hen. Perkin a king? a king!
Urs.　　　　　　　　　　My gracious lord?
Hen. Thoughts busied in the sphere of royalty
　　　Fix not on creeping worms without their stings,　　　95
　　　Mere excrements of earth. The use of time
　　　Is thriving safety, and a wise prevention
　　　Of ills expected. We're resolved for Salisbury. *Exeunt omnes.*

[IV. v]

　　A general shout within. Enter [PERKIN] WARBECK, DALYELL,
　　　　　　　　KATHERINE, *and* JANE.

War. After so many storms as wind and seas
　　　Have threatened to our weather-beaten ships,
　　　At last, sweet fairest, we are safe arrived
　　　On our dear mother earth, ingrateful only
　　　To heaven and us in yielding sustenance　　　5

93. king? a king!] King? a King? *Q.*

89–91.] These lines strongly suggest that Ford wants us to think that Henry's letters from Fox have brought him the news of Warbeck's plans, and that this has helped to turn Henry's attention to Cornwall and the West; see note on l. 83 above. Henry can create the impression of foresight for which simpler men admire him because his sources of information are good.

96. *excrements*] superfluous outgrowths (*O.E.D. s.v.* excrement[2] 2).

96–7. *The . . . Is*] i.e., the proper employment of time results in (Pickburn).

IV. v. Location] Whitesand Bay, near Land's End (Bacon, p. 163), from where Warbeck proceeded immediately to Bodmin.

　　Historical Time] 7 (10) September—see note to l. 41 below.

　　1–6.] can be vaguely paralleled by Richard's landing in Wales, *Richard II*, III. ii. 1 ff.

To sly usurpers of our throne and right.
These general acclamations are an omen
Of happy process to their welcome lord;
They flock in troops, and from all parts with wings
Of duty fly, to lay their hearts before us.   10
Unequalled pattern of a matchless wife,
How fares my dearest yet?

Kath.   Confirmed in health:
By which I may the better undergo
The roughest face of change; but I shall learn
Patience to hope, since silence courts affliction   15
For comforts, to this truly noble gentleman—
Rare unexampled pattern of a friend!—
And my beloved Jane, the willing follower
Of all misfortunes.

Dal.   Lady, I return
But barren crops of early protestations,   20
Frost-bitten in the spring of fruitless hopes.

Jane. I wait but as the shadow to the body;
For, madam, without you let me be nothing.

War. None talk of sadness, we are on the way
Which leads to victory. Keep cowards thoughts   25
With desperate sullenness! The lion faints not
Locked in a grate; but, loose, disdains all force
Which bars his prey; and we are lion-hearted,

---

7. omen] OMEN *Q*.   15–16. affliction For comforts,] *Q;* affliction, For
comforts *W;* affliction, For comforts, *G*.

---

8. *process*] progress (*O.E.D.*, 8, 9).

14–16. *but . . . gentleman*] I shall teach to this truly noble gentleman the
patience to hope, since silence will persist in asking affliction for comfort.
learn is 'teach' (*O.E.D.*, 4), a common signification; *silence* and *affliction*
are abstract-poetic for personal-concrete, in a manner very characteristic
of the style of the play, *silence* being the silent Dalyell and Jane, *affliction*
the afflicted Katherine herself. With the punctuation of Q altered in l. 15
(as by all editors since Weber) the lines make no sense.

19. *return*] yield.

20. *early protestations*] premature avowals.

22. *wait*] attend.

27. *grate*] cage (*O.E.D.*, 7).

Or else no king of beasts. (*Another shout.*) Hark, how they
    shout,
Triumphant in our cause! Bold confidence   30
Marches on bravely, cannot quake at danger.

Enter SKELTON.

Skel. Save king Richard the Fourth, save thee, king of hearts!
    The Cornish blades are men of mettle; have proclaimed
    through Bodmin and the whole county my sweet prince
    monarch of England; four thousand tall yeomen, with   35
    bow and sword, already vow to live and die at the foot of
    King Richard.

Enter ASTLEY.

Ast. The mayor our fellow-counsellor is servant for an em-
    peror. Exeter is appointed for the rendezvous, and
    nothing wants to victory but courage and resolution.   40
    Sigillatum et datum decimo Septembris, anno regni regis
    primo, et cetera; confirmatum est. All's cock-sure.

31.1. SKELTON] *Sketon Q.*   34. Bodmin] *D; Bodnam Q.*   37. King
Richard] KING RICHARD *Q.*

---

29. *Or . . . beasts*] or else not a 'lion' at all; *king of beasts* is used as a
synonym for 'lion' but with an allusion to Warbeck's claims; cf. *Richard II*,
v. i. 34.
    32. *Richard the Fourth*] Cf. IV. ii. 63. All the sources say that he assumed
this title in Cornwall, Bacon and Gainsford supposing that it was the first
time he had done so, although he had used it already in his proclamation in
Northumberland in 1496 (Gairdner, pp. 306, 326; Lumby ap. Bacon, p.
285).
    33. *The Cornish . . . mettle*] Struble points out the echo from Bacon, p.
166: 'the Cornish men were become like metal often fired and quenched,
churlish, and that would sooner break than bow'. Ford quibbles on *blades*
('good fellows') and *mettle/metal*; the two senses of the latter were not distinguished by spelling, each being spelt either way.
    35. *four thousand*] Gainsford's figure, larger than Hall's or Bacon's.
    40. *wants*] is lacking.
    41–2. Sigillatum . . . est] sealed and dated on 10 September in the first
year of the king's reign, etc.; confirmed.
    41. decimo Septembris] Although Astley is only making the gestures
appropriate to a scrivener, Ford must have had some warrant for this date,
which is about right (see Gairdner, p. 326). The other sources mention

War. To Exeter! to Exeter, march on!
  Commend us to our people; we in person
  Will lend them double spirits; tell them so.   45
Skel. and Ast. King Richard, king Richard!
         [*Exeunt* SKELTON *and* ASTLEY.]
War. A thousand blessings guard our lawful arms!
  A thousand horrors pierce our enemies' souls!
  Pale fear unedge their weapons' sharpest points,
  And when they draw their arrows to the head,   50
  Numbness shall strike their sinews; such advantage
  Hath majesty in its pursuit of justice
  That on the proppers-up of truth's old throne
  It both enlightens counsel and gives heart
  To execution; whiles the throats of traitors   55
  Lie bare before our mercy. O divinity
  Of royal birth! how it strikes dumb the tongues
  Whose prodigality of breath is bribed
  By trains to greatness! Princes are but men
  Distinguished by the fineness of their frailty,   60
  Yet not so gross in beauty of the mind,
  For there's a fire more sacred purifies

---

46. *Skel.*] *She: Q.* 46.1.] *W; not in Q.*

---

only the month; Stow's *Annales*, 481/1/25, gives the correct date for Warbeck's landing, 7 September.

 42. *cock-sure*] absolutely certain (*O.E.D.*, 1).

 53. *on*] i.e., in respect of, in.

 58–9. *bribed . . . greatness*] bribed by the retinues attendant upon greatness, i.e., the servants of a monarch such as Henry (*train*, 'retainers',
O.E.D., *s.v. sb*² 9). The picture is of persons free with their political opinions and influence being wooed by Henry's partisans. Pickburn takes *trains*
as 'stratagems' (*O.E.D.*, art. cit., 1); but his 'won over [by stratagems] to
the side of greatness' involves a strained interpretation of *bribed to. greatness* in either case is political (see note on I. i. 77) and specifically (abstract
for personal) Henry.

 59–61.] *frailty* is a virtual synonym for 'mortal condition'. All men, including princes, are frail mortals; but the 'frail' (in this sense) state of
princes can be distinguished from that of other men by its relative fineness.
The argument continues: princes admittedly, like all men, are gross, yet
not so gross as other men are, because of the beauty of their minds . . .

 62–3. *there's . . . mixture*] The 'dross' (worthless matter) is a metaphor for

The dross of mixture. Herein stands the odds:
Subjects are men on earth, kings men and gods.

Exeunt omnes.

63. stands] *Q;* stand *G.*   64. Subjects] "Subjects *Q.*   men on earth,]
G; men, on earth *Q;* men; on earth *W.*

---

the human condition of the princes (cf. Isaiah i. 25); *mixture* is the hetero-
geneous or contaminating element in it (see *O.E.D.*, 5), i.e., its human
'frailty'. Warbeck muddles his metaphor from iron-manufacture by de-
scribing the object being purified as 'dross', whereas dross is normally what
is thrown off from the object in the process of purification. This muddle no
doubt arises from the equation of sinful human nature with 'dross' having
been so automatic as scarcely to seem metaphorical; but the sentence means
only that frail humanity is by a more sacred fire purified of its human frailty.

63. *Herein . . . odds*] i.e., this is what constitutes the differences (for *odds*,
O.E.D., 2). There is no warrant for altering Q's *stands* to *stand* as has been
done by most edd. except Anderson since Gifford; cf. *Antony and Cleo-
patra*, IV. xv. 66.

Act V

[v. i]

Enter KATHERINE *and* JANE *in riding-suits, with one* Servant.

Kath. It is decreed; and we must yield to fate,
    Whose angry justice, though it threaten ruin,
    Contempt, and poverty, is all but trial
    Of a weak woman's constancy in suffering.
    Here in a stranger's and an enemy's land,   5
    Forsaken and unfurnished of all hopes
    But such as wait on misery, I range
    To meet affliction wheresoe'er I tread.
    My train and pomp of servants is reduced
    To one kind gentlewoman and this groom.   10
    Sweet Jane, now whither must we?
Jane.   To your ships,
    Dear lady, and turn home.
Kath.   Home! I have none.
    Fly thou to Scotland, thou hast friends will weep
    For joy to bid thee welcome; but, O Jane,
    My Jane, my friends are desperate of comfort,   15

Act V] *Actus Quintus: Scæna prima.* Q.

v. i. Location] St Michael's Mount, Cornwall, specified by the sources
as the place where Katherine was left after Warbeck's landing.
    Historical Time] September 1497.
    0.1. riding-suits] Imogen asks for a riding-suit (*Cymbeline*, III. ii. 75),
but it is not clear what would differentiate the suits so clearly from ordinary
dress as to convey a useful message to the audience. Struble thinks that
they were here a form of disguise and cites Gainsford's 'transhaping her
selfe into one of her seruants habits, she had gone quite away to her
ships' (sig. Pᵛ). But the main theatrical purpose here is to suggest that the
ladies have just dismounted in the course of their journey.
    7. *range*] wander about.

As I must be of them; the common charity,
Good people's alms and prayers of the gentle,
Is the revenue must support my state.
As for my native country, since it once
Saw me a princess in the height of greatness   20
My birth allowed me, here I make a vow
Scotland shall never see me being fallen
Or lessened in my fortunes. Never, Jane,
Never to Scotland more will I return.
Could I be England's queen—a glory, Jane,   25
I never fawned on—yet the king who gave me
Hath sent me with my husband from his presence,
Delivered us suspected to his nation,
Rendered us spectacles to time and pity.
And is it fit I should return to such   30
As only listen after our descent
From happiness enjoyed to misery
Expected, though uncertain? Never, never!
Alas, why dost thou weep, and that poor creature
Wipe his wet cheeks too? let me feel alone   35
Extremities, who know to give them harbour;
Nor thou nor he has cause. You may live safely.

Jane. There is no safety whiles your dangers, madam,
Are every way apparent.

Servant.   Pardon, lady;
I cannot choose but show my honest heart;   40
You were ever my good lady.

Kath.   O dear souls,
Your shares in grief are too, too much!

Enter DALYELL.

Dal.   I bring,
Fair princess, news of further sadness yet

---

26. *fawned on*] aspired to; the only example of this use in *O.E.D.*, **3** b.
gave me] i.e., gave me away, to a husband.
28. *his*] Warbeck's.
31. *listen after*] eagerly listen for.

Than your sweet youth hath been acquainted with.

Kath. Not more, my lord, than I can welcome; speak it;　　45
　　The worst, the worst I look for.

Dal.　　　　　　　　　　　All the Cornish
　　At Exeter were by the citizens
　　Repulsed, encountered by the earl of Devonshire
　　And other worthy gentlemen of the country.
　　Your husband marched to Taunton, and was there　　50
　　Affronted by king Henry's chamberlain—
　　The king himself in person, with his army,
　　Advancing nearer to renew the fight
　　On all occasions. But the night before
　　The battles were to join, your husband privately,　　55
　　Accompanied with some few horse, departed
　　From out the camp, and posted none knows whither.

Kath. Fled without battle given?

Dal.　　　　　　　　　　　Fled, but followed
　　By Daubeney, all his parties left to taste
　　King Henry's mercy—for to that they yielded—　　60
　　Victorious without bloodshed.

Kath.　　　　　　　　　O, my sorrows!
　　If both our lives had proved the sacrifice
　　To Henry's tyranny, we had fallen like princes,
　　And robbed him of the glory of his pride.

Dal. Impute it not to faintness or to weakness　　65

45–61.] This account is a brief abstract of much lengthier narratives in the sources.

46–9. *All . . . country*] Warbeck attacked Exeter on 17 and 18 September and was driven back by the citizens and by troops brought by Sir E. Courtenay (whom Henry had created earl of Devon at his coronation) and by local gentry.

50. *Taunton*] reached on 20 September.

51. *Affronted*] confronted (*O.E.D.*, 2, 3).

54. *On . . . occasions*] at every opportunity. Historically, the troops led by Henry never made any actual contact with the rebels.

55. *battles*] battalions (*O.E.D.*, 8).

57. *posted*] rode post, rapidly.

59. *parties*] detachments of soldiers, or bodies of adherents (*O.E.D.*, 6, 7).

Of noble courage, lady, but foresight;
For by some secret friend he had intelligence
Of being bought and sold by his base followers.
Worse yet remains untold.

Kath.   No, no, it cannot.

Dal. I fear you're betrayed. The earl of Oxford   70
Runs hot in your pursuit.

Kath.   A' shall not need;
We'll run as hot in resolution gladly
To make the earl our jailor.

Jane.   Madam, madam,
They come, they come!

Enter OXFORD *with followers.*

Dal.   Keep back, or he who dares
Rudely to violate the law of honour   75
Runs on my sword.

Kath.   Most noble sir, forbear.
What reason draws you hither, gentlemen?
Whom seek 'ee?

Oxf.   All stand off. With favour, lady,

66. foresight] *Q;* to foresight *G.*   73–4. Madam . . . they come] *so W;*
one line in Q.

67–8.] Gainsford (sig. O3) says that after his failure at Exeter many of
Warbeck's followers went home, for various reasons (weariness, fear, failure of the country to rise, 'politikely forecasting for the worst'). Hall (p.
484) reports similarly, and adds that when he saw his supporters with-
drawing Warbeck 'put small trust and less confidence' in those that were
left because they were badly armed and trained. But in suggesting deliberate betrayal these lines go a good deal further than any of the sources and
are probably Ford's palliation of Warbeck's flight, which Gainsford (sig.
O4) regarded as dishonourable. Hall (p. 485) says about it: 'Whether
Perkyn dyd this for feare, *least his men should forsake hym,* or for the
cowardenes of his awne tymorous courage . . . is . . . vncerteyne.' It is just
possible that the sentence which I have italicized gave Ford a hint, or that
Katherine's fate did (see note on l. 70 below).

67. *intelligence*] news.

70. *earl of Oxford*] The sources record the capture of Katherine by a
party of horsemen (Gainsford, sig. P^v, says that she was delivered up to
them by some of her own followers), but do not attribute any part in it to
Oxford.

From Henry, England's king, I would present
Unto the beauteous princess, Katherine Gordon,   80
The tender of a gracious entertainment.
Kath. We are that princess, whom your master-king
Pursues with reaching arms to draw into
His power. Let him use his tyranny,
We shall not be his subjects.
Oxf.   My commission   85
Extends no further, excellentest lady,
Than to a service; 'tis king Henry's pleasure
That you, and all that have relation t' ee,
Be guarded as becomes your birth and greatness.
For rest assured, sweet princess, that not aught   90
Of what you do call yours shall find disturbance,
Or any welcome other than what suits
Your high condition.
Kath.   By what title, sir,
May I acknowledge you?
Oxf.   Your servant, lady,
Descended from the line of Oxford's earls,   95
Inherits what his ancestors before him
Were owners of.
Kath.   Your king is herein royal,
That by a peer so ancient in desert
As well as blood commands us to his presence.
Oxf. Invites 'ee, princess, not commands.
Kath.   Pray use   100
Your own phrase as you list; to your protection
Both I and mine submit.
Oxf.   There's in your number

85–6. My . . . lady] *so W; one line in Q.*   99. us] VS *Q.*

---

81. *tender*] offer.
83. *reaching*] far-reaching; cf. the proverbial 'Great men have **reaching**
hands' (*2 Henry VI*, IV. vii. 76).
88. *all . . . t' ee*] i.e., all that are in your service, your dependents and connexions.
93. *condition*] rank (*O.E.D.*, 10).

O

A nobleman whom fame hath bravely spoken.
To him the king my master bade me say
How willingly he courts his friendship; far   105
From an enforcement more than what in terms
Of courtesy so great a prince may hope for.

Dal.   My name is Dalyell.

Oxf.   'Tis a name hath won
Both thanks and wonder from report; my lord,
The court of England emulates your merit,   110
And covets to embrace 'ee.

Dal.   I must wait on
The princess in her fortunes.

Oxf.   Will you please,
Great lady, to set forward?

Kath.   Being driven
By fate, it were in vain to strive with heaven.   *Exeunt omnes.*

[v. ii]

Enter King HENRY, SURREY, URSWICK, *and a guard of* Soldiers.

Hen.   The counterfeit, king Perkin, is escaped;
Escape, so let him; he is hedged too fast

---

105. friendship;] *W;* friendship. *Q;* friendship: *A.*   106. enforcement]
this ed.; enforcement, *Q.*   107. courtesy] *D;* courtesie, *Q.*

v. ii. 2. Escape,] *Q;* Escape *W;* Escape! *G;* Escap'd! *D.*

---

103. *bravely spoken*] i.e., spoken splendidly of.

105–7. *far . . . for*] Edd. who retain Q's comma after *enforcement* presumably take the lines to mean: 'it's far from a compulsion, but it's rather more
than so great a prince might expect [as due to him] from mere courtesy'.
This seems a much less likely and less courtly sentiment than the one
yielded by the removal of Q's commas after *enforcement* and *courtesy*: 'it's
far from being a compulsion more than what so great a prince might expect
[as due to him] by way of mere courtesy', i.e., the only element of compulsion lies in the prince's reasonable expectation that his own courtesy
will be reciprocated. The whole clause is dependent upon ll. 104–5 and
qualifies 'willingly courts': if your friendship is sought by a great prince,
that puts you under an obligation to him—and to that extent there's an
element of 'enforcement' in the situation.

v. ii. Location] The scene combines two events which in the sources are

Within the circuit of our English pale
To steal out of our ports or leap the walls
Which guard our land; the seas are rough and wider　　5
Than his weak arms can tug with; Surrey, henceforth
Your king may reign in quiet. Turmoils past,
Like some unquiet dream, have rather busied
Our fancy than affrighted rest of state.
But, Surrey, why, in articling a peace　　　　　　　10
With James of Scotland, was not restitution
Of losses, which our subjects did sustain
By the Scotch inroads, questioned?

Sur.　　　　　　　　　　　　　　Both demanded
And urged, my lord; to which the king replied,
In modest merriment but smiling earnest,　　　　15
How that our master Henry was much abler
To bear the detriments than he repay them.

Hen. The young man, I believe, spake honest truth;

---

separated by days or weeks and reverses the sources' order of them: Henry's
interview with Katherine and Warbeck's being brought into his presence
for the first time. Hall says that Warbeck was brought before Henry at
Exeter, and Hall and Gainsford can be read as implying that Henry reached
Exeter before he first saw Katherine; Bacon implies the opposite, and is
not sure whether Warbeck was seen by Henry at any point (see note on l. 31
below). None of the sources gives any warrant for the 'Salisbury' location
of all edd., which derives from IV. iv. 98 (and see note on IV. iv. 83): Salisbury was one of the few Western towns Henry did *not* visit. Historically, he
was at Woodstock near Oxford when he heard the news of Warbeck's flight
(l. 1) and at Taunton when Warbeck was first brought before him (ll. 31 ff.;
see Gairdner, p. 328, Rowse, pp. 133–4). Historically, too, Warbeck and
Katherine were eventually brought together at Exeter in his presence,
when Warbeck was made to confess his imposture before her (Gairdner,
p. 329).

　Historical Time] between 21 September and 4 October 1497.
　3. *our . . . pale*] our dominion of England (*O.E.D.*, 4).
　9. *rest of state*] government tranquility.
　10–17.] from Bacon; see IV. iii. 58 and note.
　10. *articling*] arranging by treaty (*O.E.D.*, 5).
　13. *questioned*] inquired about (*O.E.D.*, 6).
　17. *detriments*] losses (*O.E.D.*, 1).
　18. *young man*] James was twenty-five.

  A' studies to be wise betimes. Has, Urswick,
  Sir Rhys ap Thomas and Lord Brooke our steward   20
  Returned the Western gentlemen full thanks
  From us for their tried loyalties ?

Urs.   They have;
  Which, as if health and life had reigned amongst 'em,
  With open hearts they joyfully received.

Hen. Young Buckingham is a fair-natured prince,   25
  Lovely in hopes and worthy of his father:
  Attended by an hundred knights and squires
  Of special name, he tendered humble service,
  Which we must ne'er forget. And Devonshire's wounds,
  Though slight, shall find sound cure in our respect.   30

   Enter DAUBENEY, *with* [PERKIN] WARBECK, HERON,
     JOHN A-WATER, ASTLEY, SKELTON.

Dau. Life to the king, and safety fix his throne!

19. Has, Urswick,] *W;* Ha's *Vrswicke, Q.* 22. *Urs.*] *W; Sur: Q.* 30.2.
SKELTON] *Sketon Q.*

---

 19. *betimes*] early in life (*O.E.D.*, 1).
 Has] See Abbott § 335.
 20.] Bacon mentions the names in the corresponding context, but not
that Brooke was steward, which is in Hall and Gainsford. For Brooke see
III. iv. 92; Rhys (Rice in Q) ap Thomas (1449–1525), the greatest of
Welsh magnates under both Henries, went over to Henry before Bosworth:
see *Richard III*, IV. v. 12.
 25–9. *Buckingham . . . forget*] Edward Stafford, third duke (1478–1521);
the account of his retinue echoes Gainsford (sig. O3ᵛ). His father (l. 26)
was the 'high-reaching Buckingham' of *Richard III*. *Lovely in hopes*,
'splendidly promising'.
 28. *special*] distinguished (*O.E.D.*, 1 d).
 29. *Devonshire's wounds*] the earl's (see v. i. 48) not the county's; he was
wounded in the arm with an arrow at Exeter (for the Cornish bows, cf.
III. i. 61–2).
 30. *respect*] esteem.
 31.] The play was bound to stage a meeting between Warbeck and
Henry, and there is full historical warrant for it (Rowse, p. 134). Ford's
authority was Gainsford; Hall merely says that Warbeck 'committed hym
selfe to the kynges pleasure'; Bacon (p. 169): 'Perkin was brought to the
King's court, but not to the King's presence; though the King, to satisfy
his curiosity, saw him sometimes out of a window, or in passage'. See
Appendix, p. 174.

    I here present you, royal sir, a shadow
    Of majesty, but in effect a substance
    Of pity; a young man, in nothing grown
    To ripeness but th' ambition of your mercy: 35
    Perkin, the Christian world's strange wonder.
Hen.   Daubeney,
    We observe no wonder; I behold, 'tis true,
    An ornament of nature, fine and polished,
    A handsome youth indeed, but not admire him.
    How came he to thy hands?
Dau.   From sanctuary   40
    At Beaulieu, near Southampton, registered,
    With these few followers, for persons privileged.
Hen. I must not thank you, sir! you were to blame
    To infringe the liberty of houses sacred:
    Dare we be irreligious?
Dau.   Gracious lord,   45
    They voluntarily resigned themselves
    Without compulsion.
Hen.   So? 'twas very well;
    'Twas very, very well. Turn now thine eyes,
    Young man, upon thyself, and thy past actions!
    What revels in combustion through our kingdom   50
    A frenzy of aspiring youth hath danced,

36–7. Daubeney . . . true] *so W; one line in Q.*   44. To] *Q; T' D.*

---

34. *young man*] He was about twenty-three.
35. *ambition of*] ardent desire for (*O.E.D.*, 3).
39. *admire*] wonder at (*O.E.D.*, 1).
41. *Beaulieu*] The normal modern spelling of Q's Beweley, in Hampshire, then a Cistercian monastery. There are Bewleys (so spelled) in Durham and Westmorland.
42. *for*] as being.
43–5.] a departure from the sources, flattering to Henry; see Appendix, pp. 173–4 for Gainsford; Bacon (p. 168) shows how Henry and his council debated as to whether it was worth risking the obloquy of breaking sanctuary and finally decided to bribe Warbeck to come out 'by promise of life and pardon, and other fair means'. The right of sanctuary in criminal cases was abolished in 1625.
50. *combustion*] violent commotion (*O.E.D.*, 5).

Till, wanting breath, thy feet of pride have slipped
To break thy neck.
War.   But not my heart; my heart
Will mount till every drop of blood be frozen
By death's perpetual winter. If the sun   55
Of majesty be darkened, let the sun
Of life be hid from me in an eclipse
Lasting and universal. Sir, remember
There was a shooting in of light when Richmond,
Not aiming at a crown, retired, and gladly,   60
For comfort to the duke of Bretagne's court.
Richard, who swayed the sceptre, was reputed
A tyrant then; yet then a dawning glimmered
To some few wand'ring remnants, promising day
When first they ventured on a frightful shore   65
At Milford Haven—
Dau.   Whither speeds his boldness?
Check his rude tongue, great sir!
Hen.   O, let him range:
The player's on the stage still, 'tis his part;
A' does but act. What followed?
War.   Bosworth field:
Where, at an instant, to the world's amazement,   70
A morn to Richmond and a night to Richard
Appeared at once. The tale is soon applied:
Fate, which crowned these attempts when least assured,
Might have befriended others like resolved.

61. Bretagne's] *this ed.; Britaines Q; Bretaine's W.*

59–72.] The references to Henry's early career have no counterpart in
the corresponding contexts in the sources, although they were common
knowledge. Henry was taken to Britanny by his uncle the earl of Pembroke
in 1470 when he was thirteen.

66. *Milford Haven*] on 7 August 1485 when the future Henry VII began
his successful invasion; see *Richard III*, IV. iv. 535.

68–9. *The player's . . . act*] As Brereton (*Sources*) points out, this metaphor is applied five times to Warbeck by Bacon (pp. 145, 161, 166, 169,
178); Speed (965/2) had called him 'an imaginary and Stage-play Prince'.

72. *at once*] simultaneously.

Hen. A pretty gallant! Thus your aunt of Burgundy,   75
    Your duchess-aunt, informed her nephew; so,
    The lesson, prompted and well conned, was moulded
    Into familiar dialogue, oft rehearsed,
    Till, learnt by heart, 'tis now received for truth.
War. Truth in her pure simplicity wants art   80
    To put a feignèd blush on. Scorn wears only
    Such fashion as commends to gazers' eyes
    Sad ulcerated novelty, far beneath
    The sphere of majesty. In such a court,
    Wisdom and gravity are proper robes   85
    By which the sovereign is best distinguished
    From zanies to his greatness.
Hen.   Sirrah, shift
    Your antic pageantry, and now appear
    In your own nature, or you'll taste the danger
    Of fooling out of season.
War.   I expect   90
    No less than what severity calls justice,
    And politicians safety; let such beg
    As feed on alms. But if there can be mercy
    In a protested enemy, then may it
    Descend to these poor creatures, whose engagements   95

---

77. *prompted*] It is usually the pupil rather than the *lesson* that is 'prompt-ed' (see *O.E.D.*, 2). Milton's 'prompted Song' (*P.R.*, i. 12) means 'inspired', but there is no evidence for *prompted* as 'inspired' in the pejorative sense as here.

77–8. *moulded . . . dialogue*] The image is of Warbeck's lesson being rendered into the form of an *easily understood* (familiar, *O.E.D.*, 6 c) *dialogue* (between master and pupil), such as was common in the school grammars.

78. *rehearsed*] repeated.

87. *zanies to*] mimics of (*O.E.D.*, 2 b). Zanni was originally the comic servant or attendant in Italian popular comedy (see A. Nicoll, *The World of Harlequin*, pp. 82 ff.); cf. Marston, *Antonio's Revenge*, ed. Hunter, 1965, IV. i. 49.

shift] change (a metaphor from changing clothing).

88. *antic*] absurd, grotesque.

94. *protested*] publicly asserted (*O.E.D.*, *s.v.* protested 1).

95–6. *engagements To*] involvements with a view to; see Abbott § 186.

> To th' bettering of their fortunes have incurred
> A loss of all; to them, if any charity
> Flow from some noble orator, in death
> I owe the fee of thankfulness.

Hen.   So brave!
> What a bold knave is this! Which of these rebels   100
> Has been the mayor of Cork?

Dau.   This wise formality.
> Kneel to the king, ye rascals!   [*They kneel.*]

Hen.   Canst thou hope
> A pardon, where thy guilt is so apparent?

a-Wat. Under your good favours, as men are men, they may
> err. For I confess, respectively, in taking great parts,   105
> the one side prevailing, the other side must go down.
> Herein the point is clear, if the proverb hold that
> hanging goes by destiny, that it is to little purpose to
> say, this thing or that shall be thus or thus; for as the
> fates will have it, so it must be, and who can help it?   110

Dau. O blockhead! thou a privy councillor?
> Beg life, and cry aloud, 'heaven save king Henry!'

a-Wat. Every man knows what is best, as it happens. For
> my own part, I believe it is true, if I be not deceived,
> that kings must be kings and subjects subjects. But   115
> which is which—you shall pardon me for that; whether
> we speak or hold our peace, all are mortal, no man
> knows his end.

Hen. We trifle time with follies.

Her., a-Wat., Ast., Skel.   Mercy, mercy!

Hen. Urswick, command the dukeling and these fellows   120

---

102. ye] *W;* 'ee *Q.*   S.D.] *W; not in Q.*   119. *Her. . . . Skel.*] *D;*
Omnes Q; All W.

97–9. *to . . . thankfulness*] If any charity flow to them from some noble
orator, I, dying, owe [him] the fee of thankfulness.

101. *wise formality*] i.e., 'pompous idiot'.

105. *respectively*] respectfully (*O.E.D.,* 2).

108. *hanging . . . destiny*] See Tilley W 232.

To Digby, the lieutenant of the Tower:
With safety let them be conveyed to London.
It is our pleasure no uncivil outrage,
Taunts or abuse be suffered to their persons;
They shall meet fairer law than they deserve.   125
Time may restore their wits, whom vain ambition
Hath many years distracted.

War.   Noble thoughts
Meet freedom in captivity. The Tower—
Our childhood's dreadful nursery!

Hen.   No more.

Urs. Come, come, you shall have leisure to bethink 'ee.   130

Exit URSWICK *with* PERKIN [WARBECK] *and his* [*followers*].

Hen. Was ever so much impudence in forgery?
The custom, sure, of being styled a king
Hath fastened in his thought that he is such.
But we shall teach the lad another language;
'Tis good we have him fast.

Dau.   The hangman's physic   135
Will purge this saucy humour.

Hen.   Very likely;

133. he is such] HE IS SVCH *Q.*

121.] In history, Warbeck was not imprisoned in the Tower until nine
months later, in June 1498, after his attempt to escape from the 'keepers'
who looked after him at court (Gairdner, p. 232). In this scene and the next
Ford greatly telescopes the last two years of Warbeck's career: see also
note on v. iii. 13–19. Digby's name and office are mentioned in the sources'
description of Warbeck's attempt to murder him and escape, November
1499.

123–4.] suggested by Gainsford's 'diuers dared to put in practise many
vndecencies . . . had not the reuerence of his Maiesties presence diuerted
their inconsideration, and commanded no further rumour, gazing vpon
him, or violent threatnings' (sig. P3). Bacon (p. 170) describes Warbeck's
hostile reception when he was paraded from Westminster to the Tower
and back, 'but not in any ignominious fashion'.

131. *forgery*] deceit, fraudulent imitation (*O.E.D.*, 2, 3).

132–3.] Cf. Bacon, p. 111: 'himself, with long and continual counterfeiting, and with oft telling a lie, was turned by habit almost into the thing
he seemed to be; and from a liar to a believer' (Brereton, *Sources*).

Yet we could temper mercy with extremity,
Being not too far provoked.

Enter OXFORD, KATHERINE *in her richest attire,* [DALYELL], JANE,
and Attendants.

Oxf.   Great sir, be pleased
With your accustomed grace to entertain
The princess Katherine Gordon.
Hen.   Oxford, herein   140
We must beshrew thy knowledge of our nature.
A lady of her birth and virtues could not
Have found us so unfurnished of good manners
As not, on notice given, to have met her
Half-way in point of love. Excuse, fair cousin,   145
The oversight. O fie, you may not kneel;
'Tis most unfitting; first, vouchsafe this welcome,
A welcome to your own, for you shall find us
But guardian to your fortune and your honours.
Kath. My fortunes and mine honours are weak champions,   150
As both are now befriended, sir; however,
Both bow before your clemency.
Hen.   Our arms
Shall circle them from malice. A sweet lady!

143. us] VS *Q.*   148. us] VS *Q.*

137.] One would expect the nouns to be transposed, but *temper* is 'mix'
(*O.E.D.*, 3), *extremity,* 'extreme severity' (*O.E.D.*, 6).

138.1. richest attire] Struble compares Gainsford (sig. P^v): 'they gaue
her leaue to adorne her selfe, and brought her ... to the King'.

141. *beshrew*] greatly blame (for its inadequacy); *O.E.D.*, 2.

144–5. *met ... love*] It may be that Henry intends to express no more than
the relatively meaningless sentiment 'we would have met her half-way in
the matter of affection'; but if he means that he would literally have met her
half-way (instead of having her brought to him) *in point of* must be loosely
used for a phrase like 'as an expression of'.

146. *may*] must; see Abbott § 310.

153–6.] Gainsford, 'improving' on Hall, suggests that Henry became
completely infatuated with Katherine; Bacon says that he received her
with affection, 'pity giving more impression to her excellent beauty' (p.
168). Ford turns this into Henry's technique for overriding with a flood of
generosity Katherine's attempts (ll. 155, 162) to mention Warbeck.

Beauty incomparable! Here lives majesty
At league with love.

Kath.   O sir, I have a husband.   155

Hen. We'll prove your father, husband, friend, and servant,
Prove what you wish to grant us. Lords, be careful
A patent presently be drawn for issuing
A thousand pounds from our exchequer yearly
During our cousin's life. Our queen shall be   160
Your chief companion, our own court your home,
Our subjects all your servants.

Kath.   But my husband?

Hen. By all descriptions, you are noble Dalyell,
Whose generous truth hath famed a rare observance.
We thank 'ee; 'tis a goodness gives addition   165
To every title boasted from your ancestry,
In all most worthy.

Dal.   Worthier than your praises,
Right princely sir, I need not glory in.

Hen. Embrace him, lords. [*To Katherine*] Whoever calls you
mistress

169. S.D.] *B; not in Q.*

157. *Prove . . . us*] It is uncertain whether *prove* is 2nd pers. sing. or 1st pers. plural: 'we will make trial of whatever you care to grant us [in return for our favours]', or 'do you make trial of . . .' In either case, the run of the sentence is somewhat unexpected, as is the repetition of *prove* in a different sense from that in l. 156; more likely would have been a sentence meaning 'make trial of anything you would like *us* to grant *you*'. Q may be corrupt, or Ford may be making Henry hint that he expects Katherine to become his mistress (see preceding note); such a hint might lie behind her extreme foreboding at ll. 171–2, though this is partly belied by ll. 169–70.

158. *patent*] an open document signifying the order (equivalent to 'letters patent').

presently] immediately.

159. *A thousand*] Ford seems to have made this figure up, although Bacon says that Katherine received an 'honourable allowance' (p. 168).

164.] whose noble loyalty hath rendered famous a fine piece of dutiful service. This is like saying 'your loyalty has made your loyalty famous'.

165. *addition*] Cf. IV. iv. 20 and note.

167–8. *Worthier . . . in*] I have no need to boast of anything more than being [an object worthy of] your praises.

Is lifted in our charge: a goodlier beauty   170
Mine eyes yet ne'er encountered.
Kath.   Cruel misery
Of fate, what rests to hope for?
Hen.   Forward, lords,
To London. Fair, ere long I shall present 'ee
With a glad object, peace, and Huntly's blessing.

Exeunt omnes.

[v. iii]

Enter Constable *and* Officers, [PERKIN] WARBECK, URSWICK, *and*
LAMBERT SIMNEL *like a falconer. A pair of stocks.*

Const. Make room there! Keep off, I require 'ee, and none
come within twelve foot of his majesty's new stocks, upon
pain of displeasure. Bring forward the malefactor. Friend,
you must to this gear, no remedy. Open the hole, and in
with his legs, just in the middle hole, there, that hole.   5
[*Warbeck is put in the stocks.*] Keep off, or I'll commit you
all. Shall not a man in authority be obeyed? So, so there,
'tis as it should be. Put on the padlock, and give me the
key; off, I say, keep off!
Urs. Yet, Warbeck, clear thy conscience; thou hast tasted   10
King Henry's mercy liberally; the law

v. iii. 3. malefactor] *this ed.;* Malefactors Q.   6. S.D.] *W (after l. 9); not
in* Q.

---

170. *lifted . . . charge*] raised up as an object of our special care (Pickburn).
172. *rests*] remains.

v. iii. Location] Edd. give 'Tower Hill', but Warbeck was put in the
stocks at Westminster Hall and Cheapside and executed at Tyburn.
Historical Time] Warbeck was executed on 23 November 1499. This
scene is imagined as taking place just before, but also stages incidents (the
stocks) which occurred on 15 and 18 June 1498.
0.2. falconer] His special glove, satchel, and stave (see illustrations in
Shakespeare's England, II. 353, 364 opp.) might make him immediately
recognizable as such to an audience.
3. *malefactor*] Because there is only one, Q must be altered.
10. *Yet*] even now.

Has forfeited thy life; an equal jury
Have doomed thee to the gallows; twice, most wickedly,
Most desperately, hast thou escaped the Tower,
Inveigling to thy party with thy witchcraft   15
Young Edward, earl of Warwick, son to Clarence,
Whose head must pay the price of that attempt—
Poor gentleman, unhappy in his fate,
And ruined by thy cunning!—so a mongrel
May pluck the true stag down. Yet, yet, confess   20
Thy parentage; for yet the king has mercy.
Lamb. You would be Dick the Fourth; very likely!
Your pedigree is published; you are known
For Osbeck's son of Tournay, a loose runagate,
A landloper. Your father was a Jew,   25
Turned Christian merely to repair his miseries.
Where's now your kingship?
War.   Baited to my death?

---

12. *equal*] impartial. Warbeck was not tried by jury.

13–19.] The two attempts to escape were from his 'keepers' at court in
June 1498 (see note on v. ii. 121) and from the Tower in November 1499.
Only the second implicated the earl of Warwick (on whom see III. iii. 53–9
and note). Bacon and Gainsford both make it clear that Henry was glad of
the opportunity to get rid of Warwick; Bacon mentions the common
scandal (accepted by modern historians, Gairdner, pp. 333–4) that Henry
had used Warbeck as a bait to entrap Warwick, who was beheaded on 29
November.

19–20. *so . . . down*] not an improvement on Bacon's metaphor (p. 176):
'it was ordained, that this winding-ivy of a Plantagenet should kill the true
tree itself'.

23–6.] Warbeck had to read out his confession of his 'Pedigree and
Original' (Gainsford) publicly in London on 'diuers scaffolds' after his
first attempted escape in 1498; Bacon refers to his confession being
'printed and dispersed abroad' (and cf. Speed, 968/2). For the details here
see Biographical Index, *s.v.* Warbeck.

24–5. *runagate . . . landloper*] Both words mean 'vagabond' and derive
from Bacon; cf. III. iii. 50 and Bacon (p. 105): 'such a wanderer, or, as the
King called him, such a land-louper'.

25–6. *a Jew . . . miseries*] a detail from Bacon (p. 106), not in Gainsford;
based on Speed's misunderstanding of an earlier document and historically
untrue (see Gairdner, pp. 271–2).

27. *Baited*] tormented.

Intolerable cruelty! I laugh at
The duke of Richmond's practice on my fortunes.
Possession of a crown ne'er wanted heralds.   30
Lamb. You will not know who I am?
Urs.   Lambert Simnel,
Your predecessor in a dangerous uproar;
But, on submission, not alone received
To grace, but by the king vouchsafed his service.
Lamb. I would be earl of Warwick, toiled and ruffled   35
Against my master, leapt to catch the moon,
Vaunted my name Plantagenet, as you do.
An earl, forsooth! whenas in truth I was,
As you are, a mere rascal. Yet his majesty,
A prince composed of sweetness—heaven protect him!— 40
Forgave me all my villainies, reprieved
The sentence of a shameful end, admitted
My surety of obedience to his service;
And I am now his falconer, live plenteously;
Eat from the king's purse, and enjoy the sweetness   45
Of liberty and favour, sleep securely;
And is not this now better than to buffet
The hangman's clutches, or to brave the cordage
Of a tough halter, which will break your neck?
So then the gallant totters; prithee, Perkin,   50
Let my example lead thee; be no longer
A counterfeit; confess, and hope for pardon!
War. For pardon! Hold, my heart-strings, whiles contempt
Of injuries, in scorn, may bid defiance
To this base man's foul language. Thou poor vermin,   55
How darest thou creep so near me? thou an earl?
Why, thou enjoy'st as much of happiness

---

29. *practice*] trickery.
35. *ruffled*] did battle; cf. I. ii. 10.
42–3. *admitted My surety*] accepted my pledge.
47. *buffet*] contend with.
50. *totters*] swings from a rope, is hanged (*O.E.D.*, 1).
54. *injuries*] calumnies (*O.E.D.*, 2).

As all the swinge of slight ambition flew at.
A dunghill was thy cradle. So a puddle
By virtue of the sunbeams breathes a vapour   60
To infect the purer air, which drops again
Into the muddy womb that first exhaled it.
Bread and a slavish ease, with some assurance
From the base beadle's whip, crowned all thy hopes.
But, sirrah, ran there in thy veins one drop   65
Of such a royal blood as flows in mine,
Thou wouldst not change condition to be second
In England's state without the crown itself.
Coarse creatures are incapable of excellence.
But let the world, as all to whom I am   70
This day a spectacle, to time deliver,
And by tradition fix posterity,
Without another chronicle than truth,
How constantly my resolution suffered
A martyrdom of majesty.

Lamb.   He's past   75
Recovery; a Bedlam cannot cure him.
Urs. Away, inform the king of his behaviour.
Lamb. Perkin, beware the rope; the hangman's coming.

                              Exit [LAMBERT] SIMNEL.
Urs. If yet thou hast no pity of thy body,
Pity thy soul!

            Enter KATHERINE, JANE, DALYELL, *and* OXFORD.

Jane.   Dear lady!
Oxf.   Whither will 'ee,   80

61. To] *Q;* T' *D.*   78.1.] *so G; after* 'soule' (*l. 80*) *in Q.*

---

58. *swinge*] driving-power, impetus (*O.E.D.*, 3).
59. *A dunghill*] Brereton (*Sources*) compares Hall (p. 430) on Simnel: 'a
dongehyll knaue and vyle borne villeyne'.
60. *breathes*] exhales.
72.] by transmission [of the story] settle the conviction of posterity; see
O.E.D., s.vv. tradition 4; fix 2 c.
74. *constantly*] steadfastly.

Without respect of shame?
Kath.   Forbear me, sir,
And trouble not the current of my duty.
O my loved lord! Can any scorn be yours
In which I have no interest? Some kind hand
Lend me assistance, that I may partake   85
Th' infliction of this penance; my life's dearest,
Forgive me; I have stayed too long from tend'ring
Attendance on reproach, yet bid me welcome.
War. Great miracle of constancy! My miseries
Were never bankrupt of their confidence,   90
In worst afflictions, till this; now I feel them.
Report and thy deserts, thou best of creatures,
Might to eternity have stood a pattern
For every virtuous wife, without this conquest.
Thou hast outdone belief; yet may their ruin   95
In after-marriages be never pitied
To whom thy story shall appear a fable.
Why wouldst thou prove so much unkind to greatness
To glorify thy vows by such a servitude?
I cannot weep, but trust me, dear, my heart   100
Is liberal of passion. Harry Richmond,

91. this; now] *D; this now, Q.*

---

81. *respect of*] consideration for.
81–184.] Katherine's behaviour may be compared with Bacon's highly
suggestive comment that she 'in all fortunes . . . entirely loved [Warbeck];
adding the virtues of a wife to the virtues of her sex' (p. 167). Speed (967/2)
also refers to her 'wiuely faith'; see note on III. ii. 139–86 and Introduction,
pp. xl–xli.
81. *Forbear me*] leave me alone (*O.E.D.*, 4 c).
85–6. *partake Th' infliction of*] i.e., share in being inflicted with.
88. *reproach*] not exactly 'object of reproach'; Warbeck becomes a
personified abstract, 'Disgrace'.
92. *Report . . . deserts*] thy fame combined with thy merits (implying also
'the fame *of* thy merits').
94. *conquest*] moral victory (over others and myself).
96. *after-*] subsequent.
98. *greatness*] her own greatness of rank.
99. *servitude*] i.e., to duty (her marriage-vows), or to 'me'.

A woman's faith hath robbed thy fame of triumph.

Oxf. Sirrah, leave off your juggling, and tie up
    The devil that ranges in your tongue.

Urs.   Thus witches,
    Possessed, even to their deaths deluded, say   105
    They have been wolves and dogs and sailed in egg-shells
    Over the sea and rid on fiery dragons,
    Passed in the air more than a thousand miles
    All in a night; the enemy of mankind
    Is powerful but false, and falsehood confident.   110

Oxf. Remember, lady, who you are; come from
    That impudent impostor.

Kath.   You abuse us:
    For when the holy churchman joined our hands,
    Our vows were real then; the ceremony
    Was not in apparition, but in act.   115
    Be what these people term thee, I am certain
    Thou art my husband, no divorce in heaven
    Has been sued out between us; 'tis injustice
    For any earthly power to divide us;
    Or we will live or let us die together.   120
    There is a cruel mercy.

War.   Spite of tyranny,
    We reign in our affections, blessed woman!
    Read in my destiny the wrack of honour;
    Point out, in my contempt of death, to memory
    Some miserable happiness: since herein,   125

---

105. to] *Mitford conj. (1811)*, G; *not in* Q.   110. falsehood] Q; false-
hood's G.

104–10.] The passage is dependent upon R. Scot's *Discoverie of Witchcraft* (1584); see L. Babb in *Modern Language Notes*, LI (1936), and Introduction, pp. lxxvi–lxxvii.

113.] See note on II. iii. 86–90.

115. *apparition*] semblance, sham; cf. IV. iii. 13.

act] accomplished fact (*O.E.D.*, 2).

118. *sued out*] To *sue out* is to make application before a court for a legal
process: see *O.E.D.*, 12.

121. *There . . . mercy*] i.e., it would be merciful to kill me along with him.

P

Even when I fell, I stood enthroned a monarch
Of one chaste wife's troth pure and uncorrupted.
Fair angel of perfection, immortality
Shall raise thy name up to an adoration,
Court every rich opinion of true merit,   130
And saint it in the calendar of virtue,
When I am turned into the self-same dust
Of which I was first formed.

Oxf.   The lord ambassador,
Huntly your father, madam, should a' look on
Your strange subjection in a gaze so public,   135
Would blush on your behalf, and wish his country
Unleft for entertainment to such sorrow.

Kath. Why art thou angry, Oxford? I must be
More peremptory in my duty. Sir,
Impute it not unto immodesty   140
That I presume to press you to a legacy
Before we part for ever.

War.   Let it be, then,
My heart, the rich remains of all my fortunes.

Kath. Confirm it with a kiss, pray.

War.   O, with that
I wish to breathe my last! Upon thy lips,   145
Those equal twins of comeliness, I seal
The testament of honourable vows.   [*Kisses her.*]
Whoever be that man that shall unkiss

---

145. last!] *W* (last:); last *Q*.   147. S.D.] *G; not in Q.*

130.] Win favour of every rich estimate of true worth, i.e., please the best judges.

131. *saint it*] i.e., enrol her name as that of a saint: cf. Brome's *Novella* (1632), IV. i: 'Lovers shall saint thee; and this day shall be / For ever callender'd to Love and thee'.

136–7. *his . . . entertainment to*] that he had not left his country in order to experience.

139. *peremptory*] resolute (*O.E.D.*, 4).

141. *to*] for, with a view to; see Abbott § 186.

148. *unkiss*] cancel with another kiss; cf. *Richard II*, v. i. 74; the parting-scene between Isabel and Richard slightly influences Ford's scene.

This sacred print next, may he prove more thrifty
In this world's just applause, not more desertful.   150
Kath. By this sweet pledge of both our souls, I swear
To die a faithful widow to thy bed—
Not to be forced or won. O, never, never!

Enter SURREY, DAUBENEY, HUNTLY, *and* CRAWFORD.

Dau. Free the condemnèd person, quickly free him.
What has a' yet confessed?
Urs.   Nothing to purpose;   155
But still a' will be king.
Sur.   Prepare your journey
To a new kingdom, then. Unhappy madam,
Wilfully foolish! See, my lord ambassador,
Your lady daughter will not leave the counterfeit
In this disgrace of fate.
Hunt.   I never pointed   160
Thy marriage, girl, but yet, being marrièd,
Enjoy thy duty to a husband freely.
The griefs are mine. I glory in thy constancy;
And must not say I wish that I had missed
Some partage in these trials of a patience.   165
Kath. You will forgive me, noble sir?
Hunt.   Yes, yes;
In every duty of a wife and daughter
I dare not disavow thee. To your husband—

157. then. Unhappy madam] *W;* then, (vnhappie Madam) *Q;* then,—unhappy madman *G.*

---

149. *thrifty*] thriving; cf. III. ii. 186.

157.] I restore Weber's reading, which is Q's, except that the second bracket got misplaced in Q after *Madam* instead of after *foolish.* Surrey exclaims when he sees Katherine's persistence, then turns to Huntly to expostulate.

160. *disgrace of fate*] disfavour of fate; cf. 'disgrace of fortune' (*O.E.D.,* *s.v.* disgrace 2).

pointed] appointed, prescribed.

165. *partage*] share; cf. III. iii. 14.

168. *disavow*] disown, repudiate (*O.E.D.,* I).

For such you are, sir,—I impart a farewell
Of manly pity; what your life has passed through,   170
The dangers of your end will make apparent.
And I can add, for comfort to your sufferance,
No cordial but the wonder of your frailty,
Which keeps so firm a station. We are parted.

War. We are. A crown of peace renew thy age,   175
Most honourable Huntly. Worthy Crawford,
We may embrace; I never thought thee injury.

Craw. Nor was I ever guilty of neglect
Which might procure such thought. I take my leave, sir.

War. To you, lord Dalyell—what? Accept a sigh,   180
'Tis hearty and in earnest.

Dal.   I want utterance:
My silence is my farewell.

Kath.   Oh—Oh—

Jane.   Sweet madam,
What do you mean? My lord, your hand.

Dal.   Dear lady,
Be pleased that I may wait 'ee to your lodging.

> *Exit* KATHERINE, [*supported by*] DALYELL [*and*] JANE.

Enter Sheriff *and* Officers [*with*] SKELTON, ASTLEY, HERON *and*
> JOHN A-WATER, *with halters about their necks.*

Oxf. Look 'ee; behold your followers, appointed   185
To wait on 'ee in death.

---

175. are . . . renew] *G;* are a crowne of peace, renew *Q;* wear a crown of
peace. Renew *W.*   176. Crawford,] *Crawford? Q.*   184.1.] *G (subs.);*
Exeunt Daliell, Katherine, Iane Q.   184.2. SKELTON] Sketon *Q.*   184.3.
JOHN A-WATER] Mayor *Q.*

---

172. *sufferance*] suffering.
173–4. *but . . . station*] i.e., except amazement that you, a mere frail
mortal, can make so firm a stand; *your frailty* is the abstract-for-personal
substitution so frequent in the play, and implies only that Warbeck has the
'frailty' pertaining to all men.
177. *thought . . . injury*] intended you any harm.
185–6.] In history, only a-Water and his son were executed with Warbeck.

War.   Why, peers of England,
    We'll lead 'em on courageously. I read
    A triumph over tyranny upon
    Their several foreheads. Faint not in the moment
    Of victory! Our ends, and Warwick's head,   190
    Innocent Warwick's head—for we are prologue
    But to his tragedy—conclude the wonder
    Of Henry's fears; and then the glorious race
    Of fourteen kings, Plantagenets, determines
    In this last issue male; heaven be obeyed.   195
    Impoverish time of its amazement, friends,
    And we will prove as trusty in our payments
    As prodigal to nature in our debts.
    Death? pish, 'tis but a sound, a name of air,
    A minute's storm, or not so much; to tumble   200
    From bed to bed, be massacred alive
    By some physicians for a month or two,
    In hope of freedom from a fever's torments,
    Might stagger manhood; here, the pain is passed
    Ere sensibly 'tis felt. Be men of spirit,   205
    Spurn coward passion! So illustrious mention
    Shall blaze our names, and style us Kings o'er Death.

---

194. kings, Plantagenets] *G; Kings* PLANTAGINETTS *Q.*   207. Kings o'er
Death] KINGS O'RE DEATH *Q.*

---

191. *Innocent . . . head*] See note on ll. 13–19 above; the sources imply
that Warwick was also *Innocent* in the sense of 'imbecile', because of his
long imprisonment.
    191–2. *prologue . . . tragedy*] See note on v. ii. 68–9.
    193–5.] echoes Bacon's 'this was also the end . . . of the line male of the
Plantagenets, which had flourished . . . from the time of the famous King
. . . Henry the second' (p. 179).
    194. *determines*] terminates.
    196–8.] The general sentiment of ll. 197–8 is 'we will faithfully pay the
great debt [of life] which we owe to nature'; but the meaning of l. 196 may
be: 'Make the times to come poor in their power of amazement by exhausting that power now by our conduct'.
    201. *massacred*] mutilated, mangled (*O.E.D.*, 3).
    205. *sensibly*] acutely (*O.E.D.*, 2).
    207. *blaze*] proclaim (*O.E.D., s.v.* blaze v^2 2).

Dau. Away—impostor beyond precedent.
　　No chronicle records his fellow.
　　　　　　　　Exeunt [Sheriff], *all* Officers *and Prisoners.*
Hunt.　　　　　　　　　　I have
　　Not thoughts left; 'tis sufficient in such cases　　　　　210
　　Just laws ought to proceed.

　　　　　Enter King HENRY, DURHAM, *and* HIALAS.

Hen.　　　　　　　　　We are resolved.
　　Your business, noble lords, shall find success
　　Such as your king importunes.
Hunt.　　　　　　　　　You are gracious.
Hen. Perkin, we are informed, is armed to die;
　　In that we'll honour him. Our lords shall follow　　　215
　　To see the execution; and from hence
　　We gather this fit use: that public states,
　　As our particular bodies, taste most good
　　In health, when purgèd of corrupted blood.　　*Exeunt omnes.*

FINIS.

218. As] "As *Q.*　　219. In] "In *Q.*

---

212. *success*] a result.
217. *use*] moral benefit (*O.E.D.*, 16).
218. *taste*] experience.

Epilogue

Here has appeared, though in a several fashion,
The threats of majesty, the strength of passion,
Hopes of an empire, change of fortunes; all
What can to theatres of greatness fall,
Proving their weak foundations. Who will please,   5
Amongst such several sights, to censure these
No births abortive, nor a bastard brood—
Shame to a parentage or fosterhood—
May warrant by their loves all just excuses,
And often find a welcome to the muses.   10

FINIS.

1. *several*] suitable for each (*O.E.D.*, 8 b).

3–4. *all . . . fall*] all which (for *What* see Abbott § 252) belong to the scenes where great events of state are acted out. *theatres of greatness* is a metaphor for 'states' or 'kingdoms', and it is they that have 'weak foundations'; see note on v. ii. 68–9.

6. *censure*] judge.

9.] By their kindness may provide justification for all the excuses we may reasonably offer.

10. *to*] to the company of.

Extracts from Thomas Gainsford's *True and Wonderfull History of Perkin Warbeck*

Note

Gainsford's book was first published in 1618 and reprinted in 1809 in a volume of the *Harleian Miscellany*. It is this very inaccurate reprint that Miss Struble prints in the Appendix to her edition of the play. Nearly half Gainsford's book is occupied with a long account of Lambert Simnel's enterprise and with accounts of the Duchess of Burgundy and of Warbeck's early days in Ireland (see Biographical Index). The extracts that follow comprise most of the rest of the work, and are printed from photographs of the copy in the Durham University Library (Routh Collection). Long 's' has been modernized, and contractions expanded. Obvious misprints have been corrected, and a few glosses have been inserted in square brackets.

Captain Thomas Gainsford (d. 1624) served in Ireland, to which there are several allusions in his writings. He was a voluminous journalist and 'gazette-maker', and is referred to in the latter capacity in Jonson's *Staple of News* (1626), Fletcher's *Fair Maid of the Inn* (1625/6), Shirley's *The School of Compliment* (1624/5), and Jonson's masque *Neptune's Triumph* (1624). Amongst his works is *A Vision and Discourse of Henry VII concerning the Unity of Great Britain*. See *D.N.B.*, H.C. Hart in *Notes and Queries*, 10th ser., II (1904), 184–5, *Ben Jonson*, ed. Herford and Simpson, II. 173–5, VII. 691, X. 265, 667, *Works of John Webster*, ed. Lucas, IV. 204, 229, Jean Robertson, *The Art of Letter Writing* (Liverpool, 1942), pp. 39–42, J. J. O'Connor in *Modern Language Notes*, LXX (1955), 566–8.

CONTENTS

Introductory: Stanley's Conspiracy

A. *Warbeck in Scotland, 1495–6:*
  His Arrival and Reception by King James IV
  Warbeck and Lady Katherine Gordon
  The Scots invade England

B. *The first Cornish Rising, 1497*

C. *Affairs in Scotland and Northumberland:*
  Norham and English Counter-measures
  Peace between Scotland and England
  King James dismisses Warbeck

D. *Warbeck's Invasion of England:*
  The Assaults upon Exeter and Taunton
  Warbeck's Flight: Katherine's and Warbeck's Capture

E. *Events of Warbeck's Last Years:*
  His Confession, 1498
  His Last Enterprise, 1499

Introductory: Stanley's Conspiracy

[I] The King thus turmoiled euery way, repaired for diuers reasons to the Tower of *London*, whither shortly after came *Sir Robert Clifford* vnto him, partly trusting to the Kings promise, partly mistrusting his owne company and *Perkins* weakenesse: But the chiefest polecie of his resiance [residence] in the Tower was to secure himselfe, and lay hold of all others suspected, or accused in this conspiracy, who thither resorting to the Councell, might with ease and without any tumult be committed to prison, as it presently fell out: For after the King had admitted Sir *Robert*, and insinuated with him in excellent positions of Diuinity, and morality by way of disceptation [discussion], vrging the loue and fauour of his Prince in his true obedience and reconciliation, he not only related the manner of *Perkins* proceedings, but on his knees with teares in his eies discouered the matter to be weake and impossible, if it had not factious supportation from some of powerfull houses of *England*, and very neere his Maiesties person, whereof though many were punished, and the rest dissipated and diuided: Yet Sir *William Stanley* remained vnsuspected, and his heart trembled to accuse him: But when the King heard Sir *William Stanley* named, he started back amazed and in a manner confounded, that Sir *Robert* was affraid he had done him more harme in the relation, then good in the detection.

At last he burst out, what my bosome friend? my Councellor? my *Chamberlaine*? then I see there is no trust in men, nor as the *Psalmist* saith confidence in *Princes*: For as we shal not want instruments to goe forward with what enterprise we please, as *Dauid* had his *Ioab*: so shall we not lack enemies [IIᵛ] let them be neuer so carefull and desirous to fauour the least deseruer, but I may well now cry out, *Heu cadit in quenquam tantum scelus!* and with the kingly Prophet exclaime, It was not mine enemies abroad, but my companions, and such as eate at my table betraied me: What Sir *William Stanley*? he hath the gouernment of my Chamber, the charge and controlment of all that are next my person, the loue and fauour of our Court, and the very keyes of our treasurie. He made me a conquerour in the field, and by his hand I scourged tyrannie out of his Throne, therefore it is impossible, and I cannot belieue it. But when a second reply brought him to the sight of fairer particulars, and that he saw the smoake, though it was but a smother, came from some fire, he quickly recollected his spirits, and with these verses of *Euripides*, set himselfe downe at the table of preuention and reposednesse:

Ex amicis autem alios quidem non certos video amicos
Qui vero sunt rectè, impotentes sunt vt iuuent:
Talis res est hominibus ipsa infœlicitas,
Qua nullus vnquam (quicunque vel mediocriter amicus mihi)
Assequatur amicorum examen certissimum, ——*

The same night vpon better consideration my Lord *Chamberlaine* was restrained from his liberty within the quadrant Tower, and confined to his owne Chamber for a season: but when the crime was openly prooued, and the Councell had as it were with a charming hand of *Hecate* turned his inside outward, and found all his excuses to consist in distinctions, and his reasons of defence manifest astipulations [confirmations] of the matter, he grew out of all patience, and knew not what to say, or to doe: For one way like an Noble Prince commiserating his subjects, he feared lest his brother Lord *Thomas Stanley* the life of his first roialty, as a man should say take it grieuously. Another way he misdoubted, lest in remitting the fault, some other might abuse his lenity and mercy, and be the bolder to runne forward in the dangerous courses of further treasons: At last by the aduise of his Councell, and general vouge [approbation] of the Court, seuerity (considering the perill [I2] of those daies) tooke place, and mercy was put backe: so that after a solemne arraignment, he had iudgement to dye, and accordingly was brought on the 16. of *February* to Tower-hill, and had his head struck off.

The principall point of his enditement consisted in this, that Sir

* *Eurip. Herc. furens.* [Gainsford's note.]

William Stanley sware and affirmed, that he would neuer fight nor beare Armor against the yong man *Peter Warbeck*, if he knew of a truth that he was the indubitate sonne of *Edward* the fourth, whereupon arose a coniecturall proofe, that he bare no good will to King *Henry*.

A. Warbeck in Scotland, *1495–6*

HIS ARRIVAL AND RECEPTION BY KING JAMES IV

[K3] . . . they thought it more meete and expedient to passe into *Scotland*: *Gens semper inuisa Britannis*, and there make triall of a new friendship, casting vp a forward account of their happinesse, in this manner: First they were assured of the naturall and generall hatred betweene the Nations, which vpon very small occasions and probable opportunite, would burst out into flames of despight. Next, they proiected, that the nature of the businesse would allure them to his assistance, vpon hope of vaine-glory, and a reputation of so charitable a worke, as to help a Prince in distresse. Thirdly, they relied on this hope, that if no other cause would be inductiue to his supportation, yet the desire of spoile would quickly incite them to warre against so plentifull a Country. Fourthly, they perswaded themselues, that the *Scots* had a good opinion of the house of *Yorke* euer since the cruelty of the Lord *Clifford* against *Rutland*, for which they vtterly abandoned *Henry* the sixt and the Queene. And last of all, they concluded to promise them the surrendring of *Barwick*, and to enlarge their territories if he preuailed by their assistance, which was a sure motiue to draw them into any action whatsoeuer: whereupon he departed from *Corck* and landed on the West of *Scotland*, from whence he prepared himselfe to go to the King with some solemnitie, wherein his [K3ᵛ] instructions preuailed with his fortune, because for the most part the masse of people are guided by showes and ceremonies, rather then matter of substance and truth, and so he trauelled to *Edinbourgh*, whose Citizens vnaccustomed to such glorious showes, began already to commiserate his fortune and distresse: yea, the King himselfe assembled his Lords and Courtiers, as their manner then was to entertaine him and giue him audience; which when *Perkin* percieued to fall out to his good liking and hearts desire, he thus framed his speech vnto him, or if you will reduced his instructions to a manner of attracting Oratory.

*M*Ost mighty and renouned King:

Iudicis officium est vt res, ita tempora rerum quærere———

and therefore I come not to you altogether like a cast away or ban-querout, to recouer my estate by a cosening agreement with my creditours for a trifle, when there may be sufficient to pay the prin-cipall: nor like a run-away from a hard-hearted Master: or if you will, to take my liberty the better, to cast of the yoake of honest and ciuill obedience, where there is a duty and necessity of seruice im-posed: but as a stranger subiect to shipwrack, and the hassardous endurances of a tempest; I am enforced to your refuge, as much enduced with your Princely delight in deeds of charitie and hospi-tality, as my owne wants or recouery: I might adde your famous actions, renowne, and heroicke commiseration of a dis-esteemed Prince, but *Pudor est vlterior a loqui:* And although I may confesse my selfe to resemble the man in the Gospell that fell amongst theeues, whom diuers looking vpon passed by without reliefe: yet, at last he found one *Samaritan* to pay the cost and defray the charges of the Surgerie: so haue I done a worthy aunt, friend, and noble kins-woman to acknowledge her afflicted Nephew, who hath helped me accordingly: so that I make no question, that from the example of a woman your Princely commiserati[K4]on and powerful coadiute-ment shall open their larger embraces, considering that you aboue all other Princes haue beene made acquainted with the distractions of our family, and from time to time know how the house of *Yorke* hath beene dilacerated, and torne in peeces by the cruell hand of Tyrants and home-bred Wolues, which whether it were the permission of God or the secrets of his diuine Iustice; I will not now dispute vpon: Only, I must be bold to say, that when my father obtained the Crowne, and reuenged his fathers wrongs and death, there were signes of Gods fauour and assistance in the faire issue prepared, and sweet fruit of such a flourishing tree, namely two sonnes and fiue daughters, who were simply committed to the tutelage and protector-ship of an vnnaturall Vncle, who proued a tyrant and destroier of our blood and progeny, so that I may well cry out as *Ariadne* to *Theseus:*

Mitius inueni, quam te, genus omne ferarum:

Notwithstanding, *Most mighty King*, how euer my Princely Brother miscarried, as swallowed vp in the iawes of cruelty and slaughter, It should seeme the murtherers were affrighted at that they had done already, and desisted from a full prosecution of the Tyrants com-mand, or confounded with compunction of spirit spared me, and secretly conueied me out of the hands of such an homicide and blood sucker (for so I hope without offence I may rightly tearme him) and although by this meanes and the supportation of high borne *Bucking-ham* he obtained the Diadem: yet did God follow him with the swift-est pace of wrath and anger, and at last I must needs say, scourged

him with rods of vengeance indeed; for he presently lost his sonne,
and his friend and coadiutor lost himselfe: what afterwards chanced
vnto me, as my strange deliuerance, my bringing vp in *Tornay* vnder
certaine supposed parents of honest reputation, my trauailes into
forraine Countries, my aduentures abroad, my endurances at home,
with such like; it would be to tedious to relate, and therefore I desist
to put you now to further wonder and amasement at the same, because I haue them as it [K4ᵛ] were registred in a scedule, which at
your Princely pleasure you may ouer-looke, with the Duches and
Councels of *Burgundies* hand, to confirme the same: so that I confesse
when the King of *France* sent for me out of *Ireland*, I was in a manner
secure of my estate, and thought vpon no further assurance, then his
gratious apprehension of my indubitate claime. But it should seeme
(most gratious King) that you are reserued for the glory of this businesse, and euerlasting memory of so remarkeable an action, wherein
I submit my selfe, ships, and people to your guidance and direction,
Oh doe not then annihilate my confidence, nor reiect my demands.
For next to the high controuler of mens actions, I haue put my selfe
vnder the shadow of your supportation, and altogether rely on the
vnity of your willingnesse and power, to beare me through the
difficulties of this passage.

When he had made an end and giuen them cause of some amasement at his yeares and tendernesse of experience to deliuer yet his
minde so freely, and with some illustration of words and readines of
gesture, the King without any further scruple or diffidence cheered
him, telling him plainly he would assist him, and what-euer he was,
or intended to be, he should not repent him of his comming thither,
& so concluding with a speech of *Medea* to *Iason:*

Hinc amor, hinc timor est, ipsum timor auget amorem:

he gaue order for his entertainment accordingly, whereby he had
time with his wearied people to repose himselfe, and the King, occasion to thinke of many matters: yet rather for custome then to be
diuerted from his resolutions, he called his Councell and disputed
the matter with them; they again, (as it happened to *Rheoboam*, and
shall be with all the Princes in the World) grew to contradiction; and
deuided themseelues, some standing for their Countrie, some for
their priuate affection, some to please the Prince, and some to enioy
a good opinion of polecie, and wisedome. The grauer sort and
greatest experience disannulled all the former intimation of the
Prince, with the impossibility of the busi[L]nesse, as if he were but
a bare assumer of titles indeed. The quieter sort and such as had
smarted with the dissentions betweene *England* and *Scotland* dis-

claimed any further warre, and were weary with that which had passed. The yonger sort apprehended it, as a worthy enterprise, and though it had but colour of commiseration, yet considering he was befriended from the Emperour, King of the Romains, and the whole state of the Low-Countries, it could not choose but help them with many friends. There was another sort, who confessing the pouerty of their Countrie, concluded, that by this meanes by forraging, spoiling and getting good booties in *England*, much wealth might inrich them without losse or hindrance of their owne, and so cared not how the warre began, nor how long it continued. The last sort consisted of such, who because they would haue their credit enlarged from an opinion of States-men, and high reaching capacities, argued (as we say) on both sides, *pro & contra*, and from a kind of Enthymema raised profit and emolument to the Kingdome out of their sophistry: That if the Duke were assisted and preuailed, *Scotland* was sure to confirme their owne conditions: If he were countenanced, though not preuailing, the King of *England* would accord to any offers or demands, rather then King *Ieames* should take part with his aduersarie and so strange a competitor.

Whereupon it was resolued, that without further diffidence, or drawing the Duches of *Burgundies* businesse in question, the King should entertaine the Prince, who presently honored him accordingly, and caused him to be proclaimed the Duke of *Yorke*, shewing him all the fauours the Countrie could afford, and affording him such entertainement, as they imagined was both befitting his person and condition: He againe, as if that *spes bona dat vires* cheered himselfe, and assumed a new kind of behauiour, both tempered with grauity, and yet commended for cheerefull and well becomming: so that by the way of solace and inuitation to pleasure and delight, he hauked and hunted, yea, the Ladies of the Country graced the Court, and came [L^v] with all conueniencie and befitting their estates to the Citie. For vnderstanding so great a Prince; in possibilitie to be one of the mightiest Kings of Europe; not full eighteene yeares of age, yong, wise, and in the compleate strength of beauty, was resident amongst them, they conceiued matters beyond the Moone, and thought themselues happy if he would fancy or fasten vpon any of them. What should I say, although with the Poet:

Tarda solet magnis rebus inesse fides:

WARBECK AND LADY KATHERINE GORDON

Yet heere was no mistrust, nor any way giuen to feare and displeasure, but as the time, businesse, and place afforded, shewes, masques, and sundry deuises inuited him to his contentment, and the present ouercomming all pensiuenesse: so he courted with some, danced with others, iested with the rest, and was acceptable to all, till at last (the King giuing way to the motion) he fancied the Lady *Katherine Gourdon* daughter to *Alexander* Earle of *Huntlie* nigh kins-woman to the Crowne: and because she should not thinke him barren of education, nor heart bound to his ambitious designes, he tooke an opportunitie thus to discouer his loue vnto her, and good opinion of her.

Lady (said he) and the first of Ladies, that euer vsurped my libertie, or taught my tongue to pronounce the accent of affection or liking, If I proceed not so passionate as your sex expects, or you may imagin is the custome of Courtiers, I pray you impute it to the multiplicity of my businesse and greatnes of my affaires: besides, it is not seemly with Princes to betray their high spirits into the hands of deceit and ouerworking fancy; yea, foppishnes either of words, or gesture: yet, concerning your person, I can say with *Paris* to *Helena,*

Si tu Venisses pariter certamen in illud,
in dubium Veneris Palma futura fuit: *

and touching my good will; If I liue, I will make you as great in the World as my selfe, and desire no more but that you keep you within the limits of loue and obedience, that our children may be our owne, and the Common-wealth reioice they bee not mocked or deceiued with extraneall en[L2]heritors: What I am, you now see, and their is no boasting in distresse: what I may be, I must put it to the triall and submit to the diuine prouidence: If you dare now aduenture on the aduersity, I sweare to make you partaker of the prosperity; yea, lay my Crowne at your feet, that you shall play with me as *Apame* did with *Darius,* to command and I obey: Take me now then into your embraces, and I will adore and reuerence your vertues, as you com-miserate my misfortunes: Oh giue me leaue to say no more, lest I be transported to vndecencies; be now conformable, and let me be the seruant of your desires, and you shall be hereafter the Mistris of my performances; If I preuaile, let this kisse seale vp the contract, and this kisse be a witnesse to the endentures, and this kisse, because one witnesse is not sufficient, consummate the assurance, and so with a kind of reuerence, and fashionable gesture, after he had kist her thrise, he tooke her in both his hands crosse-wise, & gazed vpon her with a kind of putting her from him and pulling her to him, and so againe and againe rekissed her, and set her in her place with a prety manner of enforcement.

The yong Lady pleased as well with the complement of his be-hauiour, as the matter in hand (which was the hope of one of the

* *Ouid. Epist. Helena Paridi.* [Gainsford's note.]

greatest Diadems in the World) whether as louers, who in a simpathy of liking, applauding any thing from their *amorosos*, seemed pleased with the very accent of his voice, and variety of the Court-ship: or vnaccustomed to such wooers, she remained glad of the opportunity: or taught before-hand what to doe, she resolued to cast away all peeuishnesse and nicety: or indeed rauished with the thing proposed, she was loath to be silent, considering she was pleased, and could not be displeased, considering he had begun so kindely with her, and therefore answered him with a pretty blushing modesty, to this effect.

My Lord, If I should act a true womans part, I might play the hypocrite in standing a loofe off from that I most desire, and cry out with *Ariadne* against *Theseus*:

Non ego sum titulis surripienda tuis:

[L2ᵛ] whereupon some resemble vs to lapwings, that make a great eiulation [ululation] farthest from their nests: But I meane not to deale so with you, but come as neere as I can in my answere to that which consorteth with reason and probabilitie: If I were then absolutly at my owne disposing, I would thanke you more then I doe, and thinke you for your gentlenesse and faire demeanour worthy of any creature, or thing you could desire. As for your disclaiming deceitfull words and flattering Oratory concerning our beautie, comelinesse, vertues, and such like baits to draw vs into the net of selfe-loue, and amasement: I like it the better, and wish that all women were of my minde to marry vpon faire and reasonable conditions, and not be hurried away sometimes to their ouerthrowes with the violence of passion and affection, which is the best excuse they can make for their folly, yea many times simplicity. But you see I am the Fathers daughter, and the Kings cosin, so that I will in no sort preferre my owne will before their directions, and disposing of me: If then it pleaseth them to hazzard me, or (as you please) to bestow me in this sort, I shall be proud to call you mine, and glad if you vouchsafe to esteeme me yours: Lay then your foundation on them, and you shall see the frame of the building erected to your owne liking: For belieue it, such *Wardes* as my selfe, may well be resembled to delicate plants in rich grounds which either grow too rancke and out of order for want of pruning and looking to: or thriue not in their situation for lack of refreshing and manuring, all wich is reformed by the discretion of a skilfull gardner and aduised ouerseer: Therefore noble Sir repaire I say to the Master of the family, leaue is light & know their pleasures for your admission into this Nursery, and then shall I be glad to be a flower of your owne choise, whether it be for profit, pleasure, or ex-ornation [embellishment].

What need more words? the mariage was consummated, and

Q

poore *Perkin* transported in his owne contemplation for ioy, that if
he proceeded no further, his fortune had conduced him to such a
harbour, kissing the ground, which he [L3] trode vpon, and swearing,
the verie place was the seat of his Genius:

Ipse locus misero ferre volebat opem:

THE SCOTS INVADE ENGLAND

But when he more and more perceiued, that the Scots (like a peece of
wax) were rolled together by his warming hand, and fashioned to
what forme hee pleased, hee then made no question to hammer out
his designes on the anuile of preuailing, to their euerlasting glory,
and his establishment: yet heerein hee went beyond himselfe, and
deceiued both them and himselfe, by warranting powerfull aydes in
his assistance, from all the parts of the Realme, as soone as he should
set footing in England: notwithstanding, they prepared all things for
an inuasion, and euery man was ready to please the King and pleasure
the Prince: yea, they were so forward, that in hope of gaine, spoile,
victory, renowne, and reuenge, they cared not whether the Dukes
title were good or no, and so with a well appoynted army and sufficient forces, they marched towards the confines and borders of the
North. But the King (out of discretion) loth to make more haste then
good speed, and vnderstanding policy, coniecturing that the English,
by reason of *Perkins* being in Scotland, might alwaies haue an army
in readinesse, or raise sudden troops to lie in Ambuscado in the
borders, by way of preuention: sent forth diuers Stradiots and
Scowtmasters [horsemen and spies], to discouer the Countrey, and
the behauiour of the English, who returned with full assurance of the
coasts cleerenesse, and (for any thing they saw) they might make both
incursions and excursions at their pleasure: which although in some
cases made the King the rather to wonder, as if England were secure
from any idle proiect, or indeede scorned *Perkins* title and claime:
yet because it was generally accepted for good newes, he would not
be a contrary amongst so many: but made the more haste, and so with
fire and sword, as if hee did *arma virumque canere*, entred Northumberland, proclaiming the title of the Duke of Yorke, by the name of
Richard the fourth, and promising both pardon and preferment to all
such, as would submit themselues to the yoke of [L3ᵛ] his obedience:
the deniall whereof was accompanied with such spoile, cruelty, and
insulting, that neuer before or since did they euer triumph ouer vs,
or prooued so tyrannous: so that I may well cry out, as the Poet doth
against *Scilla.*

Intrepidus tanti sedit securus ab alto
Spectator sceleris: miseri tot millia Vulgi

Non piguit iussisse mori: congesta recepit
Omnia Tyrrhenus Sullana cadauera gurges. *

Wherein questionlesse they had gone forward, but that they perceiued no ayde or succour to come from any parts of England to
restore this titular Duke. Besides, the souldiers (full of spoile and
bloud) would goe no further, till they had sent their presents to their
wiues and children, or returned themselues to gratifie one another,
after such a victory: but in truth the King resoluing it would bee
reuenged, determined rather to retire with this assured victory, then
to tarry the nuncupatiue [so-called] Dukes vnsure and vncertaine
proceedings, and so reculed into Scotland againe.

   Some remember, that at this time (though it was but a very simple
policy) *Perkin* vsed a certaine kind of ridiculous mercy and foolish
compassion toward the English people, as though that rather mooued
the Scots to the retreat, then any thing else: whereupon, lest his
cozening and illusion should bee discouered, by reason so few resorted vnto him, he thus complained to the Scottish King, and (as it
were) exclaimed of himselfe. O wretch and hard-hearted man that I
am, thus remorselesse to forage my natiue countrey, and purchase
mine enheritance with such effusion of bloud, cruelty and slaughter.
For now I see, ere this businesse can be brought to any good passe,
houses must bee fired, countries depopulated, women rauished,
virgins defloured, infants slaine, the aged murthered, the goods
rifled, and the whole Kingdome subiect to deuastation, which (to my
greefe of soule) I must needes deplore. Therefore, great King, I request you from henceforth, doe not afflict my people, nor deforme
my country, in such a lamentable and remorselesse a manner. For
questionlesse, I shall neuer endure it with a [L4] peaceable soule and
conscience, and had (in a manner) rather lose my part and interest
therein, then purchase it with such losse and excruciation of minde,
especially effusion of bloud and barbarous enforcement.

   Surely, replied the King of Scots halfe angry, and more than halfe
mistrusting his dissembling, yea fully resolued on his weaknesse and
pusillanimity:

           ————fletus quid fundis inanes ?
           Nec te sponte tua sceleri parere fateris ?
           *Vsque adeo ne times, quem tu facis ipse timendum ?***

Me thinkes your care is rather ridiculous then superfluous, to bee
thus dolent for another mans possessions: yea, I see not, but your
claime is so remote and disanulled, that it must be an Herculean

---

* *Lucan. lib. 2.* [Gainsford's note.]
** *Lucan. lib. 3.* [Gainsford's note.]

labour to settle you in any of their cities and petty prouinces. But for calling England your land and Realme, and the Inhabitants your people and subiects, it is as wonderfull to me, as displeasing to your selfe, that in all this time, neither Gentleman, nor man of worth hath extended a daring hand, or (if you will) commisserable arme of assistance toward you: nay, though the warre was begun in your name, for your sake, and within your Realme, of which you say you are the indubitate heire, and inuited to the same by your owne people and faction.

Alas, replied the Prince, I confesse as much as you say: but if it will please you to acknowledge the truth, the falling backe of the King of France, yea, when I was in the speed of my iourney, the failing of many promises to mine aunt the Duches of Burgundy, and the defect and protraction of my businesse, by the losse of an hundred Lords & Knights, some in their liberties, some in their liues, some from their owne good motiues and intents, and all from their true hearts and endeauours, by the Kings forces and vigilant eye ouer them, hath not onely deceiued my expectation; but (in a manner) peruerted my fortune. Besides, you know with what difficulty the nature of aduersity and men in distresse, attaine vnto any credit and estimation: so that wee and you both haue had wofull experience of many great [L4ᵛ] Princes deposed from their thrones, and left friendlesse, succourlesse, and quite destitute of releefe in the hands of their enemies: and therefore, as mischeefe and misery are of mine olde acquaintance, so am I not now vnprepared to entertaine the same, but must submit to the calamity, and attend the appointment of the highest God, concerning my lowest deiection, and so I con-clude with an ancient saying of *Euripides:*

> ——*Turbam enim recipere me puduit,*
> *Vt oculis viderent hunc meum turpem habitum*
> *Occultans præ pudore meum infortunium: quando enim vir*
> *Habuerit malê magnus, in ineptias*
> *Cædit deteriores, eo qui fuit dudum infœlix.* *

Although this came roundly of, and sauoured somewhat better then the former: yet the King replied not at all, but was content with his first reproofe, being more fearefull euery day then other, that this intricate businesse would be a worke of wonder, and to fashion the lump of such deformity, to any handsome or substantiall proportion, must be dangerous and preiudiciall for euer to the Scottish crowne.

After the Nobles had been thus startled in Northumberland with the clamours of the people, and saw the Inhabitants flie euery way from the fury of the Scots, they fortified their holds, mustred their

* *Eurip. Helena.* [Gainsford's note.]

forces, followed the enemies, and certified the King of all this enterprize and inuasion, who not a little abashed at the same, as more fear-
ing the naturall subiect for starting out of the sphere of his allegeance,
then any forraine comet in the greatest radiance, and presages, he
presently tooke order for the repressing of such tumults and insurrec-
tions: but assured of the Scots retreat, and that they were returned
loden with spoiles and great riches, he resolued vpon another course,
hauing in the meane while so great occasions of displeasure against
Scotland, that all men either to please themselues, or animate the
King in his willing reuenges, cried out to armes, to armes, and this
was the eleuenth yeeres worke.

B. *The first Cornish Rising, 1497*

The twelfth yeere began with a Parliament, both for the [M] settling
the vncertaine affaires of the Kingdome, and the obtaining a subsidy,
or other disbursements of money for the furnishing an army into
Scotland, to which all the Nobility and Gentry opened willingly
their cofers, and cheerefully their hearts, exclaiming against their
immanity [enormity], and proclaiming their loyalty and endeauours,
to prosecute them with all reuenge, that durst so affright the Kingdome, and affront the peace and tranquility of the Commonwealth.
Of this army, was *Giles* Lord *Dawbney*, the Kings Chamberlaine,
made Lieutenant Generall, a man of no lesse wit then experience,
of no lesse experience then hardinesse, of no lesse hardinesse then
moderation and gouernment. But see the changes of human life, and
the mischeefes to which the best men and greatest Princes are subiect, as if the Poet were againe to cry out:

Heu non est quicquam fidum: neque certa fœlicitas:

As he was marching forward with his forces, a strange innouation
called him backe againe. For, as if Fortune meant to play the wanton
with *Perkin* on the one side, and bring him (as wee say) into a fooles
paradise, and misfortune on the other side try the Kings patience: A
new rebellion in the West, had like to haue beene as a heauy burthen
on his shoulders, and set in combustion the whole Commonwealth.
For when the Parliament was dissolued, and that Commissioners
were speedily sent to gather in the money, this *excandescens populus*,
to whom such taxes and impositions was a kinde of drawing bloud
from their very life veins, began to rebell, especially the Cornish men,
inhabiting the remotest parts of the Kingdome westward, who not
onely complained on their owne penurie and wants, as liuing in a
barren and sterile soile, ouercome with labour, watches and toyles in
the mineralls, and getting a poor maintenance out of the cauerns of

the earth, with fearefull endurances: but threatned the officers, deny-
ing the taxes, and began temerariously to speake of the King himselfe: yea, when there seemed by the Iustices & others in authority,
a dam to be cast vp against this fearefull inundation, they desisted
from wo[M^v]manish exclaimes, lamentings, and eiulations, and fall
inconsiderately to malicious calumniation, threatning the Councell,
and naming *Thomas Moorton* Archbishop of Canterbury, and S^r.
Reinold Brey, as principall directours & setters forward of these impositions against them, saying plainely, it was a shame, that a small
incursion of the Scots, which was not onely customary, but as soone
extinguished as kindled, should raise such exactions, and incite the
Kingdome to vnsufferable turmoiles, with a generall warre and
tumultuous hurliburly: to which things, when the Commissioners
would haue gently answered, and honestly maintained the Kings
purposes and prerogatiues, *Thomas Flamock* a Gentleman learned in
the Lawes, and *Michael Ioseph* a Black-smith, tooke vpon them the
defence of the Commons, threatning without further reasoning the
matter, both the receiuers, and all such, whom they imployed as inferiour officers vnder them.

By which occasion, according to that saying, *Res vehemens multi-
tudo, improbos cum habuerit præfectos:* he became a monstrous head to
these vnruly bodies, exhorting the people to arme themselues, and
not be afraid to follow them in this quarrell. For they intended neither
hurt to any creature, nor spoile to any place, but meerely a reforma-
tion of the disorder, and correction on such persons, as were the
authors of their greefe and vexation, and when any seemed to im-
pugne and reprooue these seditious and vnreasonable courses,
affirming plainely, that (from all examples and times) treasons and
commotions haue ended with lamentable effusion of bloud, both of
the authors themselues, and many innocents made accessaries,
through constraint and wicked instigation, they were called base
dastards, cowards, fooles, and louers of ease and surquedry [surfeit],
more then renown, and their countries honour and liberty: so that
what with shame of taunts and rebukes, and what with feare of the
losse of their liues and goods, they vnited themselues to this outragious company, and made vp a strong party well armed, and too
well enstructed: for the Captaines not only praised [M2] and extolled
the hardinesse of the people, but rewarded such as assisted and releeued the souldiers, whereby (after a generall muster of 40000.) they
came forward to Taunton, where they slew the Prouost of Perin,
principall Commissioner for the subsidy in those parts, and from
thence to Wells, intending to goe forward to London, where the
King was resident, and such Councellours as they maligned.

.   .   .   .   .

[M2ᵛ] When the King was aduertized of these troubles and ex-
orbitant attempts, which gathered like a clowd, threatning a tempest
round about him, and saw into what perplexity he was now detruded,
hauing warre on euery side, he compared himselfe to a man rising in
a darke night, and going into an vndrest roome, hitting his head
against that post, running against that table, meeting with his
shinnes such a stoole or forme, and staggering vp and downe against
one blocke or another: and so stood (for the time) amazed, not knowing what to say, what to do, or with whom to find fault, till with a
kind of sigh he vented out this saying of *Euripides*.

—— *Similes sumus nautis, qui*
Tempestatis cùm effugerint sæuam vim,
Prope terram appulerunt, deinde à terra
*Flaminibus pelluntur in pontum iterum.**

But to complaine of God or men, would rather aggrauate his greefe,
then procure his redresse, and therefore although he well knew that
Princes were the tennis-bals of fortune, [M3] and subiects of muta-
bilitie and alteration, whereas he must submit to the diuine prouidence: yet, he also vnderstood there was no lying still in this deplora-
tion without the ordinary practice of such remedies as God had
appointed in their seuerall workings, and therefore prepared his
Armies either to bring this disturbance to a quiet attonement, or
whip the Rebellion with the scourges of fire and sword: But when
againe he considered the Scots were his enemies, and must be suppressed; the Westerne Rebels were at his doores and must be re-
pugned: *France* was wauering, and must be looked vnto: *Flaunders*
threatning, and must be appeased: *Perkin Warbeck* lay at aduantage,
and must be watched; yea, ouer-watched as indeed the principall
fire-brand, that set all this on a blase, and in the midst of these hurli-
burlies came ouer Embassadours from the *French* King, who must
be answered; he grew somewhat perplexed againe, till shaking off all
the hindrances of his amasement, he fell to practise and orderly performances.

Whereupon he called his Councel together, & they without any
great difficulty determined the busines in this manner: To attend
vpon the Scots, *Thomas Howard* Earle of *Surrey*, a puissant and
politike Captain, prisoner at the ouerthrow of King *Rich*. the 3. and
within two yeares set at liberty, and after *Iohn* Lord *Dinham* made
high treasurer of *England*, was appointed to muster the forces of the
Countie Palatine of *Durham*, & the borders round about, & so attend
that seruice. To represse the Western Rebels, the Lord *Dawbney*
with his whole power prepared for *Scotland*, was recalled to march

* *Eurip. Heraclidae.* [Gainsford's note.]

against them wheresoeuer they encamped; to look vnto *France*; *Calice* and *Guisnes* with the Garisons were much augmented, and prouided for. To preuent *Flaunders*, the Nauy was prepared, & the Staples for the Merchants setled: To keep *Warbeck* from comming into *England* & ioining with the Rebels, the whole nobility combined themselues, especially the earle of *Essex*, & Lord *Montioy*; who came of purpose to *London* to offer their seruice to his Maiesty, & so all places were looked vnto with a vigilant eye, & manned with strength of soldiers: [M3ᵛ] and to answere the Embassadors of *Charles* the *French* King, he sent honourable persons to receiue them and con-ueigh them to *Douer*, and there a while to detaine them, till some of these tumults and rebellions were extinguished and suppressed, which indeed was so wisely and politikely handled, that none of the Embassadors were troubled so much as with the rumors of these commotions.

But see the horror of despight, and with what a contracted brow misfortune can looke vpon Kings themselues: so that a man may well say to this Rebellion, as *Ouid* did to *Cupido* in his first booke of *Elegies*:

> *Sunt tibi magna puer, nimiumque, potentia regna:*
> *Cur opus affectas ambitiose nouum*:

For, as these Rebels and Cornish men departed from *Wels*, they entertained for their chiefe Captaine *Iames Twichet* Lord *Audley*, whose countenance and authoritie in the Countrie strengthened them much. For, by this occasion they went without intermission to *Salsbury*, and so to *Winchester*, and from thence into *Kent*, hoping for further and further assistance; but they were deceiued in their expectation: For the Earle of *Kent*, *George* Lord *Aburgaueny*, *Iohn Brooke* Lord *Cobham*, Sir *Edward Poinings*, Sir *Richard Guilford*, Sir *Thomas Burchier*, Sir *Iohn Pechy*, *William Scot*, and many others with a well mustred army were not only ready to defend their Countrie from al mischiefe and destruction: but determined to offend them in their facinorous attempts, and preiudiciall intrusion, which loialtie somewhat rebated the forwardnesse of the Cornish-men, and they began to suspect themselues, being so farre from their Countrie, and remote from any supply. Notwithstanding, loth to dishearten their spirits with any depressing humor, they cast away all doubts, and presuming on their owne strength and forces, as also animated by their leaders and conductors, they were now asmuch exasperated against the Kentish-men for deceiuing their assistance, as against the King for vsurping their liberty: swearing reuenge against both: In which rage and heat of repining, they came as farre as *Black Heath* with[M4]in foure mile of *London*, and tooke a field in an arrogant ouer-daring manner on the top of an hill, supposing all things consortable to their arrogancy and deceiuable hopes, because as yet they passed and repassed without fighting, or strong encounters: But alas,

Blanditiæ Comites tibi erunt terrorque, furorque,

and they were abused with a vale of ignorance and couering of obstinacy: For the King disposed of his affaires with great policie and circumspection, not determining to giue them battaile, or exagitate them at all till he had them farre from their proper dwellings and flattering friends, till they were in despaire of reliefe and wearied with long and tedious iournies, till their treasure was spent, their vitaile [victuals] consumed and prouision failing, till their company dropped from them like rotten hangings on a moistned wall, and their whole designes and expectation quite disanulled; and then, when he imagined their soules vexed with the terror of a guiltie conscience, their fury asswaged with compunction and penitency, their spirits daunted with repentance and remorse, and all their army affrighted with madnesse and doubtfull extacies, would he set vpon them, and in some conuenient place circumuent and inuiron them to his owne best aduantage, and their irrecouerable damage and destruction.

As for the Citie of *London:* I cannot but remember and compare it vnto *Rome,* both when *Hannibal* passed the *Alpes* to threaten the Monarchy being yet farre off himselfe, and also *Marius* and *Silla* couered her fields with armed men, and trampled on the bosome of their Countrie with ambitious steps, and cruell feet of vsurpation: then spake the Poet in this manner,

——— *Quoties Romam fortuna lacessit,*
Hàc iter est bellis, gemitu sic quisque latenti,
Non ausus timuisse palam: Vox nulla dolori
Credita:———*

There was chaining the streetes, shutting vp the shops, making strong the gates, doubling the watches, hiding their treasure, cries, feares, terrors, and euery one more disturbed [M4ᵛ] for the losse of his priuat goods, then the encumbrances of the Common-wealth. Here was mustering of soldiers, watching all day in armor, staccadoing the riuer, filling the streets with companies of horse and foot, cutting down the Bridge, locking vp their dores, shutting the Gates, and what else named before, to be put in practise with aduantage of many peeces of ordnance both in Southwarke and the Suburbs, and the strength of the Tower which they knew was re-

* *Lucan. lib. 1.* [Gainsford's note.]

serued for the King himselfe. Notwithstanding, such was the instabilitie of the Citizens being a little disturbed from their quietnesse and rest, their dainties and ease, their banquetings and meetings, their feasts and sumptuousnesse, their pastimes and pleasures, that they rather complained on the King and his Councell for the first occasion of these tumults, then exprobrated the rebell for ingratitude and disobedience: But the King without further disputing against their peeuishnesse, or laying open the abuses of such refractary people, deliuered them of this feare: For he presently sent *Iohn* Earle of *Oxford*, *Henry Burchier* Earle of *Essex*, *Edmond de la Poole* Earle of *Suffolke*, Sir *Rice ap Thomas*, *Humphrey Stanley*, and other worthy martiall men, with a company of Archers and horsemen to enuiron the Hill where the Rebels were encamped round about: Himselfe with the maine battaile and forces of the Citie, much ordnance and great prouision tooke S^t. *Georges* field; where, on a Friday at night he quartred himselfe, and on the Saterday very early in the morning he poasted Lord *Dawbney* to *Dertford*, who by breake of day gat the bridge of the Strand in despight of resisters, which manfully defended it a while, shooting arrowes a full yard long, and demeaning themselues like scholerly and eloquent Orators, pleading for the time in a bad cause with good words, and handling an ill matter too-too well. From thence he went couragiously against the whole company, and what with the former Earles assaulting them on the one side, and his owne charges on the other side, as knowing how the Kings businesse stood to make an end of the warre, the battaile began apace, and not a man but prepared himselfe to [N] fight it out, till at last the Lord *Dawbney* engaged himselfe so farre, that he was taken prisoner: but whether for feare, or through his owne wit and pollicie, they quickly released him, and he as quickly dispatched the matter, and made an end of the warre: For he put them all to flight, so that a man may well say vnto them:

> ————*Via nulla salutis,*
> *Non fuga, non virtus, vix spes quoque mortis honestæ*:

and I may truely report of the contrary: neuer was a battaile so well fought and so quickly determined. For before the King was ready to goe to dinner, there were slaine two thousand Rebels, and many more taken prisoners, the rest hardly escaped home; who for all their defeature, and vncomfortable newes to the people, were rather accelerated to reuenge their companions wrongs, then exanimated from further attempts, or seemed grieued at the King and Countries molestation, shewing sad lookes, but stomachous hearts, and so remained intoxicated in their braines, and ready vpon euery occasion to a new rebellion, as you shall heare hereafter.

When this battaile was ended, and so delicately contriued (for the King lost not aboue foure hundred men) some imputed it to the Kings policy, who appointing the same on Monday, by way of anticipation fell vpon them on Saterday, and so taking them somewhat vnprouided, had the fortune to preuaile and thriue in his aduantage: Such as were taken and apprehended had their pardon, except the principall and fire-brands of the mischiefe: For the Lord *Audeley* was drawne from Newgate to the Tower-Hill in a Coat of his owne armes painted vpon paper reuersed and all to torne, and there beheaded the 28. of *Iune*. *Thomas Flamoch* and *Michael Ioseph* were executed after the order of Traitors, and their quarters sent into *Cornwall* for the terrifying of the people, some were dispatched at sundry Townes as they deserued: amongst whom the Smith, and diuers others of his immodest friends had no excuse to make for this rebellion, but whether they preuailed [N^v] or no, they were sure to be registred to eternity for daring to doe somewhat in behalfe of their Countries liberty, and bidding battaile to Kings and Princes at their Pallace Gates, and before the Citie Wals, euen *London* it selfe, that great Citie, the Chamber for their treasury, and strength of their roialtie: which makes me remember a saying of *Lucan*:

> ————*Sed me vel sola tueri*
> *Fama potest rerum, toto quas gessimus orbe,*
> *Et nomen, quod mundus amat:*————*

And in another place:

> ————*Quid plura feram? tum nomina tanto*
> *Inuenies operi, vel famam consule mundi:***

and this was the end of the twelfth yeare.

C. Affairs in Scotland and Northumberland

NORHAM AND ENGLISH COUNTER-MEASURES

In this time you must know, that the King of Scots lay not idle, but meerely vpon supposition of what would follow, prepareth himselfe, nor was so ill befriended, but he had secret intelligences of all King *Henries* purposes, and intendments, whereupon he enlarged his Army, barracadoed his passages, entrenched and fortified the holds, kept good Watch and Ward, and stood on the pinacles of a high presumption to encounter with the proudest forces of *England*; yea, to give defiance if need were to the King himselfe. Notwithstanding,

* *Lib. 8.*   ** *Lib. 9.* [Gainsford's notes.]

he now lay a while only at defence, watching with what warde the English would breake vpon him, and wondring at my Lord *Dawbneis* retraction, and why he came not forward as his espials had aduertised: but when he vnderstood of the Westerne rebellion, he then coniectured the truth, and a while reposed himselfe, till a Messenger of these Westerne men came vnto *Perkin* and profered their obedience and endeuours, if he would come and ioine his Army with theirs, and so as their Prince and Captaine, reuenge there wrongs: this was motioned to King *Ieames*, who for all he confessed, that if they would ioine with the Cornish men, there might be a gate open indeed to preuaile, and walke in the fields of Victorie: yet he would by no meanes aduenture his people so farre, and confessed plainly he wanted ships for transporting so great an Army into those [N2] parts: Only, because he would be doing to please the supposed Prince, he meant to take this opportunitie of the King of *Englands* disturbance, and once againe aduenture into his territories, and so with a sufficient preparation he attempted the Castle of *Norrham* standing vpon the Riuer of *Twede*, deuiding *Scotland* and *England*. But *Richard Fox* Bishop of *Durham*, a man of great learning, courage, experience and fidelitie, suspecting as much, had well stored and fortified the same, and was in it with such power, munition and prouision as he was able to raise, sending the King word of the siedge, and inuiting the Earle of *Surrey* to come to his reskue with all expedition: The Earle was mustering of men in York-shire, when this newes extended it selfe, and like a worthy seruitor hastend his iourney the rather, and so with twelue Earles and Barons of the North Countrie, one hundred Knights and Gentlemen of name, and twentie thousand Soldiers well ordered, and armed he came to raise the siedge, in which his braue Prelate was so engaged: Besides, he furnished a hansome Nauy at Sea, whereof the Lord *Brooke* was Admirall to giue their attendance whatsoeuer should chance: But when the King of Scots and his counterfet Duke of *Yorke* had full and certaine notice of the Earle of *Surreis* approach, and that the Lord *Dawbenies* army was also integrat and vnbroken, yea, ready to march forward as a second to the former, they thought it better to retire with securitie, then to tarry the aduenture with certeinty of losse, if not hazzard both of life and honour, and so by a voluntary consent they raised their campe and returned vnder colour of commiseration of the people whom they knew in the best war, must be subiected to slaughter or captiuitie: and to this purpose they could yield a reason out of our Poet to certain spirits, that wondred at their affrightings and drawings back, seeing no perill apparant, nor hearing of any stedfast reports, concerning a more forcible enemie, and so calling for a book reading to them this lesson of satisfaction.

—————*Potuit tibi Vulnere nulla*
Stare labor belli, potuit sine cæde subactum,
[N2ᵛ]   *Captiuemque ducem, violatæ tradere paci ?*
Quis furor ó Cæci scelerum, Ciuilia bella
*Gesturi metuunt, ne non cum sanguine vincant ?**

This answere of the Kings did rather harme then good to poore
Perkin. For, they perceiued the King was weary of this warre, and
loth to take his part any longer, and so they rested a while dis-
pleasingly pleased.

But the truth was the Earle of *Surrey* was so enraged at the brag-
ging and ouer-daring Prince, that he followed him at the heeles, and
in reuenge of many mischiefes perpetrated by him in such audacious
manner, he entred *Scotland,* defaced the Castle of *Cundrestins,* de-
uasted the Tower *Hedonhall,* vndermined the Tower of *Edington,*
ouerthrew the *Pile* of *Fulden,* and sent *Norey* King of Armes to the
Captaine of *Haiton* Castle, the strongest fortification betweene
Barwick and *Edinborough* to deliuer the same, which he absolutely
denied, vntill the worthy Generall set himselfe downe before it,
made his approches, and cast vp a strong rampart or battery for the
expugnation, preuailing so farre, that at last it was surrendred, their
liues onely saued: who were no sooner departed according to the
conditions, but our General quite ouerthrew and demolished the
same.

The King of Scots was within a mile of the siedge, and yet durst
not reskue the same, only by way of ostentation, he sent *Marchemount*
and another Herrald to the Earle of *Surrey* with a kind of defiance,
and challenge either to encounter with him Army to Army, or body
to body; conditionally, that if the victory fall to his maiesty, the
Earle should deliuer and surrender for his ransome the Towne of
Barwicke with the fish-garthes of the same, if the Earle againe were
Victor, the King would pay 1000. pound sterling for his redemption.
The noble Generall welcommed these Herralds, and like a couragious, yet vnderstanding Captaine: quickly answered all the points of
their commission: First, he was ready to abide the battaile in the
plaine field, and would if he pleased for the same purpose [N3] lay
open the trenches, and make the passages so easie, that victory
should haue comfort of comming amongst them. Secondly, he
thought himselfe much honoured, that so noble a Prince and great a
King, would vouchsafe to descend to so low a degree of contention,
as a priuate *duello* with him, for which he would not only repute him
heroike and magnanimous: but setting his loyalty to his Prince aside,
performe all good offices, which belonged to the sweet contract of a

* *Lucan. lib. 7.* [Gainsford's note.]

perpetuall amity, if it were possible, betweene them. Thirdly, for the towne of Barwicke, it was none of his, but the King his masters, which hee would not so much as coniecture vpon without his consent and aduice, as he himselfe might well iudge in the affaires of Princes, what was to bee done. Fourthly, hee thought his owne life worth all the townes of the world, and so would gladly hazard himselfe; yea, was proud (as hee said before) that so great a Maiesty would parallel him in such a kinde, onely he desired pardon for a little vaine-glory, that if hee conquered the King, hee would release him freely; if the King vanquished him, hee would either yeeld him his life, or pay such a tribute and competency, as is befitting the state and degree of an Earle, to all which he was the rather induced, because he was confident that,

Causa iubet melior superos sperare secundos:

But it should seeme, these affronts were meere flourishes: For neither battell, nor combat, nor any enterprize worth the recording was put in practise, although the English forces had layen long in the Countrey to the same purpose: whereupon the Lord Generall, loth to spend his time so inconsiderately, and somewhat wearied with the distemperature of the Climate, and vnseasonablenesse of the weather, the Countrey affoording nothing but mists and foggs at this time of the yeere, raised his camp, and retired to Barwicke. But when the truth was further enlarged, the King commanded him so to doe by his letters of priuate intelligence. For now came a time, in which the windowes of heauen seemed to open, and the God of mercy thought to [N3ᵛ] recompence his patience and goodnesse, with a quiet end of his troubles, and happy successe in his enterprizes, which fell out vpon this occasion.

PEACE BETWEEN SCOTLAND AND ENGLAND

Ferdinando King of Spaine, and *Elizabeth* his wife, hauing a purpose to marry their daughter Lady *Katherine*, to *Arthur* Prince of Wales, and very loth that any contention between the King of Scots, whom he much fauoured, and the King of England, whom he highly respected, should be (as it were) a wall of partition betweene their proiected amity and royall affinity, especially that either probability of an interest, or counterfet deuice of the issue-male from the house of Yorke, should cast any blockes or hinderances in the way of these pretences, he most prouidently sent one *Peter Hialos* a man of great learning, experience, and prudency, as an Embassadour to *Iames* King of Scots by way of mediation to contract a league of peace and absolute amity betweene the King of England and him, who proceeded with such faire conditions, and preuailed so well in his proposed message, that hee perceiued a glimmering sun-shine of this peace a farre off, but that there were certaine thickning clowds of mischeefe and disturbance, which by some effectuall heat from the King of Englands breath must bee remooued and dissipated, and therefore hee wrote to King *Henry*, that if it would please him to send some worthy man to be his associate in this enterprize, he perswaded himselfe, that an honest oratory would quickly conclude the profitable articles of amity. For the Poet had assured him, and hee found by some experience, that

> *Addidit inualidæ rebus facundia causæ,*

And for an entrance into the same, he assured the King, that there was great likelihood to lay downe the bloudy colours of defiance, and flourish the pleasant ensignes of tranquility. For the King of Scots had already protested, hee was onely emulous of King *Henries* vertues, and not maligned or despighted his person, and for *Perkins* title he made it a matter of conscience and charity. For he knewe him the right heire, if he were the right creature, and the Cleargy warranted the [N4] actions as meritorious. The better sort disclaimed all tyrannous prosecutions: For except their obedience to the King, they spent and consumed their estates, and onely returned with teares and lamentations for the losse of their friends. The inferiour sort imputed all to the superiour commands, and as for the formidable effects and bloudy issue of warre, it was only the chance and fortune of encounters, the action of fury, and the vengeance or curse appropriate to dissentions, according to that worthy author of excellent sentences and propositions.

> ——— *Sed mentibus vnum*
> *Hoc solamen erat, quod voti turba nefandi*
> *Conscia, quæ patrum iugulos, quæ pectora fratrum*
> *Sperabat, gaudet monstris, mentisque tumultum,*
> *Atque omen scelerum subitos putat esse furores.**

Whereupon King *Henry* boasting of the character of Prince of peace, so that he might not be branded with ignominy of basenesse, pusillanimity and dishonour, quickly consented to such agreement, and for the same purpose sent *Richard Fox* Bishop of Durrham, who still lay in the battered Castle of Norrham, as his cheefe Commissioner, who accordingly associated himselfe with *Peter Hialos*, at the towne of Iedworth in Scotland, whither the Embassadour from King *Iames* likewise repaired. Heere were many matters disputed vpon, many conditions layd open, many difficulties raised, many greeu-

* *Lucan. lib. 7.* [Gainsford's note.]

ances vrged, and many conclusions argued: but because they failed
in the maine poynt, nothing was determined. For the King of England required *Perkin Warbeck* to bee deliuered into his hands, as the
principall fountaine of this venomous streame, the cheefe occasion
of his vnquietnesse, the perturber of his Realme, the seducer of his
subiects, and the author of many rebellions. But the King of Scots
(like a Prince indeed) would not buy his peace with the bloud of
Innocents, especially a man comming to him for succour, shewing
all the markes of a distressed and abused Prince, allied vnto him by
marriage, commended by the Emperor, assisted by the Duches of
Burgundy, & in him[N4ᵛ]selfe of faire demeanour, sweet behauiour,
and of a most royall and well esteemed spirit. Therefore (I say) he
would by no meanes betray him into the hands of his enemies, that
was so long admitted into the bosome of his friends, nor should it
bee sayd, that in any such degree, for any worldly respect whatsoeuer,
King *Iames* of Scotland would bee base or perfidious, which he had
learned from the example and punishment of *Prusias* King of Bithynia, whom the Romans deposed, for consenting to betray *Hanibal*
into their hands, though they had promised large rewards, and
threatned seuere vengeance.

The Commissioners answered directly, that they intended not by
way of defamation, or contumelious discouery of the vanity of the
man, or impossibility of his businesse to make him odious or corrob-
orate their owne purposes, by the destruction of so silly a creature,
or discrediting so poore a businesse: but meerely to shew the truth,
and vnfold the secrets of the deceit, that such a Prince as King *Iames*,
might not be colluded [fooled] with shadowes and apparitions, but
orderly drawen into this holy and generall league, wherein both
Emperour, France and Spaine desireth a combination of amity with
England, onely there wanted himselfe to make the number compleat,
that the horne of *Achelous* might bee sent from nation to nation,
from kingdom to kingdom. For I can assure you, the Marchants of
England haue been receiued into Antwerp with generall procession,
the Emperor is pleased with this combination, the King of Spaine
pretendeth a marriage, the King of France endeauoureth a league,
and all the Princes of Europe seeke after a true confirmation of quietnesse. Therefore once againe, be not an enemy to the good of all
Christendome, nor so aduerse to this holy combination, that the
world shall rather esteeme you wilfull and preiudicate, then wise
and considerate.

Notwithstanding all this forcible and effectuall intimation, the
King of Scots would not consent to deliuer *Perkin* vpon any condition, but as hee came to him for refuge, hee should depart vntouched,
and not by his occasion bee in [O] worse case then the bruit beasts,

or vildest condition of men, as he had learned long since out of that ancient Tragedian:

> *Habet confugium bellua quidem petram*
> *Serui verò aras deorum: ciuitas verò ad ciuitatem*
> *Fugit, calamitatem passa: Rerum enim humanarum*
> *Non est quicquam perpetuò beatum.**

Yet with much adoe hee was brought to a truce for certaine yeeres, and condescended to this, that *Perkin* should bee no longer succoured, harboured, or maintained by him, or in his territories and dominions: with which answer, and orderly ratification of the same the Embassadours departed, the Armies retired, the Souldiers discharged, the King of England satisfied, the Orators of France (who from Douer had audience at London about the same purpose) rewarded, and of all others the worthy *Peter Hialos*, as principall worke-man in this intricate businesse, liberally and bountifully recompenced.

KING JAMES DISMISSES WARBECK

Only poore *Perkin*, whose glorious meteor began now to bee exhaled, seemed disconsolate and exanimated at this newes and determination, especially when King *Iames* began to expostulate and reason the matter with him. First, from a repetition of the benefits and fauours receiued by his Princely liberality and gentlenesse. Secondly, from his consanguinity, in marrying his kinswoman vpon dangerous hopes and triuiall aduentures. Thirdly, from his many trialls of sundry conflicts in England, proouing all his promises winde and smoke, and his best enterprizes triuiall & fanaticall. Fourthly, vpon the now combination of amity with all the Princes of Europe, which could not be done without the King of Englands consent and agreement. Fiftly, vpon the fatherly regard of his Countrey, which had neede haue some breathing time of ease and rest, and must questionlesse take a loue-day of consolation and desisting from turmoiles. Last of al, from the care of the Religion & Mother-Church, vnto whose obedience and regard hee was now absolutely sworne: Therfore he desired him to take some other course, and depart out of his Realme. For (as hee heard) hee was [O^v] now interested [had a share in] in the confederacy of the peace of Christendome, and vnlesse hee should bee a periured and perfidious Prince, hee could in no sort infringe the conditions, nor breake the truce combined by a firme and vnseparable adiuration.

When *Perkin* had heard him out, although euery word was worse

* *Eurip. Supplices.* [Gainsford's note.]

R

then the croking of some night-rauen or scrich-owle, and the amazement (for the time) might haue much disabled him: yet loth to discredit his cause by any demisnesse or pusillanimity, and seeing all answeres were superfluous, and the very messengers of despaire and disconsolation, he raised himselfe with some outward cheerefulnesse, and as well to auoyd ingratitude toward so great a Benefactour, as to countenance himselfe and his businesse, he thus casting away all feare and abashing timidity, replied.

Most worthy Prince:

Mortale est quod quæris opus: mihi fama perennis.

And therefore God forbid, that my commorance [tarrying] in your Court and Kingdome, or the weakned cause of my attempts should prooue disaduantagious or ominous vnto you, both in regard of the many fauours your Princelinesse hath heaped vpon me vndeserued, and mine owne willingnesse not to bee too too troublesome or offensiue vnto so benigne a Maiesty, which rather then it should bee hazarded for my sake without a cheerefull and liberall willingnesse, the fame and glory of the enterprize shall be sufficient for mee, and I will not onely disclaime my right and interest in the Kingdome of England, my lawfull inheritance by descent: but poure out my selfe, and spend my life most profusely for your sake. Onely this I must entreat at your hands, to giue me leaue to rigg and calcke vp my ships, and gather together that dispersed company I haue, or such as would willingly and voluntarily attend me. Which seeming but reasonable, and no way repugning the former agreement with the Embassadours, was quickly condescended vnto: so with many gifts, and royall furniture for his wife and family, he tooke his leaue & sailed backe the same way he came into Ireland, [O2] determining (as the last anchor-hold of his fortunes) either to vnite himselfe with the Cornish-men, whom he knew not fully appeased, or to retire to Lady *Margaret* his most worthy aunt and faithful coadiutrix.

D. *Warbeck's Invasion of England*

THE ASSAULTS UPON EXETER AND TAUNTON

He had not beene long in Ireland, but his false fortune began once againe to play with him, as flattering him with assured confidence and warrantize, that the Westerne men would welcome and entertaine him, from whom he had this notice: that they could not forget their former iniuries and slaughters, nor determine a setled and true obedience to the Lancastrian family: whereupon because something must be done, or else he should be for euer discredited: or that God in his Iustice derided all such enterprises to scorne: or else in his mercy would giue King *Henry* a breathing time to set his other Princely qualities of wisedome, magnificence, quietnesse, religion, charitie, gouernment and pollecy on worke: he sailed out of *Ireland* with fiue small Ships, and two hundred men, his wife and attendants, his substance and wealth, and in a word all that he had.

But when he was to conferre about his landing and setting forward his designes, he had such poore Councellors, as a man would smile at for pity, rather then laugh at for scorne. For his principall friends were now *Iohn Heron* a mercer, and banquerout: *Iohn* of *Water* sometimes Maior of *Cork*: *Richard Sketon* a Tailer: and *Iohn Astley* a Scriuener: men in generall defame for dishonest actions, and in particular reproach, for vnderstanding nothing but what consorted to their own wilfulnesse, and outragious appetites; of whom I may say, as *Ouid* complaines in another case in his Elegies:

> *Non bene conducti vendunt periuria testes,*
> *Non bene selecti Iudicis arca patet:*

With this crue about the month of *September* he landed at a place called *Bodnam*, and there so sollicited, and excited the multitude and wauering people, that when they heard him proclaimed *Richard* the fourth, as the indubitat sonne [O2ᵛ] of *Edward* the fourth, whom the Duke of *Glocester*, or if you will, *Richard* the Tyrant determined to murther, but that he escaped by the prouidence of God, they flocked vnto him to the number of 4000, and according to the nature of children running after newfangled toies or painted pictures: submitted to his princelines, and sware with all allegeance to maintaine his dignity & royaltie: with which confidence & company after they had taken the musters of his Army, and concluded to get some strong Townes into their possession, that so they might not only augment their forces, but still haue places of supportation and refuge to retire vnto, they went directly to *Excester*, and besiedged it. But because they wanted ordnance to make a battery, and other prouision to raise their trenches, and approches, or indeed if you will, were ignorant of martiall discipline, and the secrets of a true Soldiers profession, they spent the more time against the Gates, and endeauoured nothing but a forcible entrance, assaulting the same with great peeces of timber like the Roman rammes, crowes of yron, fire-brands, and impetuous violence of great stones cast at them, and amongst them. But the Citizens manfully defended themselues, and held it out to their perpetuall fame, letting ouer the walls in secret places diuers in baskets with strong cords to post to the king & acquaint him with their distresse. In a mean while seeing a fire made vnder their Gates, and that the enemies fury encreased, they suspected themselues, & had no other shift but to put force to force, & with one fire extinguish, or if you will deuoure another, and so they caused great store of faggots & timber combustible to be brought close to the posternes and greater gates, where the mischiefe began, and set the same on fire, which encreased with a filthy smoake, and smother, and at last burst out into a flame and blazes, so that neither the enemies could come in, nor Citizens goe out: but all were compelled to desist from that worke and apply themselues to more new and necessary labours. For the Rebels assaulted the most weake and broken places of the Wall, and the Citizens ranne to the expulsions, and repaired the brea[O3]ches as fast as they were made; besides, they had leasure to cast vp great trenches vnder their Gates, and by strong bankes rampering [fortifying] the same made them more difficult passages then before: The wals were mightely and impetuously assaulted, but the worthy Citizens defended them with that courage, and countermanding: that they slew aboue two hundred Soldiers in that fury, and behaued themselues as if they determined to obtaine a perpetuall name of renowne, and vnmatchable Trophe of honor: so that I may well and briefely say of them:

──*Serpens, sitis, ardor, arenæ*
Dulcia virtuti: gaudet patientia duris.

When *Perkin* and his associats saw so strong and strange opposition, they seemed both amased and defatigated at the same, whereupon betweene rage and despaire, he retired his lowsie and distressed Armie to the next great Towne called *Taunton*, where he mustred them a new, but found a great want of his company: For many of his desperate followers were slaine and cut off: many of the honester and ciuiler sort, seeing the Towne of *Excester* so well maintained, and that very few resorted vnto him, contrarie to his former flourishes, and ostentation; fell from him, and retired themselues home: many wery of the wars, and coniecturing an impossibility, to remoue a king so firmely established, or terrifyed with the punishment impending on Treason, and presumptuous rebellion, left him to his fortunes, and many politikely forecasting for the worst, seeing not one of the nobility or better sort to afford a helping hand to the lifting vp of this frame, were contented to dispence with former testations, and so prouided for themselues, whereby (as I said) as if the prouerb were verified:

Non habet euentus sordida præda bonos.

he came short of his reckning, and the Items of his accounts were much curtailed of their former length and computation.

But in truth the posts of the Country brought comfortable tidings of the Kings Army approaching, of which the [O3ᵛ] Lord *Daubney*, a fortunate and successfull man in all his enterprizes, was Generall: yet in the meane while had Lord *Edward Courtney* Earle of Deuonshire, Lord *William* his son, Sir *Edmund Carey*, Sir *Thomas Trenchard*, Sir *William Courtney*, Sir *Thomas Fulford*, Sir *Iohn Hatwell*, Sir *Iohn Croker*, *Walter Courtney*, *Peter Egecomb*, *William Sentnaure*, and diuers others, brought forward the forces of the countrey, to raise the siege of Ex[c]ester, which not onely animated and encouraged the Citizens, but rebated the fury of the contrary, and diuerted them from that sore and outragious manner of assaulting the walls, where in the last onset, the noble Earle, with diuers others, were hurt with arrowes; he wounded in the arme, and the rest in seuerall parts of their bodies, but very few slaine: And so with much adoe, this famous and honour-thirsting City, with the honest Inhabitants of the same, were deliuered and releeued.

By this time, the royall standards of King *Henry* were aduanced in sight of the City, and the drums beat vp their accustomed marches, to the joy and fulnesse of contentment, both of the towne and Countrey: But when the King was aduertized of their returning to Taunton, he hasted thither: But first he welcommed *Edward* Duke of Buckingham, a young, noble, and well regarded Prince, in whose company came along an hundred Knights and Esquires of speciall name and credit in their countries, amongst whom Sir *Alexander Bainham*, Sir *Maurice Barckley*, Sir *Robert Fame*, Sir *Iohn Guise*, Sir *Robert Points*, Sir *Henry Vernon*, Sir *Iohn Mortymer*, Sir *Thomas Tremaile*, Sir *Edward Sutton*, Sir *Amias Paulet*, Sir *Iohn Bickwell*, Sir *Iohn Sapcotes*, Sir *Hugh Lutterel*, and Sir *Francis Cheny* were principall. O what a glorious thing it is, to see a Noble-man either stand by the chaire of the Prince, as a Court starre and Supportation: that (at last) the King may aske, what shall be done to the man hee meanes to honor: or mooue in his own orb, that is the loue and credit of his Country, firme to the State, and gracefull in all his actions and proceedings, still hauing a care to the gouernment of the people, and an eye [O4] to the dignity of the Common-wealth.

·　　　·　　　·　　　·　　　·

WARBECK'S FLIGHT: KATHERINE'S AND WARBECK'S CAPTURE

When the King approached the towne of Tawnton, whether out of policie not to hazard the whole army at once, or out of suspicion of some reuolters in his company, or humbly considering there might be a turning of Fortunes wheele, as still *Rota fortunæ in Gyro* in the encounters of a battell, or harping vpon some stratagem and enterprize, as prouidently forecasting both the worst and best, which might chance: Hee sent before him *Robert* Lord *Brooke* the Steward of his house, *Giles* Lord *Daubney*, and S^r. *Rice app Thomas* to giue the onset and beginne the battell, that hee with the rest, as a strong Ambuscado and releefe, might come to the reskue, if they were wearied and defatigated. But little needed this policy, or procrastination: For poore *Perkin* (desperate of his fortunes, and quite exanimated to encounter with the Kings forces, in so war-like a manner and fearefull a preparation, contrary to all the motiues of a true Roman Honour, and without knowledge of his army) about midnight, accompanied with sixty horse, departed in wonderfull celerity to a Sanctuary towne [O4^v] besides Southampton called Beudly, where he, *Iohn Heron, Thomas a Water*, and others, registred themselues as persons priuiledged.

.   .   .   .   .

[P^v] But all this was nothing in comparison of that which followed: For his [King Henry's] horsemen prosecuted the chase so diligently and honestly, that they pursued the Lady *Katherine Gourden* wife to this *Perkin*, euen to *Michaels* Mount; who, notwithstanding, had she not been betraied by some of her owne followers, might haue escaped: For transhaping her selfe into one of her seruants habits, she had gone quite away to her ships: But that some pittying the distresse of the King, and turmoiles of the Kingdome; and perceiuing the end of the warre and pacification of these troubles to depend vpon her surprising, would by no meanes giue way vnto new disturbances, but tooke her and presented her to the Kings Commissioners: what should I say, when shee herselfe said nothing, but perceiuing them Gentlemen of worth with *Hipsiphile* to *Iason*, she cried out.

Si vos nobilitas, generosaque nomina tangunt.

I know you will vse me like your selues, and vnderstand I am a Prince euery way, so they gaue her leaue to adorne her selfe, and brought her like a bond-woman and captiue to the King, who wondring at her beawtie and attractiue behauiour, lifted vp his hands to Heauen in her behalfe to see so great a worth betraied to fanaticall hopes, and freneticall deceit, thanking God for himselfe, that he had such a Trophe of his endurances and victories in his hands, nor was the Emperour *Aurelius* more proud of *Zenobia*, then he reioiced in this aduenture: some say he fantasied her Person himselfe, and kept her neere vnto him, as his choisest delight; yea, so doted on her perfections, that he forgat all other things, then the contentment, which he receiued by her, insomuch that ma[P2]ny dared to libell against him with that saying of *Deianira* to *Hercules*.

Quem nunquam Iuno, seriesque immensa laborum
fregerit, huic Iolen imposuisse iugum:

Some report, he durst not let her marry for feare of ambitious tumors in such, as could attaine to such a fortune: Some confirme, that she was of that greatnesse of spirit, that she scorned all others in regard of her selfe, both by the priuiledge of her birth-right, and the possibility of her greatnesse. Howsoeuer, he intreated her most honorably and amiably (such a power hath beauty and comlinesse euer in distresse) and sent her to the Queene so maiestically attended, as if she had been a Queene indeed.

In the meane while my Lord *Dawbney* imploied himselfe and his company so effectually, that enuironing the sanctuary wherein *Perkin* was with two companies of light horse, who were vigilant, cautelous, strong and couragious, and so lay in the aduantage of watching the place, that *Perkin* could no way escape: but the King was not satisfied with this protraction [delay], and therefore loth to loose him, or giue him liberty to runne with the blinde mole into further cauerns of the earth to cast vp heaps and little hills of commotion and affrighting his estate and yet daring not to infringe the priuiledge of these holy places (such a hand had superstition, and the Popes fulmination got ouer all the Princes of Europe) he went more politikely to worke, and sent diuers persons of account to perswade his submission, and render himselfe wholly into the Kings hands, who not only promised him pardon of life, but comfort of liberty, yea, honourable maintenance vpon the easie conditions of desisting to perturb the Commonwealth any further, and disclaiming so iniuriously to pretend any title to the Diadem.

When *Perkin* saw to what streights his Barke was driuen, and that he must either split on the rocks of despaire, or retire back againe into the troublesome Ocean [P2ᵛ] of despight, according to the nature of cowardly and irresolute men, he chose the worst part to saue his life, and submit to the Kings acceptation, not remembring, because he was neuer acquainted with the secrets of maiesty, that he, which hath beene once a Prince, must neuer looke for a setled quietnesse in a priuat estate (because he is still subiect to the Conquerors pleasure) but an ignominious life, then which, an honourable death is tenne thousand times better, which made the noble *Hecuba*, as a worthy patterne to al vnfortunate Princes, thus answere the proudest conquerors themselues.

> *Porrigam collum cordatè intrepidè,*
> *Liberam vero me, vt libera moriar,*
> *Per deos queso dimittentes occidite: Apud manes enim*
> *Serua vocari: Regina cum sim, pudet me:* *

But as I said he now only recounted the difficult passages of his for-

* *Eurip. Hecuba.* [Gainsford's note.]

mer trauailes, the dangers escaped, the deceit pretended, the perill imminent, and the misfortune too-too apparant, as being in no securitie in the place, he was fled vnto, nor hauing any confidence in the persons, he had chosen: For though he knew there was a reuerence appropriate to sanctuaries; yet kings, if they pleased, will be tied neither to law nor Religion, but performe what they list, or vnder colour of their owne security, say they are compelled vnto: Therefore without any further aggrauation, relying on the Kings Pardon, and those honourable conditions propounded, he voluntarily resigned himselfe, and came to his maiesty, as a messenger of glad tidings, that now all warres, troubles, and commotions were by this meanes ended and determined.

The King not much wondred at him: for he only found him superficially instructed of a naturall wit, of reasonable qualities, wel languaged and indifferent apprehension, but farre from that highnesse of spirit, or heroick disposition to deserue the character of a Prince, or lay claime to a Diadem: yet loth with any boisterous strength to [P3] handle a bruized arme, or draw the fellow into a new selfe-loue, or good opinion of himselfe, hee passed ouer his examination the slightlier, and brought him immediately to London, being met all the way with great concourses of people, who both came to gratifie him and his auspicious successe, and to see *Perkin* like some strange meteor or monster: or, if you will, because wee will deale more cleanlier with him, like a triumphant spectacle, to mooue amazement, delight and contentment, according to that saying of our Poet:

Nocte pluit tota, redeunt spectacula manè:

But when they began to capitulate [specify], that being a stranger and an alien borne, hee durst not onely abuse so many Princes and Common-wealths with lies, fictions, and abominable deceit: but euen bid battell to Kings and Princes: yea, bring Kings and Princes into the field for his assistance, they fell from wondring at him, to raile and abuse him, both with checkes and opprobrious taunts: yea, diuers dared to put in practise many vndecencies, both of rage and indignation, had not the reuerence of his Maiesties presence diuerted their inconsideration, and commanded no further rumour [outcry], gazing vpon him, or violent threatnings against him. To conclude, the King brought him quietly to London, and for all he had giuen him life, and affoorded him a kinde of liberty: yet did hee set a guard ouer him, that hee could neither haue free conference, nor doe what he wantonly listed without them.

E. Events of Warbeck's Last Years

HIS CONFESSION, 1498

[P4ᵛ] For hee was first taken and brought to Westminster with all scorne and reproch, then set in a paire of stockes with contumelious derision, then carried through all the streets of London like a prodigious spectacle, then put to the racke, which made him not only confesse his pedigree and originall, but write it with his owne hands: Last of all, mounted on diuers scaffolds he read it in publike, and that so disgraciously, as in the commemoration was able to torment a looker on so that hee might well crie out

> ————Vitamque per omnem
> *Nulla fuit tam mæsta dies: nam cætera damna*
> *Durata iam mente malis, firmaque tulerunt:**

In some of your Chronicles you haue this confession at [Q] large, as in *Grafton*, which to make the story compleat, I haue a little contracted, and thus expose the same.

B E it knowen vnto all men, that I was borne in the towne of Tourney in Flanders, my father *Iohn Osbeck* Controller of the said towne, and my mother *Katherine Haro*, my grand-father *Direck Orsbeck*, after whose decease my grand-mother married *Peter Flamine* Receiuer of Tourney, & Deane of the boat-men ouer Lescheld; my mothers father was called *Peter De Faro*, which kept the keyes of Sᵗ. *Thomas* gate within the said towne. I had also an vnckle Mʳ. *Iohn Statime* of Sᵗ. *Pias* Parish, with whom I dwelled very young, hee married mine aunt *Iane*, and brought me vp very well; yet my mother not contented, as being very chary of mee, had mee to Antwerp to learne Flemish more exactly to a kinsman of my fathers *Iohn Steinbeck*, with whom I remained a full halfe yeare, but by reason of the wars I returned to Tourney, where I was placed with Mʳ. *Barlo*, who within another yeere carried me to the mart at Antwerp, where I fell sicke awhile, and so was boorded in a Skinners house much conuersant with the English nation, whereby I learnt the language, as you see. From thence I went to Barrow mart, & lodged at the Old Man: Afterward, Mʳ. *Barlo* left me at Middleborough with *Iohn Strew* a Merchant, who first made be beleeue, I was better then I was. From Antwerp I sailed into Portugall with my Lady *Brampton* in a ship called the Queenes ship, & serued a Knight in Lichborne called *Don Peter Las de Cogna*, who had but one eye; yet the manner of his behauiour and order of his house, made mee tarry a yeere. Then *Pregent Meno* a Brittaine carried mee into Ireland, and either com-

———

* *Lucan. lib. 5.* [Gainsford's note.]

S

manded so by my Lady *Margaret*, who (as shee said) was my aunt, or proiecting something for his own priuate, would needs perswade me I was a *Plantaginet* of the house of Yorke. For when I arriued in Corck, because I was somwhat handsomly apparrelled, they would needs bestow vpon me the title of the E[arl] of *Warwick* [Qᵛ] sonne to *George* Duke of Clarence formerly in Ireland, which *Iohn Le Wellin* the Maior maintained, and for as much as my deniall was contrary to their expectation, they brought me to the crosse, and made me swear: which I did, disclaiming him, or any of his kinred, vntill *Stephen Poitron*, with *Iohn a Water* came vnto me, as resolued I was King *Richards* bastard-sonne (then in the hands of the King of England) perswading mee not to bee afraid or daunted at any thing: For they would ayd me & assist me, euen to the obtaining the crowne of England; yea, they knew of their owne knowledge, the Earles of Desmond and Kildare were ready to aduenture their liues and estates for my sake: After this they carried mee into Flanders, to Lady *Margaret* Regent and Duches of Burgundy, who preuailed so far with me, that I took vpon me the person of *Richard* Duke of Yorke, second sonne of King *Edward* the fourth, and so with reasonable preparation, I returned backe againe into Ireland, where the sayd *Iohn a Water, Stephen Poinings, Iohn Tiler, Hubert de Brough*, the foresayd Earles, and many others entred with mee into a dangerous rebellion, and I was proclaimed by them *Richard* the fourth. From hence the King of France sent for me by *Loyte Lucas* and *Stephen Frian*, but making peace with England, he left me to my fortunes: Then I sayled into Flanders, where my supposed Aunt made more of me then before, so I attempted England, but was driuen backe againe into Flanders, from whence I went into Scotland, and from thence againe into Ireland, and so into England.

.   .   .   .   .

[Q2] When the King had this way satisfied himselfe, and pleased the people, as he thought: hee made no more adoe, but to preuent inconueniences, clapt him in the Tower, from whence he escaped not, vntill hee was carried to Tiborne, and there swallowed vp by the neuer satisfied paunch of Hell, for his former abuses, and intolerable wickednesse, which hapned very shortly after.

.   .   .   .   .

HIS LAST ENTERPRISE, 1499

[Q2ᵛ] *Peter Warbeck* impatient at this restraint of his liberty, and stomaching [resenting] his former disgraces & indignities, would endure no longer, but studied euery hower how to escape, not yet knowing what to do, when he did escape, to which purpose by faire promises and false perswasions, he corrupted his keepers: *Strang-waies*, *Blewet*, *Astwood*, and long *Roger* seruants of Sir *John Digby* Lieutenant of the Tower to slay their said Master: and set both *Perkin* and the true Earle of *Warwicke* at large, and so to make their fortunes, as they could either by domestike or forraine friends: to which, when the innocent Prince condiscended, as glad any way to enioy his libertie, and to be freed of his imprisonment (for you see birds kept in golden cages beat and flutter vp and downe as scorning their enclosure, to get out into their natiue Country the region of the aire) mischiefe and misfortune, which plaies the tyrant with many men all their liues long, & neuer af[Q3]fordeth one day, or breathing time to giue them a taste of any pleasure, or contentment, discouered the whole conspiracy to the King and his Councell, not leauing out any circumstance which might either exasperate his rage, or pull forward death and destruction to the delinquents. Whereupon, without further disputing the matter *Perkin Warbeck*, *Iohn a Water* sometimes Maior of *Corck*, and his sonne were the 16. of Nouember arraigned and condemned at Westminster of high Treason, and the 23. hanged at Tyburn: *Perkin* mounted on a scaffold reading his confession, and contrary to all expectation, asking the King and Country forgiuenesse, and dying penitently with great remorce of conscience, and compunction of spirit:

Et sic finis Priami——

Not long after *Edward* Earle of *Warwick*, who had been the 21. of Nouember arraigned at Westminster before the Earle of *Oxford* high *Constable* of *England* for the present, was vpon the 28. 1499. beheaded at the Tower Hill: For he quietly confessed the enditement, concerning his consent and willingnesse to obtaine his libertie, though it were by violating the law in that kinde, and breaking of prison, whose simplicity I rather lament, then condemne the offence. For it was a dangerous time for any Plantaginet to liue in, and I may well cry out:

Omne tulit secum Cæsaris ira malum:

But the King was indeed glad of this occasion, and fortune gave vertue the check, because as he had imprisoned him without a cause, he knew not what to doe with him without a fault: yet some report that the principall reason of accelerating his death was a speech of *Ferdinando's* king of *Spaine*, who should sweare, that the mariage betweene Lady *Katherine* his daughter, and Prince *Arthur* of Wales should neuer be consummated, as long, as any Earle of *Warwick* liued. For the very name and title was not only formidable to other Nations, but superstitious to the wauering, and vnconstant English: whereupon

the King was [Q3ᵛ] the gladder to take hold of this opportunitie,
wherein the conuiction of Law had cast this stumbling-block of treason in his walke and race to a longer life, and yet was there nothing
done, but by orderly proceedings, and iustifiable courses: more then
when the silly Prince submitted to his mercy, he thought it the greatest point of mercy to looke to himselfe, and so for the benefit of
his posteritie, and the sedation of all troubles both present and to come, struck off his head, and
with him the head of all diuision
and dissention.

William Warner's *Albions England*

We owe to J. J. O'Connor (*Notes and Queries*, CC (1955), 233–5) the suggestion that Ford's conception of the relation between Dalyell, Katherine, and Warbeck might be indebted to Chapters xxxv–xxxvii of Book VII of Warner's *Albions England* (first printing, 1586). Warner's account of the reign of Henry VII mentions little except the 'three Phaëtons' as he calls them (i.e., Lambert Simnel, Warbeck, and Ralph Wilford). He starts his story of Warbeck and Katherine as follows:

> He [Warbeck] wiu'd a Lady passing faire and of the Kings Allie,
> The Earl of Huntlies daughter, of Scotch-blood royall bread.
> She both before and after that her low-pris'd Mate was dead,
> When well she knew his parentage, and felt his ebbed estate,
> In onely sorrow did abound, in loue no whit abate:
> Howbeit in the *English* court prefer'd to high estate.
>   Theare (for she was of comely parts and vncompeered face)
> She, often brauely courted, yeelds no Courtier labor'd grace.
> To one amongst the rest, that most admired her answers chast,
> She said, besides the sinne, and that I so might liue disgra'st,
> A Presedent of wrong and woe did make me long since vow
> Chastly to liue the Loue of him whom Fates should me allow:
> I knew, quoth she, a Knight (a Knight he was in each respect)
> I knew a Ladie (faire she was but fouly to be chect)
> They loued long (if that to loue and leaue may loue be said)
> Till lastly she conceiued loue wheare loue should be denayd. . .[1]

There follows the lengthy cautionary tale (occupying all of Chapter xxxvi) of Erickmon and the faithless Ginetta, who ends up by being haunted by the ghosts of both her lover and her husband. The courtier to whom Katherine addresses this warning replies with a tale (occupying the whole of Chapter xxxvii) about a mouse who aspires to wings. This mouse is in fact a *bat*; it tells its tale to an owl about how it was warned by a wise old mole not to aspire too high but how it rashly disregarded this advice. The owl then eats the bat. But it is

---

[1] *Albions England* (London, 1612 edn), sig. M5^v.

resurrected by the goddess 'Pallas' and permitted to fly about in the twilight, 'to give thereby to vnderstand That to aspire is lawfull, if betwixt a Meane it stand' (sig. N5). The aspiring bat is presumably intended as a figure for Warbeck, but Katherine's wifely (or vidual—it is not clear which) loyalty to him remains unshaken. The importunate courtier is unnamed.

It is hard to agree with O'Connor that Ford could possibly have regarded any of this, if he knew it, as possessing any historical authority; but he might, as O'Connor suggests, have noted the stress on Katherine's loyalty and the faint adumbration in Warner's courtier of a person in the same relation to Katherine as Dalyell in the play. No significant verbal echoes have been detected. It must also be remembered that there are suggestions for a deeply affectionate and loyal Katherine in Gainsford (see note on III. ii. 139–86), Bacon and Speed (see note on V. iii. 81–184).

Various Enquiries

(i) *The lost play about Warbeck*

We owe our knowledge of this, oddly enough, to the same Thomas Gainsford the journalist who wrote Ford's first major source. In his *History of the Earl of Tyrone* (1619) he wrote:

> How *Perkin Warbeck* for all his exhaled vapouring, went forward assisted by the Scottish policie, Flemmish credulitie, and inueterat malice of the Duches of *Burgundy*, against the house of *Lancaster*, our stages of *London*, haue instructed those who cannot read.[1]

Gainsford gives no hint of when Warbeck was staged.[2] J. J. O'Connor has suggested that Ford might have begun his career earlier than has been supposed (i.e., before he had attained the comparatively advanced age of thirty-five in or about 1621) by writing a play about Warbeck, which later became, after revision, the play that we know. Gainsford's summary of what the lost play is about, if that is what it is, suggests a content which paid more attention to 'Flemmish credulitie' and Margaret of York than our play does; but Gainsford might have allowed his detailed knowledge of Warbeck's life, as displayed in his book printed in the previous year, to affect his account. Perhaps, on the other hand, the lost play is to be identified with *Believe It Is So and It Is So* and was by Dekker, as Abraham Hill's list states. Ford's play may be a revision of a lost original by Dekker. The existence of a lost play by either author would adequately account for the character-name Warbeck in *The Witch of Edmonton*.[3] One can imagine various other permutations and combinations, but no means of proving any of them.

(ii) *Believe As You List, Believe It Is So and It Is So*, and *Perkin*

The first two titles may be related to one another. It seems very

---

[1] Introduction, p. 4.

[2] J. J. O'Connor in 'A Lost Play of Perkin Warbeck' (*Modern Language Notes*, LXX (1955), 566–8) makes some suggestions based on the supposition that Gainsford, whose absences from England can be traced, saw it himself. [3] See Introduction, p. xxxi.

probable that there is also a connexion between Massinger's *Believe As You List*, licensed by Herbert in May 1631, for acting by the King's Men, and our play. Massinger's play is famous for several reasons. It was originally about Don Sebastian, deposed king of Portugal, and his efforts, in the teeth of Spanish opposition, to regain his throne.[1] Sir Henry Herbert, the Master of the Revels, disallowed it in January 1631, because it 'did contain dangerous matter'.[2] Massinger then rewrote it[3] as a play about Antiochus the Great, king of Lower Asia, who seeks to regain his throne after defeat in the field and a long disappearance, in the teeth of Roman opposition (represented by Titus Flaminius). The play twice presents a situation closely resembling the one in which Warbeck was involved with James IV. Flaminius, although he knows that Antiochus is who he claims to be, maintains that the king is an impostor; he persuades the Carthaginian senate to cease its support of him, although, like James IV, it refuses to surrender his person to Flaminius; later, Flaminius, by threatening him with the full might of Rome, persuades Prusias, king of Bithynia,[4] to yield up Antiochus, who has taken refuge at his court, and who is thereupon dispatched to the galleys (in the inconclusive ending he is rescued and exiled).

Massinger was indebted to two sets of sources, ranging from a pamphlet by Anthony Munday to Plutarch and Ralegh's *Historie of the World*; but the thematic resemblances to *Perkin* are striking. Antiochus is represented as a steadfast and magnanimous sufferer, stoical, and motivated (like Warbeck at Norham) by compassion for those who suffer because of him, eloquent and innately royal. Torture is used to make him confess that he is an impostor. The big difference between Warbeck and Antiochus (that the latter is genuine and the former not) makes for surprisingly little difference in the atmosphere of the two plays. Antiochus has a base comic follower Berecinthus the flamen (a major comic part, however), who combines the (in our play) very minor rôles of Frion and the bankrupts and disables a lot of Antiochus's glory; Flaminius, in some ways a convincing and powerful portrait of a Roman imperialist, combines the rôles of Henry and Hialas but has little in common with either of them as characters. The play manifests intense interest in the subject of pretenders, Flaminius remarking: 'All ages have been furnished

[1] To whom the ubiquitous Gainsford also refers, *Wonderfull History*, sig. B2.

[2] *Dramatic Records of Sir H. Herbert*, ed. J. Q. Adams (New Haven, 1917), p. 19.

[3] See C. J. Sisson's introduction to his Malone Society Reprint edition.

[4] See Gainsford again, *Wonderfull History*, sig. N4[v]; but he confuses Antiochus with Hannibal.

With such as have usurped the names And persons of dead princes.'

One can easily suppose that one of these two plays, proceeding from rival companies and rival theatres, was a deliberate attempt to match the other. The fuss made by Herbert over the original Don Sebastian draft, which must have been gossiped about in the small world of the London theatre, might have discouraged anyone else after 1631 from writing a play about a pretender, especially an English one. This might suggest that Ford's play preceded Massinger's first attempt, except that there is reason to suppose that *Perkin*, too, came under suspicion.[1] So that argument cuts both ways: would Massinger have risked a play about the Portuguese 'pretender' *after* a play about Warbeck had run into trouble ? On the other hand, the length that Massinger went to—rewriting his whole play for an Asian/Roman setting, surely an unusual act of tenacity on the part of a banned author—suggests that something was driving him on. We cannot be sure that that something was the success of Queen Henrietta's Men in a rival play about a pretender; but if we could, it would mean that Ford's play preceded Massinger's (which was rewritten presumably between 11 January, the original disallowing, and 6 May, the final licensing, 1631) but did not precede it by much, if it was currently operating as a goad or stimulus during the earlier part of 1631. Massinger may of course have been unwilling to abandon his manuscript for quite other reasons. There are, throughout the whole story, plenty of possibilities; but there is no means of telling which of the several patterns they could easily be made to form might be closest to the truth.

[1] See above, p. xvii.

Glossarial Index to the Commentary

An asterisk before a word indicates information which supplements that given in *O.E.D.* The index generally lists the form of a word that appears in the text, but the basic form is sometimes given for the grouping together of more than one occurrence of a word.

Abjects, III. i. 23
act, V. iii. 115
action, *Prol.*, 19–20, II. ii. 141
actors, *Ded. Epist.*, 6
addition, IV. iv. 20, V. ii. 165
admire, V. ii. 39
admit, I. ii. 19, III. ii. 41, V. iii. 42–3
adversity, IV. iii. 137
advisement, III. iii. 15
affronted, V. i. 51
after, V. iii. 96
Aganippe, *Commend. poem*, ii. 4
airy, III. iii. 63
allow, *Commend. poem*, v. 2
amazement, V. iii. 196–8
ambition, V. ii. 35
antic, *Prol.*, 4, I, iii. 41, V. ii. 88
apparition, IV. iii. 13, V. iii. 115
argument, I. ii. 3–4
articles, IV. i. 53
articling, V. ii. 10
as, III. ii. 98
ascent, II. iii. 55
at once, V. ii. 72
attempts, I. ii. 107, II. i. 113
avow, IV. iii. 105
Ayton, IV. i. 9

Baffled, IV. ii. 30
baited, V. iii. 27
barbèd, IV. iv. 8
battalia, II. ii. 138
batten, IV. ii. 81
battles, V. i. 55

beadsman, III. iii. 38
beard, I. iii. 39
Beaulieu, V. ii. 41
beldam, I. i. 122
beshrew, V. ii. 141
betimes, V. ii. 19
Blackheath, III. i. 21
blades, IV. v. 33
blaze, V. iii. 207
bless, II. iii. 14
blood-shrunk, I. i. 25
bonny-clabber, III. ii. 8
bravely, IV. i. 54, V. i. 103
*break forth, II. i. 15–16
——— out, II. i. 15–16
breathes, V. iii. 60
breathing, IV. i. 71
bribed to, IV. v. 58–9
broken, II. i. 15–16
buffet, V. iii. 47
bug's-words, III. ii. 111
bustling, I. ii. 183
by, II. i. 16, III. iii. 30

Careful, II. i. 22, III. ii. 146
cast a mist, III. ii. 19
catch, III. ii. 7
censure, *Epilogue*, 6
chain, IV. i. 74
challenge, II. iii. 53
chancery, II. ii. 12
change, II. ii. 92
charge, I. iii. 107, IV. iv. 51–2, 85, V. ii. 170

charmed, II. iii. 6
chats, I. ii. 15
chief, II. ii. 136–8
chough, IV. ii. 58
close, III. ii. 154–6
clownery, I. ii. 41
cock-sure, IV. v. 42
coil, II. ii. 26
collusion, *Commend. poem*, iii. 4
*colossic, I. i. 109
combination, IV. iii. 7
combustion, V. ii. 50
come home, II. iii. 176
—— in, III. iv. 22
*command, I. i. 89–90, III. ii. 179
commend, II. ii. 44–5
commendation, III. iii. 7
commissioned, *Ded. Epist.*, 9
compliment, III. iv. 28
composition, I. ii. 126–7
compounding, II. iii. 148–9
conceit, II. iii. 163, IV. iv. 45
conceited, III. iv. 31
conceive, IV. iv. 75
conclude, IV. i. 30
condition, II. iii. 119, III. iv. 101–2,
　V. i. 93
confusion, I. i. 48, II. ii. 127, III. i. 11
congees, II. iii. 46
conquest, V. iii. 94
*consort, III. ii. 78
constantly, V. iii. 74
construction, *Ded. Epist.*, 21
construe, III. iv. 51–2
contents, II. iii. 61–2
controlment, I. iii. 107
conveyance, II. i. 91
Cornish chough, IV. ii. 58
couched, *Prol.*, 14, II. iii. 2
counsel, I. i. 75, II. i. 80
countenance, *Prol.*, 5
counterpawn, II. iii. 118
country, II. iii. 143
court, V. iii. 130
courtship, II. iii. 177
cozenage, IV. ii. 25–6
create, III. iv. 104
creation, III. iii. 58
credit, *Ded. Epist.*, 8–9

credulity, III. ii. 45–7
cross-caper, II. iii. 170
curiosity, *Ded. Epist.*, 19

Date, I. ii. 34
debates, *vb*, II. iii. 187
defame, III. iv. 58
defeasance, II. iii. 119
defence, I. i. 99
deliver, III. iii. 7
demean, II. i. 99
*deserved, IV. ii. 19
desperately, III. ii. 182–3
determine, *Ded. Epist.*, 10, V. iii.
　194
detraction, II. iii. 40
detriments, V. ii. 17
device, II. iii. 155
dialogue, V. ii. 77–8
digest, II. iii. 151
directly, III. iii. 60
disavow, IV. ii. 12, V. iii. 168
discovery, I. iii. 8
discradled, I. iii. 36
disgrace, V. iii. 160
dispatch, IV. iii. 55
disputes, I. ii. 86
dissembled, I. i. 111
distinction, III. ii. 105
dolent, III. iv. 76
doubt, III. i. 57, IV. iv. 44
*dream hence, II. i. 112
dross, IV. v. 62–3
duty, II. iii. 156

Earl, IV. i. 31
early, IV. v. 20
earnest, III. iii. 47
elephants, IV. iv. 7
else, III. iii. 20
endear, *Prol.*, 24
enforcement, V. i. 105–7
engage, II. ii. 26
engagements, III. i. 108, V. ii. 95–6
engines, IV. ii. 8
entertain, II. i. 39.2, IV. ii. 47
entertainment, *Ded. Epist.*, 17, III.
　ii. 150, V. iii. 136–7
entire, III. iii. 12

equal, I. ii. 121, V. iii. 12
*Europe, II. i. 45
*example, I. ii. 130
excrements, IV. iv. 96
Exeter, V. i. 46–9
expectation, *Prol.*, 25–6
expressions, *Ded. Epist.*, 8–9
extremes, II. iii. 184, IV. iii. 101
extremity, V. ii. 137
eyelet-holes, II. iii. 145

Fadge, IV. ii. 57
faintly, III. i. 86
*faith, II. iii. 58
falconer, V. iii. 0.2
*fall on, III. iii. 22
famed, V. ii. 164
familiar, V. ii. 77–8
familiarly, II. iii. 23
famous, *Prol.*, 15–16
fate, *Prol.*, 25–6
favours, II. ii. 44–5
fawned on, V. i. 26
fawns, III. iv. 27
feathered, III. i. 51
figured, I. i. 102
fishgarths, IV. i. 32
fix, V. iii. 72
flattered, III. i. 48–50
fly upon, II. i. 81
fondly, IV. iv. 29
fool, III. iv. 67
for, I. i. 68, I. iii. 25, II. i. 109, III. ii. 58, V. ii. 42
forage, III. iv. 54
forbear, V. iii. 81
forged, *Prol.*, 17
forgery, V. ii. 131
formality, V. ii. 101
frailty, IV. v. 59–61, V. iii. 173–4
full-filed, *Commend. poem*, iv. 3
furniture, IV. iii. 106

Galliard, I. ii. 48
garboils, IV. ii. 57
gather [a] head, I. iii. 130–1
gave me, V. i. 26
generous, V. ii. 164
gentle, III. ii. 66

girl, II. iii. 35, IV. i. 31
glow-worm, IV. iv. 34
go through-stitch with, II. iii. 115
gorget, III. i. 0.1
Graiensis, *Commend. poem*, v. 7
grate, *sb.*, IV. v. 27
*great, I. i. 77
greatness, II. ii. 97, IV. v. 58–9, V. iii. 98, *Epilogue*, 3–4
greediness, I. iii. 27
*grudge, II. i. 28

Herald, III. iii. 34–5
Heydonhall, III. ii. 116, IV. i. 5–7
highest, II. ii. 18
hire, II. i. 60
Hole, II. iii. 147
honest, II. i. 6
hopes, in, V. ii. 25–9
*hubbubs, II. iii. 168
hurdle, III. i. 95

*Impartial, II. iii. 184
*impostorous, I. i. 100
impoverish, V. iii. 196–8
improved, III. i. 54
in, II. iii. 159, III. ii. 99
in point of, V. ii. 144–5
indenture, II. iii. 118
indirection, III. iii. 32
indulgence, I. ii. 126–7
infliction, V. iii. 85–6
injuries, III. ii. 49–52, V. iii. 54
innocent, V. iii. 191
innovation, IV. iv. 59
instance, I. iii. 25
*instinct, II. iii. 42
instructed, III. iv. 28
intelligence, I. iii. 31, II. ii. 148, III. iv. 83, IV. iii. 119, V. i. 67
*interest, III. iv. 105
interrupts, III. ii. 23
issue, I. ii. 153–7, II. i. 97, IV. iv. 51

Jointure, II. iii. 55
jubilee, I. ii. 141
jump, IV. ii. 56
justice, *Prol.*, 3, III. iv. 31
justifiable, *Commend. poem*, i. 0.1

justify, II. iii. 133

Kindreds, I. ii. 34
king of beasts, IV. v. 29
knacks, III. ii. 10
known, *Prol.*, 15–16

Landloper, V. iii. 24–5
leading-staff, III. i. 0.2
learn, IV. v. 14–16
lectures, III. ii. 49–52
lesson, I. ii. 80, V. ii. 77
lifted, V. ii. 170
listen after, V. i. 31
lodge, IV. iv. 42
lovely, IV. iii. 38, V. ii. 25–9

Magnificence, II. i. 98
massacred, V. iii. 201
maugre, I. i. 117
may, V. ii. 146
meet, *vb*, IV. i. 53
mention, *Prol.*, 15, I. ii. 155
mercy, II. ii. 57
mettle, IV. v. 33
Milford Haven, V. ii. 66
mines, IV. ii. 8
minions, III. i. 46
mist, cast a, III. ii. 19
*mixture, IV. iii. 44, IV. v. 62–3
mockery-king, I. i. 4
model, IV. iii. 158
monster-multitude, III. i. 91
Moors, III. iii. 11
more than, IV. iii. 126
motion, I. ii. 159, II. iii. 9, 142, 166,
    III. iv. 43
——, *vb*, IV. iii. 25
mounting, IV. iv. 74
muscadine, IV. ii. 82
must, IV. iv. 70

Nature, III. iv. 56
nearest, II. ii. 68
nearly, II. ii. 4
need, *sb.*, III. i. 31
——, for, *Prol.*, 10
new, of, *Commend. poem*, iii. 2
Newgate, III. i. 95

new-stained, *Commend. poem*, i. 11
nick, IV. iii. 35
Norham, III. iv, location
noverint, II. iii. 118

Oblige, IV. i. 80
observance, V. ii. 164
observe, II. ii. 52
occasion, upon, II. iii. 176
occasions, on all, V. i. 54
odds, stands the, IV. v. 63
officious, I. i. 65
on, IV. v. 53
once, III. iv. 100
——, at, V. ii. 72
open, III. iii. 37
opinion, V. iii. 130
oraculous, II. ii. 146

Painted, I. iii. 44
pale, *sb.*, V. ii. 3
part of, IV. iii. 29
partage, III. iii. 14, V. iii. 165
partake, IV. ii. 45, V. iii. 85–6
parties, I. ii. 69–70, V. i. 59
party, IV. iii. 71–2
passed, I. i. 88
passionate, II. i. 117
patent, V. ii. 158
*patience, III. ii. 49–52
pawns, II. iii. 58
peremptory, V. iii. 139
perfect, IV. iii. 125
personate, *Ded. Epist.*, 4
Phaëthon, II. iii. 16
Phoebean, *Commend. poem*, ii. 2
piece, *vb*, IV. ii. 36
point of, in, V. ii. 144–5
pointed, V. iii. 160
*pointed out, IV. iii. 31
ports, III. iv. 5
post, *vb and sb.*, III. ii. 118, IV. iv.
    63.1, V. i. 57
practic, *Commend. poem*, iv. 10
practice, V. iii. 29
precedent, I. ii. 144–5
prefer, I. i. 65, II. iii. 156
prerogative, II. iii. 8
present, II. iii. 137, IV. i. 34

presenters, III. ii. 109
presently, II. iii. 38, IV. ii. 58–9,
    V. ii. 158
pressing-iron, II. iii. 144
prevent, IV. iii. 119
private, IV. ii. 4
proceed in, II. ii. 40
process, IV. v. 8
progress, II. i. 57
prompted, V. ii. 77
proof (of proof), IV. iv. 36
protestations, IV. v. 20
protested, I. ii. 149, V. ii. 94
prove, III. i. 31, V. ii. 157
providence, III. iii. 13, IV. iv. 6
provision, II. iii. 61–2
purchase, *sb.*, I. i. 30

Quaint, I. ii. 91
quartan fever, III. ii. 36
quean, II. iii. 47
quenched, III. i. 70
quest, III. i. 102
questioned, V. ii. 13
quiristers, III. ii. 6

Rage, *Prol.*, 19–20, I. ii. 111
*railed, III. i. 77
rained, I. i. 23
range, II. i. 57, V. i. 7
rare, III. ii. 4, IV. iv. 55, V. ii. 164
reaching, V. i. 83
recall, I. iii. 95
redivived, *Commend. poem*, iii. 1
refer, II. iii. 61–2
rehearsed, V. ii. 78
relation, II. i. 54
relish, II. iii. 177
remorse, III. iv. 65
report, *sb.*, IV. iii. 88, 145, V. iii. 92
reproach, V. iii. 88
reproof, III. iv. 82
repute, II. iii. 38, III. iii. 8, 14
reserve, II. i. 86, III. i. 22, 72, III. ii.
    61
resolution, II. iii. 44
respect, I. ii. 134, IV. iii. 98, V. ii. 30,
    V. iii. 81
respected, IV. i. 44–5

respectively, V. ii. 105
rest of state, V. ii. 9
restore the fight, II. ii. 144
rests, V. ii. 172
retribution, IV. i. 76
return, II. i. 66, III. i. 72, III. ii. 136,
    IV. v. 19
*riding-suit, V. i. 0.1
ruffian, III. iv. 4
ruffle, I. ii. 10, V. iii. 35
rule out, III. ii. 181
run in, I. ii. 150
runagate, III. iii. 50, V. iii. 24–5

Safe, III. iii. 42
saint, *vb*, V. iii. 131
Saint George's Fields, III. i. 9
Salisbury, IV. iv. 83
search, III. ii. 181
second, III. iv. 94
secure, securely, I. iii. I, IV. i. 86
sensible, III. i. 69, IV. i. 38
sensibly, V. iii. 205
served his turn, II. ii. 38
servile, I. ii. 111
set up, I. ii. 50
several, *Epilogue*, I
shadow, III. ii. 20–1
shall, IV. i. 52
shape, II. iii. 170
shift, *vb*, V. ii. 87
*shorten, III. ii. 89, 165–6
should, II. i. 119–20, III. i. 56, IV.
    iii. 163, IV. iv. 3
side, I. ii. 113
since, I. iii. 39
so, IV. iii. 163
sometimes, I. iii. 49
sooped up, I. ii. 37
*sovereignty, II. iii. 42
special, V. ii. 28
spirits, III. iii. 63
stagger, III. ii. 166
stand, II. i. 80, II. ii. 101–2
stands the odds, IV. v. 63
state, *Prol.*, 26, V. ii. 9
state of man, II. ii. 107
station, V. iii. 173–4
stomach, II. i. 7, III. ii. 7

stomach, *vb*, IV. ii. 44
straggler, II. iii. 35
strain, *Prol.*, 18
studious, III. iii. 23–4
study, II. i. 83, III. iii. iv. 49, IV. i. 26
style, II. ii. 104
subsidies, I. iii. 129–34, III. i. 25–7, III. iv. 87
substance, III. ii. 20–1
success, V. iii. 212
sue out, V. iii. 118
sufferance, II. i. 23, II. iii. 184, III. iv. 74, IV. iii. 126, V. iii. 172
suffrage, IV. iii. 11
supported, I. i. 0.2–3
surety, V. iii. 42–3
swabber, I. i. 125–6
swinge, V. iii. 58

Tabor, III. ii. 4–5
taste, III. ii. 177, V. iii. 218
tattles, I. ii. 15
Taunton, V. i. 50
temper, *vb*, V. ii. 137
tender, *sb.*, V. i. 81
tenures at will, I. ii. 102
theatres of greatness, *Epilogue*, 3–4
things and things, IV. ii. 89–90
thought thee, V. iii. 177
thrift, IV. iv. 26
thrifty, III. ii. 186, V. iii. 149
Titans, III. i. 3
title, *Commend. poem*, iii. 9, II. iii. 55
to, III. ii. 75, IV. iii. 16, V. iii. 141, *Epilogue*, 10
toil, II. ii. 131
totters, V. iii. 50
toward, III. ii. 110
trace, III. ii. 145
tradition, V. iii. 72
traducer, III. iv. 37
train, *sb.*, IV. v. 58–9
—— takes, IV. iv. 27
translation, IV. iv. 72
*treat, I. ii. 162
treaty, III. iii. 29, IV. i. 79

trial, II. i. 26
trim, I. i. 78
trimmed, III. iv. 4
troll, III. ii. 7
trowses, III. ii. 111.1–3
truncheon, III. iv. 3.1
truth, II. i. 67, III. ii. 151, III. iv. 60, V. ii. 164
tune, I. ii. 80
twine, III. ii. 102–4
twingle-twangle, III. ii. 4–5

Unbottomed, I. i. 50
unkiss, V. iii. 148
unlodged, I. i. 104
unsuspected, IV. iii. 107
upon, I. ii. 163
use, *sb.*, III. iii. 14, IV. iv. 96–7, V. iii. 217
——, *vb*, II. iii. 40
usquebaugh, III. ii. 8
usurps, II. iii. 44

Viper, III. iv. 33
volume, II. i. 53
vulgar, I. ii. 144–5, II. i. 44

Wait, IV. v. 22
—— on, I. iii. 94
wand, *Commend. poem*, iii. 2
want, *sb.*, III. i. 31
—— *vb*, II. ii. 34, II. iii. 29–30, IV. iii. 2, IV. v. 40
warrant, *Epilogue*, 9
wheeled about, II. ii. 74
whet, *Commend. poem*, iv. 8
Whitesand bay, IV. v, location
who, III. i. 86
whoreson, I. ii. 14
will, *sb.*, III. ii. 179, IV. ii. 21
withstanding, III. iii. 51
work, *Commend. poem*, i. 4

Yet, V. iii. 10

Zanies, V. ii. 87